# FILM
## IN THE THIRD REICH

*Art and Propaganda in Nazi Germany*

*by*
David Stewart Hull

A Touchstone Book
Published by Simon and Schuster

*To*
ILSE M. BISCHOFF
*and*
CAROLA BISCHOFF TERWILLIGER

# A NOTE ON TERMINOLOGY AND TRANSLATION

The translation of the often peculiar German used during the Third Reich presents problems. I have attempted a more or less literal approach, substituting words only when absolutely necessary, for example, "Weimar Republic" for the commonly used "System Time," the latter meaningless for the American reader. The original spelling of umlauted proper names and words has been preserved, hence Göring, and Goebbels.

The rate of exchange of the dollar and Reichsmark was variable and actually meaningless. Officially, $1 equaled RM 2.50, but in practice the rates could be manipulated to $1 for RM 4, and during the war there was no rate of exchange that can be worked out with accuracy.

# CONTENTS

# PREFACE

This study of the Nazi-era film originated sometime in late 1959 when James Card, curator of motion pictures at the George Eastman House, Rochester, New York, showed me a print of *Münchhausen*. I was intrigued with the film, and wanted to find more information about it and about a film industry which, in the middle of a terrible war, could produce such an epic.

The standard reference works were of little help, and the more I read, the more confusing the situation became. It was soon obvious that most of the writings I had consulted were contradictory or evasive on even the simplest details. At this point, Mr. Card suggested that I write this book.

After nine years of research and writing, this volume is at last completed. I cannot claim that it is the last word on the subject, but I do hope that it will stimulate interest in the films of the Third Reich and will prompt future film historians to investigate the period in greater depth.

The materials in this book are based on a number of sources. First, the viewing of the films themselves in archives from Rochester to East Berlin. Secondly, interviews with directors, writers, actors, cameramen, producers, designers, and executives of the industry who worked during the period under examination. Thirdly, intensive study of the writings of and on the period, often unreliable.

I saw every film discussed, unless otherwise noted, and the opinions expressed, other than those credited to others, are mine.

Many persons and institutions have been of help to me in my research both in the United States and in Europe. I am especially grateful to Dartmouth College Films, Dartmouth College, Hanover, New Hampshire, for lending me the facilities to do preliminary research. Mr. J. Blair Watson, director of Dartmouth Films, was especially helpful, as was his assistant, Mr. Robert Gitt, who aided in numerous ways, especially in the screening of hundreds of thousands of feet of often rapidly deteriorating nitrate film, sometimes at risk of life and limb.

Of the world film archives, I must express my deep appreciation to the following institutions and personnel for their help in obtaining both films and research materials for this study:

Mr. James Card, George Eastman House, Rochester, New York; Mr. John Gillett, Miss Dorly Minich, Miss Norah Traylen, Mr. Robert Vas, and the Aston Clinton film archive staff, all associated with the British Film Institute, London, England; Herr Klaue, assistant director of the Film Archiv of the German Democratic Republic, East Berlin; Dr. Edgar Breitenbach and Mr. John Kuiper of the Library of Congress and their staff both in Washington, D.C. and at the Suitland, Maryland, archive vaults; Miss Margarita Akermark, Mrs. Eileen Bowser, and Mrs. Adrienne Mancia of the Museum of Modern Art Department of Film, New York City; Dr. Max Breucher, president of the Ufa and its subsidiary organization, Transit Film, in Frankfurt and Düsseldorf; and various persons at the Bavaria Film Studios in Munich.

Many persons were interviewed, and some have requested that their names be without mention here. My thanks go to them as well as to the following:

Dr. Herbert Maisch; Richard and Ilse Angst; Luis Trenker; Karl Hartl; Eduard von Borsody; Josef von Baky (deceased); Jürgen von Alten; Boleslav Barlog; Robert A. Stemmle; Paul Martin (deceased); Alfred Weidenmann; Ernst von Salomon; Dr. Fritz Peter Buch; Max W. Kimmich; Veit Harlan (deceased); Werner Eisbrenner; Kristina Söderbaum; Edith Hamann; Anni Selpin; Liselott Klingler; Leni Riefenstahl; Heinz Hilpert (deceased); Sepp Rist; Dr. Fritz Hippler. Both Leni Riefenstahl and Luis Trenker were of special help in arranging screenings of their films for me.

Others who aided this book in various capacities include:

Dr. Barkhausen, Bundesarchiv (Koblenz); Dr. Wilfried B. Lerg, Institut für Publizistik der Westfäler Wilhelms-Universität (Münster); E. Remani, A. Stephan and Dr. Mooshake, Transit-Filmvertrieb G.m.b.H. (Frankfurt/Main); John G. Stratford; Nathan Podhorzer, Casino Films (New York); Miss Agnes F. Peterson and Mrs. Arline Paul, Hoover Institution on War, Revolution and Peace (Stanford University); Thomas Brandon; Miss Susie Rolland; Mrs. Erika Beyfuss, Bavaria-Film (Munich); Fitzroy Davis; E. M. Hacke, Proszenium (Kemnath-Stadt/Operpfalz) was most diligent in searching out rare books and film programs of the era.

For assistance in arranging interviews in Germany, and helping me on difficult linguistic, interpretive, and logistical problems, my thanks to Bernt Kummer. For translation of exceptionally complicated materials, the enthusiastic collaboration of Mrs. René Fülöp-Miller is acknowledged with the greatest gratitude, as is the help of Mrs. Alice Weymouth.

The photographs used in this book came from many of the cited archives organizations, and individuals.

For many suggestions and corrections of details, my deep thanks to Miss Ilse Bischoff, and my editors at the University of California Press, Max Knight and Ernest Callenbach.

D. S. H.

*June 8, 1968*
*East Hampton, New York*

# PROLOGUE

The most common questions asked about films made in the Third Reich are "What was made?" and "Who made these films—how did it happen that these artists lent their services to the Nazi regime?"

This book is an attempt to give a preliminary answer: Preliminary, because it will take many more years before the mass of documents preserved from the period is properly analyzed and centrally catalogued. Preliminary also, because the discussed period of history is so recent that it can be subject to various schools of interpretation.

For the most part, an effort has been made to shun psychological analysis of personalities, for this is not the purpose of this study. Rather, by describing legislation, the films and their genesis, and the biographies of their creators, it was hoped that a factual background could be provided to give the reader an understanding of the period and those who played a part in it.

This book has been written primarily for those with little or no knowledge of film-making in the Third Reich. Very little has appeared on this subject in English, and fewer than a half-dozen films discussed here are available through normal rental sources in the United States. The problem of viewing the films themselves is going to worsen in the future. The nitrate stock used during the period is subject to decomposition; already some titles have disappeared which were available to the researcher only a few years ago. The preservation of German films made between 1933 and 1945 is a low-priority item on the budgets of even the most affluent film archives—if ever a film archive can be said to be affluent at all. Most of the color films have already deteriorated beyond the point of recovery. Unless something is done about this situation, in the next fifty years the frustrated film historian will have to add another thousand or so titles to the legion of lost films. For this reason, I felt it my duty to describe many films in detail.

The bibliography of this volume contains a fairly comprehensive listing of materials presently available on film in the Third Reich. For those whose reading knowledge is limited to the English language, only H. H. Wollenberg's short (and rare) *Fifty Years of German Film* can be recommended. That volume is generally objective and factually correct, but devotes only a small part of its content to the Nazi-era motion pictures. There is hardly anything else, save the final chapters of the late Dr. Siegfried Kracauer's *From Caligari to Hitler* and a few magazine articles.

The situation in other languages is not much better. German "histories" written during the Nazi era itself are almost unreadable and ridiculously loaded with propaganda; the major postwar histories of the German film (Heinrich Fraenkel, *Unsterbliche Filme*; Kurt Riess, *Das gab's nur einmal*) contain a wealth of anecdotal material but depend on the reader's familiarity with the movies and personalities under discussion.

The two multi-volume histories of world cinema written in French available to me allow little space to the Nazi film, and most of the information is factually inaccurate.

However, two valuable research tools are available, and without them this book could hardly have been written. The first is Dr. Alfred Bauer's great catalogue of the German film, which lists credits for virtually every feature film made in the years 1929–1950, and is amazingly free of errors, even typographical ones. The second study is Joseph Wulf's *Theater und Film im Dritten Reich* (1964), a rich collection of published and unpublished materials relating to the Nazi film. Since it is unlikely that this book will be translated into English—

although this should be done—I have relied heavily on it, particularly in tracing the complex history of the first few years of the Nazi take-over of the film industry. My debt to Dr. Wulf's scholarship can not be sufficiently expressed.

## II

Although this book is limited to the subject of the German film in the 1933–1945 period, it is probably necessary here to give a brief introduction to the German film as a whole, from its pre-World War I genesis. Such an introduction must be superficial, as the period has been taken up in detail in several easily obtainable books.

The pioneer study was the late Dr. Siegfried Kracauer's *From Caligari to Hitler* (1947). This book has always been highly controversial, because it takes as its approach the "contention that the films of a nation reflect its collective mentality. His study of the course followed by the German film from the days of Caligari to *M, Mädchen in Uniform,* and *The Last Will of Dr. Mabuse* is equally an analysis of deep-seated reasons for Hitler's ascendency," to quote the dust jacket. Whether one accepts this thesis or not—and although I admire the research, I find the second of Dr. Kracauer's premises preposterous and much of the evidence used in its support factually questionable—the book is a milestone of the "psychological study" genre. It should be read—with a large grain of salt—by anyone interested in the subject.

Still more interesting is Lotte Eisner's remarkable book, *L'écran démoniaque*, which will be available in an English translation about the time this book appears. Mrs. Eisner spends more time than Dr. Kracauer concentrating on individual films and their creators, and her observations are consistently subtle and discerning. Together with her yet untranslated study of the work of F. W. Murnau, her history of the German film before the Nazis may be regarded as the definitive work on the period.

The short background material which follows is no substitute for reading Kracauer and Eisner, but I feel it is necessary to include it if only to refresh the reader's memory on some basic details and trends of the period before 1933.

### III

Although there were German films of interest in the 1895–1918 period—and a number have been unearthed lately which prove the era was not so stale as previously supposed—the birth of the modern German cinema is normally placed at the production of *The Cabinet of Dr. Caligari* in 1919.*

The end of World War I and the ensuing revolution and chaos, proved traumatic for the arts in Germany. It is interesting that *Caligari* was made in 1919, a year which marked the publication of Hesse's *Demian*, and found Brecht working on his first major drama, *Baal*. The old order of German culture was dead or dying: the popular playwright Hauptmann had passed his peak; in music, Reger had died in 1916, Pfitzner was spent, and Richard Strauss's last major work, *Die Frau ohne Schatten*, was completed by 1917, although this puzzling composer had an autumnal renaissance toward the end of his long life. The center of modern music was in Vienna, dominated by Arnold Schönberg and his school. Only Thomas Mann seemed to be able to continue his work in an orderly fashion, with masterpieces both behind and before him.

The temporary cultural vacuum was filled by amazing creativity in the visual arts, in which painting must be joined by the motion picture in any analysis. It cannot be too strongly stressed that the cinema was respected as a legitimate art form in Germany long before it reached that position in America.

The reasons for this are interesting. From the start, the German film used established personalities of the theatre world: Paul Wegener even before World War I, and two of *Caligari*'s main players, Conrad Veidt and Werner Krauss, were highly regarded on the stage. In America, the centers of theater and film were separated by 3000 miles, which necessitated the creation of film "stars," most of them without much stage training. A few personalities were created directly by the German film industry in its early years, most notably Henny Porten and Lil Dagover, but this was the exception.

---

* To confuse cinema historians, the film was not released until February of 1920, but the 1919 date usually follows mention of the title.

The common practice was for actors to switch from one medium to the other and back again with a dexterity which would have been bewildering to their American counterparts. As the financial and popular rewards of the motion picture increased, the "Filmwelt" was created as an off-shoot of the theatrical establishment, a concept foreign to non-Germans.

Hollywood might have its "movie colony" and its "movie stars," but it never had a "Filmwelt." The term, basically, denotes the ensemble nature of the German film industry. Directors, writers, actors, cameramen, composers, set designers, and editors were united in an exclusive club, and group effort was the rule. There was remarkably little competition or professional jealousy between members of the group. Part of the reason was the lack of a true studio system in the Hollywood sense. Although there were several major studios in Berlin from the end of World War I onward, the same names would be seen at one time or another in all camps. The infant industry had to work hard to make its place firm in the world market, and cooperation was one method to attain this goal.

As Dr. Kracauer states: "Films are never the product of an individual"[1]—surely a questionable statement as far as world cinema is concerned but true in Germany. Films of the German cinema industry, silent and sound, tend to have a certain sameness within a given period. To be sure, there were highly individual directors such as Murnau or Lubitsch, whose later American pictures have much the same flavor as their earlier German work with only the passing of time and taste changing the externals.

But it is rarely possible to guess who directed what in the 1933–1945 period since the personnel involved was so inbred and interchangeable. This is not to infer that direction was poor or that there were no individual touches by this or that artist. In the American cinema of the same era, it is often possible to spot the directional style of such minor masters as Wyler, Hawks, or Walsh, but to separate the German directors whose choice of genre resembles theirs—let us say Steinhoff, Harlan or Selpin—is another matter.

The general date given for the beginning of the decline of the German cinema is 1924, when Hollywood, alarmed at the appeal of the foreign product, began to raid the best talent for its own use. The concept of a Filmwelt was shattered with this monumental exodus of directors, actors, and technicians. To counteract this, the German industry attempted to copy the style of Hollywood pictures, since this was what their public wanted. The benefit to America was marginally greater, for some of the ensemble spirit began to infect the Hollywood studios. Most importantly, the Germans taught the Americans' camera mobility, which revolutionized the industry. And the addition of world-famous names gave Hollywood a certain "class," which it desparately sought at the time.

Back in Germany, the results were less happy. Second-rate imitations of American silent films flooded German screens. This trend was opposed by a small group of directors who had resisted Hollywood's blandishments, most notably Fritz Lang and G. W. Pabst. Their films became increasingly refined, remained personal in spirit, and in some ways represent the German cinema at the height of its creative powers.

The advent of sound, coupled with the effects of the Depression, nearly finished the German film industry. The Hollywood prodigals returned home, defeated by the new language barrier and the economic cutbacks taking place in America. Ironically, it was an American of Austrian birth, Josef von Sternberg, who put the staggering industry back on its feet with *Der blaue Engel* (*The Blue Angel*), (1930). This film, partly financed with American money and made in both German and English versions, was an enormous success. The Filmwelt was able to pull itself back together again, and the last three years of the Weimar Republic marked a renaissance in the industry.

Instead of reproducing the theatre intact on the screen—the first American reaction to the sound medium—a different approach was taken. Sound was used suggestively to enhance the great visual beauty of many films, and dialogue was held to a minimum. The sophisticated use of sound in such films as *Westfront 1918* (1930), *M* (1931), and *Berlin-Alexanderplatz* (1931) is still startling today. While this appealed to viewers who attended artistic pictures, it hardly made an impression on the audience at large.

The solution to this was a curious and actually satisfying compromise—the creation of musical pictures with clever songs and amusing plot lines, often filmed in multi-language versions for export. *Die Drei von der Tankstelle* (*Three from the Filling Station*), (1930) seems to have pleased even the most sour critics, and it was quickly followed by numerous imitations, the most notable being *Walzerkrieg* (*War of the Waltzes*), (1933). This genre continued almost unabated throughout the Nazi period.

### IV

This period of frothy operettas provided a temporary relief from the increasingly sinister political situation. The Filmwelt, with a few exceptions, seems to have ignored politics as much as possible. Communism was fashionable and national socialism extremely *outré*. Yet if it meant surface acceptance of the new regime rather than a break from the Filmwelt, the average member of the group hardly hesitated long over his decision, unless he was a Jew and had no choice in the matter. The overriding concern was continuance of the artistic status quo and to hell with politics.

Here appears the most perplexing paradox. The number of Nazis in the industry of the 1933–1945 period was small. A few actors and directors were card-carrying early supporters of the regime, but very few indeed. Throughout the whole period, the Filmwelt was a hotbed —however passive—of limited resistance to the government. The cultural world still claimed a privileged position, and the Nazi bullies, suffering from the smallness of their own personal appeal, were attracted to the public's favorites. In return for keeping their mouths shut in public, members of the Filmwelt were awarded favors which would have been unthinkable in either a democratic or Communist state.

The word "opportunism" seems appropriate here, but it would be an oversimplification to accept this explanation completely. To choose between exile or stardom, a concentration camp or the veneration of sixty-six million Germans in 1933 was not hard. The fatal error, morally, was the supposition that governments come and go, but art marches on in a vacuum. Nothing could have been farther from the truth, but it was too easy to ignore reality in the plush confines of the Filmwelt.

Unlike the Soviet Union, where the axe could fall at any time on any artist, in Nazi Germany the odds were even that by playing along with the regime one's skin would remain in one piece and one's career continue unimpeded. Goebbels and his associates had no false illusions of loyalty on the part of the film colony, but accepted this in a manner which is almost unbelievable when reviewed today. In his diary entry of September 20, 1944, Goebbels' aid Rudolf Semmler reported:

All film and stage artists have been called upon to send a written tribute to Hitler. . . . Goebbels is always in favour of ideas with a demonstrative look about them. The collected tributes are to be bound in leather and presented to Hitler at Christmas on behalf of the German artistic world. Hinkel* has written personal letters to the leading stars of film and stage in which he mentions July 20th and the need to maintain loyalty to the Führer.

The answers come in hesitatingly. The whole scheme—completely misconceived from the start—is a failure. Most of the letters consist of general, meaningless phrases. They nearly all thank the Führer for the triumphs to which he has led art, the stage and the film. Emil Jannings writes a very cautious letter. Gustaf Gründgens, who had to be reminded twice, replies that he is now a soldier, not an artist, and therefore cannot take part. In almost all letters one can sense the unwillingness to be committed in the present situation. But Goebbels is thinking of using these tributes, when the time comes after the war, for a new policy towards the artists.[2]

### V

At this point we must return to the questions posed at the beginning of this prologue. First, what films were made in the Third Reich?

This is relatively easy to answer—about 1363 feature pictures, of which 208 were banned after World War II by the various Allied censorship boards for containing Nazi propaganda. In the 1951 catalogue of proscribed films[3] published by the Allied Control Commission, a viewing of 700 suspect features revealed only 141 that were politically objectionable, and some of these were restricted on admittedly slight grounds. Many of these prohibited films will be discussed in detail later in this study.

* Hans Hinkel, secretary-general of the Reich Chamber of Culture.

On the second question, the following pages will tell who made the films, but the reasons why are not so simple to record. A number of basic theories as to personal behavior of artists under the Third Reich have been advanced:

1. The "Bad Eggs in Every Basket" theory. Basically, there are enough evil or stupid persons in any country at any given time willing to carry out absurd assignments. This was true not only in Germany, but in the United States of the McCarthy period when some leading Hollywood names lent their services to childish anti-Communist films.

2. The "All People are Opportunists" theory. Anyone, given the right stimulae and incentives, will do almost anything as long as he can rationalize it later to himself.

3. The "Artists are Simply Dumb" theory. This school holds that the average member of the film colony has the intelligence of a dodo and the morals of a Hong Kong whore. Egocentricity and monstrous narcissism, coupled with susceptibility to flattery, makes the actor and his group the lowest of God's creatures.

4. The "Everyone in Nazi Germany Was a Nazi, so What Did You Expect?" line. Therefore, it follows that all films of the era, political or not, were fascist and bad. This is popular in Communist critical circles.

5. The "I was Forced" syndrome. Most attractive among postwar defendants, but definitely true only for a minority.

6. The "Art is Apolitical and the Artist Must Hold Himself Above Politics" approach. Rather similar to point five, and untenable in view of the entirely "political" anti-Semitic abominations of Nazi film-making.

These categories, flippant though they may seem, reflect the prevalent explanations of a distressing phenomenon.

# 1933: THE SUBVERSION OF THE FILM INDUSTRY

Film would hardly have played an important part in the history of the Third Reich if it had not been for the presence of Joseph Goebbels in the Party hierarchy. Hitler found films only a pleasant way to relax at the end of the day, and enjoyed the company of pretty actresses in public and private; Göring dabbled in opera and theatre and only took an interest in film when his favorites were involved (his second wife, Emmy Sonnemann, had appeared in a few movies); the remainder of the Party leadership will rarely appear in this history.

Goebbels was not only interested in but almost obsessed by films. There probably has never been another individual in the history of any modern government who devoted so much of his time to the motion picture in every possible capacity. It is startling to realize that every film made in the Third Reich had to be passed by Goebbels for public showing, including features, shorts, newsreels, and documentaries.

The reasons for Goebbels' enthusiasm for the film medium are not too hard to find. Of course, he realized the value of film as propaganda for the Nazi party, but the reasons go deeper. As a young man he was a writer and was fascinated by the stage and its actors. He grew up during the period when German films gradually gained supremacy in Europe, and their influence was felt throughout the world. Unlike most Nazi leaders, he was a well-educated and well-read man. And he was, to some extent, stagestruck.

However, nature had seen to it that he would not be an actor. An early illness had left him with a deformed foot, and he walked with a limp which he managed to minimize with great difficulty. He was short, and not particularly good looking. With these physical limitations, he attempted to enter the cultural world as an author, but his early works were turned down. The frustrations of an ambitious young man in these situations can be well imagined.

To compensate for some of these physical factors he worked on his voice. There was an initial problem here because he was a Rhinelander, with an accent which tends to be somewhat amusing to the average German. With much hard work he eliminated this and gradually developed one of the most remarkable voices in the history of modern politics.

It was a voice which cannot be described in words. Recordings do it some justice, but only in films, coupled with his demonic personal presence, can it be fully appreciated. It is not necessary to understand German to get the message of his speeches; the inflection, the modulation of a single syllable could turn a passive audience into a screaming mob. Through hard practice he was able to perfect a delivery which was equally impressive to huge gatherings and to the radio audience at home. As a public speaker, Goebbels had no peer.

Yet despite this remarkable gift, there was still a gnawing sense of inferiority underneath his snappy, fast-talking façade. He went out of his way to cultivate friends in the theatre and film circles, and not only because they could be of help to him in his political projects. His attitude toward these persons bordered on worship. They could in theory do no wrong. Many an erring actor or actress found a personal scandal hushed up by the personal intervention of Goebbels in his years of power. As his aid Rudolf Semmler observed, "His motto is like that of Frederick the Great: 'Artists must not be bothered.' "[1]

The career of Goebbels has been well documented in a number of books, and his rapid rise in the political world of national socialism can be found elsewhere.[2] Throughout his life, Goebbels kept detailed diaries, although the bulk of them vanished, apparently to points East,

in the final days of Berlin. These diaries were meant for future publication, and parts of them have already reached us in various states.
The first diary that concerns us covers the period of 1932–1933 and
was prepared for publication by Goebbels under the title *Vom Kaiserhof zur Reichskanzlei* (1934).[3] The period of 1942–1943 is covered
in a book edited by Louis Lochner under the title *The Goebbels Diaries*
(1948).[4]

What is striking about these books is the amount of material relating to films. Even on the busiest day, Goebbels found time to see at
least one film, and apparently to write about it.* There are facts about
the films of the time, gossip about this or that actress, and occasional
flights of fancy on the future of the medium. Goebbels' interest in the
motion picture went far beyond that of a "hobby" as some commentators have referred to it. He probably understood films as well as any
industry executive, and probably better.

Long before the Nazis came to power, they had friends, conscious
or unconscious, in the film industry. The late Dr. Siegfried Kracauer,
in his book *From Caligari to Hitler*,[5] would seem to advance the theory
that most of the industry sympathized with the Nazis from 1919 on,
perhaps unwittingly. There were films in the late silent period and the
early sound era which advanced nationalistic tendencies to be adopted
by the Nazi film industry; these tendencies existed also in German
literature. Some themes, when examined in the light of future events,
look suspicious, but the historian must be careful to avoid putting
the cart before the horse.

Of the German sound films made between 1929 and 1932, less
than half a dozen were banned after World War II by the Allied Military Government censorship division, which is not an impressive figure
to back up the Kracauer theory. The banned pre-1933 sound films include a couple of nationalistic and rather dull versions of events in
the life of Frederick the Great, some war films of various periods, and
so forth. Kracauer is particularly suspicious of a type that has been
called the "Mountain Film." This was a unique German genre, as

---

* The Lochner book is heavily edited from the original diaries, and apparently
many entries on film were excised because they lacked general interest for the
American reader.

Joseph Goebbels, Minister of Propaganda of the Reich.
(Photograph by Alfred Eisenstaedt.)

fully individual as the American Western. The hero is usually pitted against the mountain, which can be a maddeningly ambiguous symbol to the analyst. These films could be poetic, such as Leni Riefenstahl's *Das Blaue Licht* (1932), exciting as G. W. Pabst's *Die weisse Hölle von Piz Palü* (1929), or stirring to the nationalistic instinct as Luis Trenker's *Der Rebell* (1932), which will be discussed in detail below. In fairness to Kracauer, all three of these directors (plus Dr. Arnold Fanck, the "inventor" of the genre) went on to make films during the period of the Third Reich with some enthusiasm, although only Miss Riefenstahl and Fanck could be considered politically active in the regime.

Luis Trenker (b. 1892) presents a curious case. An actor in, and director of, nationalistic films, he was not even a German, but a Tyrolean with Italian citizenship who was discovered by Fanck in the course of one of the latter's expeditions, and put into a film as a double and stunt man, later graduating to star roles. In time he created a screen personality somewhat like that of John Wayne in the United States—the rugged outdoorsman, simple and honest, always ready to help the heroine by deeds of physical courage. His appeal was not solely to the German audience, for he was brought to the United States for several films in which he duplicated his German success.

Like so many Tyroleans, Trenker was a nationalist, and the region is rich in heroes. One of the most popular, Andreas Hofer, was to be the subject of some later Nazi films because of his exploits against the Napoleonic French. Bitter battles in the area during World War I had created a new mythology, and this had already been used in *Berge in Flammen* (1931) and its American remake, *The Doomed Battalion* (1932).

The ultimate film of this cycle is *Der Rebell*, a blood-and-thunder drama of a young patriot's fight against the French, set high in the mountains. Trenker had entered into a deal with Deutsche-Universal, a German subsidiary of the American Universal Pictures, for this film, an international cast had been gathered, and the picture was eventually released in several languages. It differed from the other films of its type only in that it had a bigger budget, better-known actors, and the advantage of more sophisticated sound-film technique.

In an oversimplification, Kracauer remarks:

There is pictorial evidence that the Trenker film was nothing but a thinly masked pro-Nazi film. Photographed by Sepp Allgeier, it introduced symbols which were to play a prominent part on the early Hitler screen. To enhance national passion, elaborate use is made of close-ups of flags, a device common with the Nazis. In the visionary concluding sequence, the resurrected student, who along with two other rebel leaders has been executed by the French, moves onward, a flag in his hand.[6]

This passage must be regarded as somewhat dubious. To call *Der Rebell* "a thinly masked pro-Nazi film" on the basis of selected visual images by Sepp Allgeier (only one of four cameramen, by the way) is far-fetched. The fact that the film appealed to both Hitler and Goebbels is in no way indicative that the National Socialist party had anything to do with the film which was, after all, financed by American money.

On January 18, 1933, Goebbels and Hitler went to see the film, and Goebbels records in his diary:

In the evening we go to see the film *Der Rebell*, by Luis Trenker. A first-class production of an artistic film. Thus I could imagine the film of the future, revolutionary in character, with grand mass-scenes, composed with enormous vital energy. In one scene, in which a gigantic crucifix is carried out of a small church by the revolutionaries, the audience is deeply moved. Here you really see what can be done with the film as an artistic medium when it is really understood. We are all much impressed.[7]

What is interesting here is that Goebbels finds the film effective for *artistic* reasons, in addition to admiring its political possibilities. The word "revolutionary" is somewhat ambiguous but revolution as a film subject was uncommon during the Third Reich, and crucifixes were seldom in evidence in Nazi films. *Der Rebell* is no prototype of the Nazi film despite Allgeier and his flags.

The situation is complicated by Trenker's later behavior. Somewhat of an opportunist, he apparently became enthusiastic about the Party during the early days of the National Socialist regime, although he was

later to change his mind violently. On August 23, 1933, *Film-Kurier*,
the German equivalent of *Photoplay*, printed an article about Trenker's
visit to Hitler:

> Trenker's favorite theme, "Leuchtendes Land" ["Glowing Land"],
> a film for which he has been fighting for years, was about to be started
> at last, probably at Universal, but in spite of everything, his efforts
> have failed. . . . Dr. Goebbels already knows parts of Trenker's favorite
> manuscript and is pleased with them. Trenker regrets that he didn't
> meet this art seeker at the Führer's country house. He thinks it would
> have been easier to talk amidst the meadows and woods than in the
> heart of busy Berlin.
>
> And now to the visit with the Führer. Hitler's country house
> "Wachenfeld" at Salzberg in Berchtesgaden is a "schiener" [dialect for
> *schöner* or "beautiful"] said Trenker, smiling. The Führer's taste, his
> understanding of the countryside, his predilection for open spaces and
> great lines are manifest in this estate which is situated in a beautiful
> region. Hitler said that he saw the film *Der Rebell* four times and each
> time with new enthusiasm. "Besides," mentioned the Führer, "the
> film is running at the moment at the Luitpold-Lichtspiele in Munich."
> Trenker was greatly surprised that the Führer was so well informed.
> He himself did not know it.[8]

This nauseating bit of writing is worth reprinting here not only as an
example of the journalistic style of the period, but as one example of
the attitude of actors toward the new regime. Few allowed themselves
to be used so thoroughly as Trenker.

Hitler was appointed chancellor by Hindenburg on January 30,
1933. On the second of February, Hitler, Goebbels, and most of the
new government attended the Berlin premiere of a film that was not
quite as innocent as *Der Rebell*, a drama of submarine warfare in
World War I entitled *Morgenrot* (*Dawn*).* This film, despite some
pacifist tendencies, had plenty of wartime action, which appealed to
the less sophisticated viewers. It is far more the prototype of the early
Nazi film than *Der Rebell*, and was directed by the Austrian Gustav
Ucicky who was later to play a prominent part in the propaganda
fiction-film production.

---

* The film actually received its premiere the previous evening in Essen, the
hometown of *Morgenrot's* leading lady.

"*Dawn* is no Nazi film,"[9] comments Kracauer, but even the somewhat naïve Berlin movie correspondent of the New York *Times* observed, "It is a film of exceptional qualities, aside from its propagandistic tendencies."[10] Propaganda for the New Germany it certainly was, and there is evidence that *Morgenrot* was made at the Ufa after some well-placed suggestions from the Party.

The film caused much trouble, most of it abroad. Because the British were not portrayed in a particularly favorable light, the British newspapers jumped on it, and, in England, Sir Charles Cayzen demanded, and got, a debate in the House of Commons. Apparently Sir Charles wished to make an official protest to the new German government. The British government, for its part, was most unwilling to stir up an already uneasy situation between the two nations, and prevailed upon the foreign secretary, Sir John Simon, to appear before the House, where he found himself in the rather odd position of having to defend a Nazi film. The motion for an official protest was effectively stifled, although the committee assigned to the matter discovered among other matters that the Ufa had borrowed a Finnish government submarine without telling the Finns what the story of the film was about.[11]

February was a busy month for the new government. It suppressed sixty Communist newspapers and seventy-one belonging to the Social Democrats. On the 27th, the Reichstag burned, with far-reaching results. Goebbels was kept busy explaining these events to the German public, but as yet he had no central means for delivery of news and propaganda.

Goebbels had full plans drawn up for an institution devoted to such activities, and pleaded with Hitler to let him carry through with them. However, the "Führer" was in no hurry to delegate so much power to Joseph Goebbels. The sheer complexity of founding such an organization was a staggering problem. *Lichtbild-Bühne*, a daily somewhat along the lines of the American *Variety*, wrote in their March 8 issue:

It was confirmed to us from reliable sources that the film will occupy an important place in the framework of the proposed establishment of an enlightenment and propaganda department; a special movie division is under consideration. Details concerning this project are being examined in various quarters.[12]

On March 13, Goebbels was appointed "minister of popular enlightenment and propaganda," four days before his thirty-sixth birthday. This
new office had been planned since the previous August. To celebrate
the opening of the Propaganda Ministry, Goebbels fell on a great idea.
He suggested to Hitler that he open the new Reichstag in the Garni-
sonskirche at Potsdam, the burial place of Frederick the Great and a
shrine that was the German equal of Mount Vernon. The date of
March 21 was selected because it was the anniversary of the founding
of the first Reichstag of the Second Reich in 1871. In celebration of
this event, *Lichtbild-Bühne* printed the following editorial:

The German film industry and its participants and co-workers can
be proud of their achievements which enable the new leadership of
the state to rely on them as instruments of national and world-wide
importance. To minimize this achievement and to point out the linger-
ing flaws is easier than to appreciate what has already been done. In-
ventors and technicians, producers and actors, directors and distributors, have called attention to the intellectual and economic values of
the German films, which now occupy a leading place in the world
market, and which are shown in the cinemas of civilized countries
around the world. Today, on the occasion of our national holiday, the
German film industry may point with justified pride to its undeniable
success, which stands in marked contrast to the loss of prestige suffered in many other realms of our national life. We express the hope
that in the future a strong and understanding leadership will create
conditions that will further our ethical and artistic goals, so that the
industry will blossom in unstained purity.[13]

On March 23, the members of the new Reichstag voted 441 to 84 for
the passage of the so-called "Enabling Act," which gave dictatorial
powers to Hitler. Democracy was now dead in Germany for the next
twelve terrible years.

Goebbels had his first official meeting with the film producers' organization on the 28th. He recorded in his diary:

Speak for the first time to the film producers at the Kaiserhof in the
evening, and successfully set forth a new programme for the pictures.
I gain the impression that all present are honestly willing to coöperate.
The film can only be re-established on a healthy basis if German na-

tionality is remembered in the industry, and German nature is portrayed by it.[14]

The last sentence gives a hint of the events of April 1, when a boycott of Jewish shops was organized as the most obvious part of the beginning of a major anti-Semitic campaign. The same day the six American film companies which had branch offices in Berlin received the following letter in the mail:

> As the commissar at the head of this cell, and by the authority given to me, I call on you to give notice of the dismissal of all your representatives, rental agents and branch managers of Jewish extraction and to give them leave of absence immediately. No more employment contracts may be entered into and so far as such have been effectuated lately from transparent causes, they shall be cancelled immediately. I emphasize that it is not religion but race that is decisive. Christianized Jews are thus equally affected. In place of these gentlemen, only members of the National Socialist Party shall be employed.[15]

The so-called *Arierparagraph* (Aryan Clause), which banned Jews from any part of the film industry, was not announced until June 30, but the events of April 1 and the week that followed gave a clear enough warning. Many of those who could leave Germany did so.

The German people were as fond of films as Americans, perhaps even more so. They supported numerous film magazines, both "trades" and those of a popular nature. The latter kind included the daily *Film-Kurier* (ceased publication in 1944); and the less prestigious weeklies *Film-Woche* and *Film-Welt* (both closed in 1942). The circulation of these magazines was enormous and one of Goebbels' first tasks in the film field was to get control. *Film-Kurier* went first, receiving a new editor on April 5, Dr. Luitpold Nusser, formerly in charge of the film press division of the Nazi party Propaganda Office. *Der Film*, the oldest professional weekly devoted to film in Germany, lost its publisher, the greatly respected Max Mattison, who was replaced by "members of the National Front who will see to it that *Der Film* will reflect the opinion of the present government,"[16] as the issue of April 15 proclaimed bluntly. The article went on to say, "*Der Film* will retain its objectivity also in the future, but there is one exception:

we will not tolerate that the German film be dragged through the gutters of unscrupulous business maneuvers, not even if this is done in the disguise of nationalism. On the contrary, *Der Film* will keep faith with the principles of government and will do all in its power to further the reconstruction of the German film art."

Needless to say, the industry was in a state of shock within a few months of the establishment of the Nazi government. The Berlin correspondent of the New York *Times* reported that on April 8 production had almost completely ceased at all studios pending the passage of expected film laws. The situation was not helped by conflicting statements on the nature of the future plans of the industry given by various Party spokesmen. At a luncheon on April 14, Hitler, who was usually content to stay out of Goebbels' film department, expressed his opinions in a slightly more earthy fashion than that favored by the propaganda minister. Although the remarks were made to the actor Tony van Eyck, apparently off the record, they were printed in the world press the next day. In part, Hitler said:

I want to exploit the film as an instrument of propaganda, but in such a way that every theatregoer may be clearly aware that on such and such an occasion he is going to see a political film. It nauseates me when I find political propaganda hiding under the cloak of art. Let it be either art or politics. The subject matter strikes me as immaterial. The artistic effort must be 100%. The saccharine gruel that has been put on the screen lately has been enough to chase away every person of judgement.[17]

Hitler's idea that propaganda and art don't mix was to be tested shortly in three films which proved beyond a doubt that film matters should have been left exclusively to Goebbels.

One of the prime offenders guilty of "saccharine gruel" was the giant Ufa company, which had been founded in 1918. In addition to producing films, it owned a large number of movie theatres including the most important in Berlin, which assured that its product received the most attention, a situation not at all to the liking of Tobis, the other major production company. In 1932, Ufa had more than 5,000 employees and workers in every field related to the film.

A somewhat peculiar situation developed between Ufa and the

Nazi government. The majority of the shares in the company were held by Alfred Hugenberg (1865–1951), a press lord who not only owned the conservative Scherl Publishing Company, but who dabbled in politics with far-reaching results. In 1931 he had signed the so-called "Harzburger Front" with Hitler on behalf of his *Deutschnationale Partei*, and had thrown a great deal of support to Hitler at a crucial time in Hitler's political career. Hugenberg was rewarded in February of 1933 with the position of head of the Department of Economics for the new regime, but his tenure lasted only until June of 1933, when he returned to his publishing and film activities. Hugenberg, with his shares in Ufa, could bring pressure to bear on the studio heads to make films which aided the Nazi cause, such as *Morgenrot* and *Hitlerjunge Quex*. However, the other stockholders and most of the actual management of the company were cool to the Nazi cause.

One of the reasons for this was that Ufa had considerable foreign exports, and the new regime gave every sign of stopping the production of the kind of film which could be profitably shown abroad for much-needed foreign currency. Insubordination to the government was shown in various ways, particularly in neglecting directives from Goebbels. The Ufa could do this because it had virtual control of an organization called SPIO, which was made up of representatives of the film producers of Germany, somewhat along the lines of the American P.G.A. (Producers Guild of America) but far more powerful in industry affairs.

The Party members at the Ufa invited Goebbels to speak to them on April 27 at the gigantic studio complex situated at Neubabelsberg to the south-west of Berlin. *Film-Kurier*, now in Nazi hands, gave a somewhat cautious report of his speech, which was apparently not well received by the independent Ufa workers.

It was to be gathered from the content of his important address that Dr. Goebbels was aware of the pessimism and low spirits in certain sections of the industry. Unrest was evident in the German production centers. He wanted to seize the opportunity to point out that he would be the last to let the German film down. On the contrary, one should know him well enough now to realize how close to his heart the movie industry is. He promised to advance the industry by various means. Until now, unfortunately, the German film industry has not fulfilled its deepest task, i.e. the task of every art: to be a pioneer fighter for national culture. Instead, it had performed disgraceful boot-blacking service and was definitely behind the times. All this was going to be changed now. In the movies, like everywhere else, *Gleich-schaltung** was a prerequisite.[18]

Cautious revolt was in the air in various artistic fields. The great conductor Wilhelm Furtwängler took public issue with Goebbels over the dismissal of the Jewish conductors Bruno Walter and Otto Klemperer from their posts with German orchestras and opera houses. Goebbels was apparently somewhat taken aback by this particular attack, but Walter and Klemperer left Germany for safer places.

The industry organizations were difficult to infiltrate and control. The first to go was the *Reichsverband Deutscher Lichtspieltheater*, a group roughly equal to the Theatre Owners of America. The report of its capitulation was published in *Film-Kurier* on March 18:

A reorganization of the *Reichsverband*, reflecting the will of the majority of associations represented in the group, took place last night. . . . Adolf Engl agreed to head the new group. The old board, realizing the signs of the times at this late hour, resigned unanimously, and empowered Engl—in a dignified manner—to take charge.[19]

The closing words of the old board, according to the article, were: "New times require new men. To clear the road is the command of the hour! We resign!"

If SPIO ignored Goebbels, DACHO, the official actors' and directors' association, challenged him. They presented the propaganda minister with a list of Jewish members who they felt should be allowed to continue their work because of distinguished service at the front during the war or because of their special service to German film. In retaliation, Goebbels disbanded the organization on July 1.

Early in May he began to take steps against both SPIO and DACHO. The members of both organizations were called together at the Kaiserhof Hotel for a series of speeches by various government figures with the aim of getting the two groups in line. Goebbels spoke

---

* *Gleichschaltung* roughly means the forced absorption of everything into the functions of the state, that is, Nazification; William Shirer translates the word as "coordination" (in quotation marks).

first, and, refraining from threats, delivered a somewhat reflective speech on what he considered to be good films.

He began by saying that he admired films greatly and simply could not understand the sudden nervousness and uncertainty in the industry because of the new government. He went on to surprise the group by giving examples of four films, by type, which he thought the German industry should try to emulate: Eisenstein's *Potemkin*, for excellence as propaganda; Lang's *Nibelungen* for showing modern themes although the setting was in remote times; *Anna Karenina* (apparently this was the German release title of the 1927 Garbo film, *Love*), an example of the purely artistic film; and Trenker's *Der Rebell* as a perfect blend of national epic with high artistic standards.

After this, Goebbels continued in his most charming manner to assure the audience that the national government would prohibit no films if the producers would do their duty. He told his listeners that amusing films were necessary and should continue to be made, but that these films had better meet certain national standards of quality, that is, Goebbels' own.

He was followed by Engl from the mentioned theatre owners' association, who laid down the hard line. He warned his audience that the "Friedrichstrasse crowd" (a reference to the Berlin street where Jewish producers had their offices) was through for good. Germany did not want to cut herself off from the rest of the world, he said, but German films must be made by Germans who understand the spirit of the German people. All non-Germans in distribution must go. He ended by declaring war on Tobis for its monopoly of the sound-film patents.

Arnold Raether, from the Ministry of Fine Arts, concluded the program. He told the disappointed audience that the government had no plans for subsidy of the industry, but it was going to issue permits to companies and cinemas, which would go only to those who in the last fourteen years had favored the Nazi principles. He made a special point that the Ufa was no friend of his office, and pointed out to those who had not already noticed it that the Ufa had not even been invited to the meeting. He further warned the absent members of the Ufa to relinquish control of SPIO immediately, or there was going to be trouble for both groups. He ended his talk by saying that the purpose of making films was twofold: to educate the people and to make propaganda for the state.[20]

In an effort to please the government, the film companies voluntarily began to ease Jewish actors and actresses out of their films, although this requirement had not yet become law. Everyone was amazed when Goebbels showed up at the premiere on May 6 of the film *Ein Lied geht um die Welt* (*A Song Goes Round the World*), featuring the Jewish radio tenor Josef Schmidt, made from a Jewish script, and directed by the Jewish director Richard Oswald, in fact about as Jewish a film as was to appear after the Nazis took power. Goebbels appeared to enjoy himself immensely. Possibly he liked Schmidt's excellent voice; perhaps he was merely playing one of his sardonic jokes. In any case, a reviewer for the *Deutsche Kultur-Wacht* expressed the more normal Party position when he wrote, "A song goes round the world all right, but it's the Horst Wessel Song!"[21] Goebbels never got around to banning the film until October 1937.

However, in case anyone thought the government was getting soft on censorship of films, particularly on grounds of "race," Goebbels banned a film called *Taifun* (*Typhoon*) only a few days later. This particular work had been directed by Robert Wiene of *The Cabinet of Dr. Caligari* fame, and starred a number of popular actors in a drama of plague and other natural catastrophies in Asia. The censorship decision is interesting as an example of the early attitudes on "race":

The tendency of this picture is to show a dispute between Germans and Asians. The racial problem is the central problem of today. The film displays a completely negative attitude. It fails to pay attention to the racial instinct of the German people and does not spare the German people the feeling of inferiority. In every way the film evades its responsibility to educate the people systematically in the field of racial hygiene. The German people would be unable to understand why a film which portrays the German people as inferior to Asians is permitted to be shown publically. In our time it is especially unbearable to show a film which runs contrary to the intentions of the national government.[22]

It was one thing to produce films which included propaganda for national socialism when the settings were in the past, but it was quite another matter to bring modern Party history (or legend) to the screen. Goebbels thought it a better idea to slip the propaganda into a film gradually rather than to announce it from the start, but the latter course was hard to avoid when the subject of a film was to be the life of a recent Party hero. In 1933, three rather blatant propaganda features were produced of this variety: *SA-Mann Brand*; *Hitlerjunge Quex*; and *Hans Westmar*.

The first, *SA-Mann Brand*, was released June 14 to profound public indifference. It was made at the small Bavaria Studio (at the time, the German equivalent of Monogram) by a third-rate director (Franz Seitz), and a cast of virtually unknown actors. The general

Manfred Kömpel-Pilot and Heinz Klingenberg as two Nazi rowdies in Franz Seitz's *S.A.-Mann Brand* (1933).

shoddiness of the whole production is indicative of the lack of importance attached to the film in high places. Despite an impressive opening night at the Gloria-Palast with thousands of SA members lining the streets, audiences preferred the American film *I Am a Fugitive from a Chain Gang* which was running at the same time in one of the Ufa cinemas.

New film laws were announced on June 30 to coincide with the enactment of the "Aryan Clause" of the same day. Starting July 1, Jews were to be completely excluded from the industry. No production by foreign companies in Germany was allowed without native-born Germans in charge or, in special cases, foreigners of German descent. In actual practice, the latter part of the law had effect only on Deutsche-Universal, since almost no foreign films were being shot in Germany at the time. July 12 brought even stricter restrictions. Workers desiring any kind of film job would have to present proof that both their parents and grandparents were "Aryans."

However, for the time being, films which had been made with Jewish actors, authors, producers or directors before the law went into effect were still allowed to be shown. If they had been prohibited, there would have been very few German-language products available.

In lieu of banning films, which was bad for the Party image abroad, it was often more convenient to stage a "popular demonstration"; the local police took the hint to have the film's exhibition stopped in the interest of public safety. A good example of this technique is revealed in the treatment accorded to the film *Wege zur guten Ehe* (*Ways to a Good Marriage*), based on ideas by the pioneer sexologist Th. H. Van de Velde, whose works had been previously banned by the Nazis. The *Deutsche Allgemeine Zeitung* of July 5 reported a "public demonstration" in the North German city of Kiel:

In agreement with the authorized city officials, the student body of Kiel started an action of protest and finally succeeded in the immediate banning of the film *Wege zur guten Ehe*. Although the highest Berlin censorship office on May 16 had cleared this film about "enlightenment" which demonstrates "love as the woman needs it," and although it has been shown without incident since then in many cinemas before large crowds, the student body of Kiel considers itself obliged to protest because the film is "poorly concealed propaganda for Van de Velde's ideas." Van de Velde's books were publicly burned during the *auto da fé* of May 10. The Kiel students argue that it is therefore intolerable that the German people should be instructed by the film of a blacklisted author whose social and sexual-ethical point of view contradicts fundamentally the life philosophy of national socialism. So as to avoid unpleasant incidents, the Kieler Lichtspieltheater has heeded the wishes of the Kiel students and has canceled future showings of the Van de Velde film.[23]

However, the film was not banned nationally until March 7, 1937; the participation of such popular performers as Olga Tschechowa, Alfred Abel, and Hilde Hildebrand probably made it impossible to ban it at once without alarming these actors and their many admirers, an action Goebbels desired to avoid.

If the work of a Jewish author could be the subject of a public demonstration, the same could happen to a Jewish actor, particularly if he was unlucky enough to have previously offended the regime. This was the experience of Max Hansen, who starred in a film called *Das hässliche Mädchen* (*The Ugly Girl*) which had been made between February and April under the direction of Hermann Kosterlitz, later to be known in Hollywood as Henry Koster. *Film-Kurier* covered the premiere in the September 8 issue:

There was applause for the movie. Dolly Haas received an ovation. When she brought Max Hansen with her on the stage for the next curtain call, whistling was heard from various sides. The applause stopped. The whistling continued. The curtain remained closed because rotten eggs were thrown at the stage. Someone called from the balcony: "We want German movies! We want German actors! We do not need Jewish actors, we have enough German actors! Aren't you ashamed, German women, to applaud Jewish actors? Oust the Jew Max Hansen, who only six months ago sang a couplet about 'Hitler and Little Cohn' in a cabaret!"[24]

Despite having all the facilities of a propaganda division of the government under his control, Goebbels was not satisfied that the affairs of the cultural world were being properly handled. Accordingly, his next project was to organize the Reich Chamber of Culture. The preliminary organization was announced in somewhat garbled form on July 23, but the actual Culture Chamber was established September 22. As one book describes it:

> Goebbels sponsored the law which created a Reich Chamber of Culture to work alongside his ministry. He was the President of this organization, and it was decreed that every worker in the cultural field had to belong to his appropriate section of it. There were seven of these sections, or sub-chambers—the chambers of broadcasting, press, literature, fine arts, theatre, music and film. Membership included not only the creative cultural workers such as writers, broadcasters, actors, and musicians, but also those whose function was to equip or to present the arts, such as publishers, radio manufacturers, and musical instrument makers. The Chamber also engulfed the cultural organizations* such as libraries, choirs, orchestras and acting schools.[25]

The Chamber of Film, or *Filmkammer*, was broken down into the following sections: General administration, politics and culture policy, artistic supervision of film production, movie economics, professional film organizations, film production, movie management in the industry, movie theatres, film technique, with professional committees, cultural and propaganda films and their display.

As time went on, modifications were made, which will be discussed later. In addition to the ten major sections, there were numerous subdivisions and local appointments. But each official was personally appointed by the president of the Reichsfilmkammer. The first to hold this office was Dr. Fritz Scheuermann, about whom more will be said later.

In October, the *Schriftleitergesetz* or "law for editors" was put into effect, which made it mandatory for all editors to obtain licences from Goebbels in order to practice their craft. These licences could be obtained only after a thorough "racial" and political investigation. Section 13 of this remarkable law read, "Editors are required to deal truthfully with their topics and to evaluate them to the best of their knowledge."

---

* For details of this enormous organization, see the establishing laws printed in *Reichsgesetzblatt 1933*, I, 483, 531 ff.

The importance for film of this law is considerable, for it had a direct bearing on film reviews and film writing, which was to remain relatively free of interference (at least in some newspapers) until 1936 when criticism of the arts was officially abolished. Film reviewers were anxious to prove their loyalty, however, as this article by one Wolfgang Ertel-Breithaupt in the *Berliner Tageblatt* (October 8) shows:

When I edited the first national film magazine, *Filmkünstler und Filmkunst*, in 1929, I applied the same standards which form the basis of our present newspaper law, for I realized that only from a truly German world view would ensue a new creation of artistic film production. It goes without saying that the greater elements of the movie industry at that time fought against me to the very end. There was no gratitude to be expected, but a true fighter fights for the benefit of his convictions and does not ask for payment. Basic creative changes have to be measured by different standards, and those who are culturally far-sighted must view these things horizontally to rediscover the true measure for their conscience.[26]

The outstanding gaffe of the year was the production of a film biography of the early Nazi martyr, Horst Wessel, prepared for the twenty-sixth anniversary of his birth. The historical Wessel was a pimp murdered in a street brawl. His major contribution to the Nazi cause was the composition of the words for the first verse of the so-called Horst Wessel Song, the anthem of the Party. (The music used was adapted from a North Sea fishermen's song.)

Since the facts of Horst Wessel's life were unsuitable for mass consumption, a revised biography by Hanns Heinz Ewers was used as the basis of the film, with this remarkable author providing the scenario.* The music was composed by Dr. Ernst ("Putzi") Hanfstängel, a crony of Hitler and Goebbels who later became the government's liaison officer for the Anglo-American press. The direction was assigned to Dr. Franz Wenzler, a mediocre craftsman who passed out of the annals of German film-making in 1935. Leading roles in this second

---

* Ewers had scripted one of the first important German films, Paul Wegener's *Der Student von Prag* (1913), and had written the sensational novel *Alraune* which has been filmed at least three times to date.

attempt at modern Party propaganda were assigned to a cast of nonentities with the exception of the great Paul Wegener, who played a Communist leader.

Under the title *Horst Wessel*, the film was previewed on October 3 at the Capitol Cinema before an invited audience, which included Göring, Wilhelm Furtwängler, Erich Kleiber, members of the SA, some actors and actresses, selected diplomats, and a few newspapermen. The special matinee passed without incident.

But on the 9th, the film was suddenly forbidden on the day of its scheduled premiere. The official communiqué reported, "The reasons underlying the decision may be summed up in the sentence: the film does justice neither to Horst Wessel, whose heroic figure it belittles through inadequate representation, nor the National Socialist move-

Emil Lohkamp as the hero of *Hans Westmar* (1933),
the slightly disguised biography of Horst Wessel.

ment, on which the state now rests. The film thus jeopardizes vital state interests and Germany's reputation."[27]

The film was sent back for reediting. An entire section concerning the origin of the "Horst Wessel Song" was removed, probably because it revealed how little Wessel really had to do with its composition. Other short cuts were also made.

Under the new title *Hans Westmar, Einer von vielenein deutsches Schicksal aus dem Jahre 1929 (Hans Westmar, One of the Multitude, a German Life Tragedy of the Year 1929)* the film went to the censor again on November 23 and was at last shown on December 13.*

The Berlin correspondent of the New York *Times*, Claire Trask, synopsized the film for her readers:

It shows a student, Hans Westmar, returning from a genial, waltz-loving Vienna to an objectionably international Berlin, where, in a bar, a Negro jazz band plays havoc with the martial rhythms of "Die Wacht am Rhein" and a Spanish dancer toys with the morals of a somewhat less martial burgher of the democratic year 1929. It shows Communism as a corroding force and its head, a Russian, a serf to Moscow. Hans Westmar sees delivery from all this and more in the tenets of National Socialism. He becomes active. His organizing gifts are extraordinary, but he believes the Party's growth to be in the masses. So he gives up his studies and becomes a manual laborer. He goes to live in the East of Berlin, the stronghold of the Communists. They plot against him, for he succeeds in winning over too many of their members. He is shot, and though he lingers a few days, the wound is fatal and he dies.

The most realistic and therefore the most vital parts of this picture are its mass-scenes. The supposed-to-be-historically-exact street fight as the funeral cortège passes the Karl Liebknecht House, the Communist headquarters, is brutally convincing and gives one the sensation of an eye-witness. In the transition from *Horst Wessel* to *Hans Westmar*, the film loses continuity and takes a knowledge of the book too much for granted. Because of this and in spite of an overabundance of close-ups, the intent of the picture is reversed—the story of Hans Westmar merely becomes background to a forcefully documented national movement.[28]

* This is the date given in Bauer's index of German films, a usually accurate source. Most other references list February 3, 1934 as the official premiere.

Despite some occasional terrible acting, the film holds up well and is one of the best propaganda films of the 'thirties. The funeral sequence is so realistic that many believed it to be a newsreel, and the crowd scenes are skillfully managed. In style, the film is far closer to the Russian models than to any German film heretofore seen on the screen. *Hans Westmar* is a film that should be seen and studied by anyone interested in mass propaganda, and it is of particular interest when compared with the Ewers book, which is fairly easy to obtain today.

The sudden banning of the film was the occasion for a number of ribald jokes by Berlin moviegoers. Those who took *Hans Westmar* seriously (not a large group) were represented by H. E. Fischer, who contributed the following to the *Berliner Lokal-Anzeiger* on December 14:

At a time when footloose men without a country are spreading lies about the New Germany in foreign countries, it has become necessary to revive in the movies the Germany of the past when these selfsame men slandered Germany within its own borders. At a time when certain foreign countries did not want to see what was hidden beneath the Brownshirts, i.e. the heart of a political fighter, the pulse of a man of faith, the holy fires of hope; today, when in the United States of America the first anti-German propaganda film is being made,* the time is ripe when a German movie shall demonstrate what it meant to conquer Germany, what it meant to be a "Nazi," what it meant to be persecuted, beaten up and yet to believe, to fight, and to conquer.[29]

Despite the enormous publicity the film received, it was poorly attended by the Berlin public, which was quickly developing a total resistance to political films.

In the meantime, the Ufa had taken Raether's warning to heart and had produced the third of the Party films, *Hitlerjunge Quex*, which, after a special preview for Hitler on November 12 in Munich, was premiered on November 19, before the first public showing of *Hans Westmar*.

---

* Apparently a reference to something called *Hitler's Reign of Terror*, a Jewell release of April 27, 1934. It ran into almost as much censorship trouble in the United States as *Hans Westmar* had faced in Germany.

Members of the Hitler Youth join in singing a song, from Hans
Steinhoff's elaborate propaganda vehicle *Hitlerjunge Quex* (1933).

Unlike *SA-Mann Brand* and *Hans Westmar*, *Hitlerjunge Quex*
was a major production of the Karl Ritter unit, lavishly financed, with
a script by K. A. Schenzinger and B. E. Lüthge from the former's
novel, which was based on the case of Herbert Norkus. Norkus was a
young boy murdered by the Communists in 1932; his assassination
occurred at a time fortunate for the Nazis, and furnished Goebbels
with an excellent excuse to make a stirring speech over the boy's grave.

The direction was given to Hans Steinhoff (1882–1945?), an important Nazi director, later to be entrusted with some of the lavish
propaganda vehicles of the early 'forties. A rather dour North German,
Steinhoff was particularly successful in biographical melodrama, although he occasionally showed a flair for stylish comedy. Unlike most
of the Nazi directors, Steinhoff had been well estabilshed even before
the coming of sound,* had directed the young Jean Gabin, and, as
a matter of curiosity, had brought to the screen one of the first scripts
of Billy Wilder, *Scampolo, ein Kind der Strasse* (1932). To borrow
a term of William Shirer, he was perhaps the first "intellectual gang-

---

* Steinhoff's directorial debut is usually credited to *Der falsche Dmitri*
(1923), with Eugen Klöpfer.

ster" of the industry, and one of the few directors during the Nazi period to be outspokenly in favor of the regime.

The leading roles in *Hitlerjunge Quex* were taken by Heinrich George, one of the best actors of the period, his wife, Bertha Drews, also a talented actress, and Claus Clausen. The story concerns an heroic boy, Quex (or Heini) (played by an otherwise unidentified Hitler Youth), whose father and mother are dedicated Communists. But Quex is drawn to the young Nazis, and is eventually murdered by a group of enraged and drunken Bolsheviks. The film has been analyzed elsewhere in great detail.[30]

The photography (Konstantin Irmen-Tschet) and art direction (Benno von Arent and Arthur Gunther) are up to the highest Ufa standards, with highly mobile cameras and beautifully designed sets. Particularly interesting is the opening sequence of the picture in which a boy attempts to snitch an apple from a grocers and sets off a riot; the only character to profit is a little girl who is shown in a number of shots, sitting in a gutter while being pelted by apples from heaven. A local carnival sequence includes an anti-Nazi *Moritat* obviously borrowed from the opening of the *Dreigroschenoper* film.

The premiere was a gala occasion, preceded by the performance of a Bruckner symphony and a speech by Baldur von Schirach, the leader of the Hitler Youth and author of the lyrics of the song used in the picture. The audience included most of the Party leaders, and their entrance to the Ufapalast am Zoo was lined by thousands of Hitler Youth in uniform.

*Hitlerjunge Quex* succeeded where the other films had failed because the producers were clever enough to select a hero with whom an audience could identify, and to set him in a story full of familiar, if somewhat violent, clichés. It has none of the neo-documentary quality of *Hans Westmar*, but it is a better film in respect to story, direction, and acting, and more typical of the type of propaganda feature favored by the Nazis in later years.

If the unfortunate Ufa had succeeded in pleasing the government with *Hitlerjunge Quex*, they fell from grace again over a rather arty little melodrama entitled *Du sollst nicht begehren* (*Thou Shalt Not Covet*). The script of the film had been written by its director, Richard

Schneider-Edenkoben, a young and talented artist. His script had been sent to Walther Darré, the incompetent minister of food and agriculture, and returned with some suggested changes; as usual, no one paid much attention to Darré's comments.

The story of the film is simply that of Cain and Abel, here called Görk and Lutz. Görk works the soil on a small farm, and is jealous of his brother Lutz, who has returned home from the city and takes up the easier job of sheep-herding. Eventually Lutz steals his brother's girl and Görk kills the pair. The film had almost no dialogue, was beautifully photographed by Werner Bohe, and had a fine musical score by Herbert Windt.

Darré went after the film as a supposed slander of his farmers. He further claimed that the actor Walter Griep in the role of Görk was made up to look like Marinus van der Lubbe, the Dutch boy who had recently fired the Reichstag. A whole list of foolish objections ended with: "We passionately object to the film. That the Ufa has brought it out in spite of earlier disapproval will prove neither a blessing to it nor the German people."[31]

The film year 1933 ended in somewhat of a stalemate. Goebbels had succeeded in infiltrating the organization of the industry but he had failed in trying to bring it around to the National Socialist point of view. Most of the actors, writers, and directors had open contempt for the regime and both the Ufa and Tobis did everything in their power to counteract its directives. Some of the best artists in the film world began to emigrate, many finding a welcome in America.

But the handwriting was on the wall. A little book by Hans Traub entitled *Der Film als politisches Machtmittel* (*The Film as a Means of Political Persuasion*), (1933), left little doubt that the film was going to be put to use by the state in new ways, principally as an organ of propaganda, as this passage indicates:

Without a doubt the film as a means of communication has outstanding value for propaganda purposes. Persuasion requires this type of language, which conveys a strong message through simple stories and vivid action. Furthermore, the moving picture occupies second place among all propaganda means. In the first place stands the living word: the Führer in his speeches. . . . Within the great realm of language, however, which approaches the listener through technical means, the most effective method is the motion picture. It requires constant attention, for it is full of surprises, sudden changes in action, time and space, and is incredibly rich in the rhythm of increasing and decreasing emotions. When we consider that movies are screened once, most twice, and at times up to four times daily in 5000 cinemas, we realize that the film has the following main characteristics of an ideal propaganda vehicle: 1) the potential subjective appeal to the "world of the emotions"; 2) selective limitations of content; 3) polemic value from the start; 4) repetition in "lasting and regular uniformity," to use Hitler's words.[32]

## II

Only a small number of films made during the Third Reich contained propaganda. The percentage rarely, if ever, went over 25 for any given year. There are two reasons for this:

First, people had to be lured into the cinema to spend money. From the start, the German public registered resistance to films which were too obviously propagandistic. Although the industry was later state-supported and state-owned, it was necessary to bring in money just as in any normal business venture. So the studios had to produce and release a large number of films that were certain to make a profit on the basis of past experience.

Secondly, it was impossible to find enough writers, directors, and actors able to make explicit propagandistic films. These films with political content, as a rule, were made on larger budgets and had more elaborate shooting schedules. For these reasons, each company could turn out only a few each year. It was simpler to inject messages into newsreels and documentary films than into features. Audiences paid to see the feature but also saw the newsreels and shorts, so in the end it came out to the same thing. To make sure that the viewers remained captive, it was common practice after 1941 to have the doors of the cinema locked during the projection of newsreels.

The year 1933 is uncommonly interesting because it marked the release of the final films made before the establishment of the Hitler government, and the first films of the new regime as well. A total of 135 films were released, the work of 73 directors (plus two American codirectors called in for export versions)—an unusually representative selection. Only eleven of these films were banned after the war by the Allied Military Government censorship, and some on casual grounds. The Nazis themselves banned nine, many of them years after the original release. Production declined by twenty-one from the 1932 total, partly because of the period when the industry virtually closed down to await directives from the new government.

Some of the films one would most like to see are unfortunately virtually unavailable. Even the largest collections of German films have holes in the 1933–1935 period partly because of the deterioration of nitrate stock and the wear and tear of time, partly because some of these films were apparently lost when the small companies that made them went out of business. It is relatively easy to find almost any Ufa or Tobis film, but it is another matter to locate something made by Edda-Film and released through an independent combine, such as Thea von Harbou's *Elisabeth und der Narr*, which sounds uncommonly interesting in the reports.

However, 1933 is better than some later years because of a lively export market that sent German films around the world; a number of titles exist in American vaults (with English subtitles), which have long ago vanished in their country of origin.

One of the most extraordinary films of the immediate pre-Nazi period is Frank Wysbar's *Anna und Elisabeth* (April 13, 1933).* Wysbar† is a director who does not fit into the pattern of the time. His specialty was the supernatural, divorced from the shock elements that characterize the genre in America. *Anna und Elisabeth* is an example of his skill in handling difficult subjects with imagination and taste.

The film again brought together the team of Dorothea Wieck and Hertha Thiele, who had scored an enormous success in *Mädchen in Uniform* (1932). Miss Thiele plays a young girl able to work miracles; she raised her brother from the dead and cured a woman with a de-

---

* Dates in parentheses indicate official premiere as listed in Bauer's index, unless otherwise indicated.

† Wysbar later emigrated to the United States, changed his name to Wisbar, and is familiar to early television viewers who saw him introduce his weekly program "Fireside Theatre." He also produced and directed numerous cheap films for PRC (Producers Releasing Corporation) during the 1940's. He returned to Germany after the war and died there in 1967.

formed neck. She is forced against her will to use her powers on a crippled and slightly unbalanced young woman (Wieck) who forms a mystical attachment to the girl and attempts to manage her life. Forced by the Church to prove her powers before an open court, Anna hesitates and fails to resurrect Elisabeth's husband, who has died during the course of the investigation. Anna failed because the man had no faith when alive; Elisabeth misunderstands and throws herself into a quarry believing the girl has betrayed her. She is rescued, but her future is ambiguous, as is Anna's.

It would have been simple to have played the film on a single note of hysteria throughout, but instead there is a mood of quiet malevolence, as though the girl's gift is perhaps not sent from heaven. The dark houses of the small town are set against a bright, sunny sky, but gradually the powers of darkness are victorious.

The film is beautifully acted, and gave Miss Thiele the best of her roles after *Mädchen. Anna und Elisabeth* was shown in the United States with English titles, but it apparently attracted little attention, and it would seem to be completely forgotten in Germany as well. It is a film that merits a revival.

The other great film of the year was Max Ophüls' *Liebelei* (March 10, 1933), based on Schnitzler's play of the same name. Since the film has virtually no connection with any Nazi-period film (although it

Hertha Thiele works a miracle in Frank Wysbar's unusual *Anna und Elisabeth* (1933).

would seem to have influenced some of Käutner's work) there is not much reason to deal with it in detail here. *Liebelei* was released without the names of either Schnitzler or Ophüls on the credits. The most ironic point about the film is that it was banned *after* the war, despite the fact that it is profoundly pacifist and hardly glorifies the military caste which it depicts. The cast included Wolfgang Liebeneiner and Gustaf Gründgens, both to be popular actor-directors during the Nazi period, and Magda Schneider, Luise Ullrich, and Olga Tschechowa, one of the most powerful line-ups in the history of German film. Ophüls' other film released during the period, *Lachende Erben* (*The Laughing Heirs*), (March 6), was a minor comedy made long before *Liebelei* and held up for obscure reasons.[33]

Fritz Lang's last pre-war German film, *Das Testament des Dr. Mabuse* (*The Will of Dr. Mabuse*) was never seen in Germany, and had its premiere in Vienna on May 12, after being refused a censor certificate on March 29. If most authorities, and Lang's own personal remarks, are to be considered, the film would properly belong in the political section of this chapter. However, the elaborate thesis that the film was meant as a parable on the Hitler regime, with Nazi stock phrases put in the mouths of gangsters, seems far-fetched, and, if true, would certainly have gone over the heads of almost all the audience. Considering that the script was by Thea von Harbou (Frau Lang at the time), a writer who left her husband for the Nazis, the legend of the film's "true meaning" seems to have no foundation in fact.

Goebbels banned the film but offered a job to Lang; the director took the next train to Paris instead. Lang makes a great point about having supervised the film's release in a French-language print smuggled to Paris, implying that the German prints were destroyed.[34] However, the film was premiered in Vienna in the original version, distributed by Deutsche-Universal.

Goebbels disliked the film, for many reasons, especially because of an aversion to crime films in general. An article in *Film-Kurier* (September 29, 1933) gives the official line on films of this genre:

"Greatness" does not dwell in a criminality tainted with Metropolis fantasies, gigantic destructiveness, and decay, but rather in the great service done for the people by the tireless exponents of speed, intelligence, and justice. The limelight of the crime film is no longer focused on gangsters who go about their dirty business with some degree of skill (as has been the case until recently), but rather on heroes in uniform or civilian clothes who fight out of duty and are motivated by professional honor.

There will remain enough tension, darkness, and adventure when the German detective film stages its fight against enemies of the people, state, and society, which is closer to the reality of today. To fight for a just cause is the important point, not the glorification of criminals.[35]

The most successful films of the year 1933 were far below the quality of the films already discussed. *Brennendes Geheimnis* (*Burning Secret*), (March 20), directed by Robert Siodmak from a story by Stefan Zweig, was notable for the delicate handling of its theme. A married woman and her thirteen-year-old son go on a holiday to Switzerland. A visiting Don Juan goes after the mother through cultivation of a false friendship with the boy. Just as the mother is about to give in, the boy flees the resort for his home, where his mother follows him. Her marriage is saved by the boy's action. The film was helped by Siodmak's fine direction and an excellent performance by Willi Forst.

*Kleiner Mann, was nun?* (*Little Man, What Now?*), (August 3), apparently owed its success to the popularity of the Hans Fallada novel on which it is based, and the presence of an all-star cast including Hertha Thiele, Viktor de Kowa, and Hermann Thimig. The film, like its American remake of the following year, seems to have disappeared. The contemporary press was enthusiastic and many writers placed the film among the best of the year.

*S.O.S. Eisberg* (*S.O.S. Iceberg*), (August 30), has survived, for it was made by Deutsche-Universal in versions in several languages, including a popular one in English. Perhaps because we have seen so many films of this kind subsequently, it lacks the excitement it originally had, and shows its age. The photography is still beautiful and the story holds our interest, but the acting is melodramatic.

The virtues of Carl Froelich's *Reifende Jugend* (*Ripening Youth*), (September 22), are still evident, although an attempt to insert some rather clumsy propaganda ends the film on a sour note. For the most part, the story revolves around a modern Romeo and Juliet, who carry on their love affair in the *Waterkant*, the flat seacoast of the Baltic, near the Gothic port of Stralsund. Heinrich George plays the school teacher who eventually straightens out the various problems. The film catapulted Albert Lieven to stardom for his performance as the young hero, but Hertha Thiele was not at her best.

Several musicals are worth mention. *Leise flehen meine Lieder* (called in America *Schubert's Unfinished Symphony*), (September 8), was the first film directed by Willi Forst, and far above the usual musical biography. Ludwig Berger's *Walzerkrieg* (*The Waltz War*), (October 4), concerning the rivalry between Strauss and Lanner, and the love affair of Victoria and Albert, was one of the last of the type of musicals made at the early sound period which proved so popular with world audiences.

However, the biggest box-office hit was Reinhold Schünzel's *Viktor und Viktoria*, (December 28), a musical about a female impersonator who loses his voice and asks a young girl to play his role in the theatre. She does so well that she becomes a great star all over the world. The film has a delightful score by Franz Doelle, and Schünzel's direction is stylish. It is ironic that in the tragic year 1933 this silly comedy should prove to be the most popular film.

# 1934: GOEBBELS SHOWS
# HIS TEETH

The year 1934 was to be one of consolidation for the Nazi regime, following the violent changes of 1933, so well described by William Shirer:

When Hitler addressed the Reichstag on January 30, 1934, he could look back on a year of achievement without parallel in German history. Within twelve months he had overthrown the Weimar Republic, substituted his personal dictatorship for its democracy, destroyed all political parties but his own, smashed the state governments and their parliaments and unified and defederalized the Reich, wiped out the labor unions, stamped out democratic associations of any kind, driven the Jews out of public and professional life, abolished freedom of speech and of the press, stifled the independence of the courts and "coordinated" under Nazi rule the political, economic, cultural, and social life of an ancient and cultivated people.[1]

If Goebbels had given a sample of what he could do in 1933, 1934 was the year when he showed his teeth to the film industry. Controls were dramatically increased, although certain liberties, unthinkable only a few years later, were still permitted. Goebbels waited only until January 18 to bring the moving-picture producers into line in no uncertain terms. This first decree was reported in the *Völkischer Beobachter* of January 19, 1934:

The Kulturfilmstelle of the Reichsfilmkammer reports the following: The authorization to produce films, either professionally or for the common good, under public or private management, is by legal definition only permitted to members of the Reichsfilmkammer. With the exception of local movie houses, all moving picture enterprises, and therefore itinerant producers, firms which produce publicity films, associations or corporations privately or publically directed, must, by February 1, 1934, at the latest, become members of the appropriate branch of the Reichsfilmkammer, the "Reich Union of German Moving Picture Departments. . . ." Establishments which are not already members of the organization may be closed down at once. After the specified date, a general control will be established.[2]

This all-embracing decree for the film industry paralleled what Hitler was to do to state governments in the so-called "Law for the Reconstruction of the Reich" which was announced on January 30, 1934.

February was to be Censorship Month in the second year of the Third Reich. Goebbels' first move was to create the position of a "Reichsfilmdramaturg," the import of which was not fully realized at first. *Lichtbild-Bühne* of February 3 described the position as follows:

Minister of the Reich Dr. Goebbels has created in the Propaganda Ministry the position of Filmdramaturg of the Reich and has nominated editor Willi Krause to this post. The Filmdramaturg of the Reich is charged with advising the movie industry in all important questions concerning production. He is to examine all manuscripts and scenarios to see to it that topics which run counter to the spirit of the time are suppressed. Thus the work task formerly handled by the drama bureau of the Reichsfilmkammer is now being handled by the Reichsfilmdramaturg. All manuscripts and film treatments are in the future to be submitted to Krause and not to the Reichsfilmkammer.[3]

Krause, the new *Dramaturg*, was an old friend of Goebbels, having served as film reviewer on *Der Angriff*, Goebbels' newspaper. However, the industry considered him a bureaucratic bungler, and his "advice" was usually ignored as much as possible. His artistic ability was nil; the reaction to the film he scripted, *Nur nicht weich werden, Susanne!* (*Don't Lose Heart, Suzanne!*), (1935), was so unanimously bad that it probably contributed to his fall from Goebbels' good graces. He was replaced by Hans Jürgen Nierentz on April 1, 1936.

The most important film decree of the Third Reich became law on February 16, 1934, when the Cabinet passed an all-inclusive censorship bill, such as had never been seen in any country outside Soviet Russia. The thirty-three articles of this law[4] completely hamstrung filmmakers, although the full import of the new legislation was not apparent for some time. A laconic press release stated: "Hitherto film censorship has been negative. Hereafter, the new State will assume entire responsibility for the creation of films. Only by intensive advice and supervision can films running contrary to the spirit of the times be kept off the screen."[5] Those who had thought Goebbels would stop with his Dramaturg were rudely awakened.

The industry did not take this law without resistance. The general opinion was that Goebbels had gone too far, for the new law simply meant that the government, without quite saying so, had completely taken over the film industry.

All censors were to be appointed by Goebbels. They would now check all earlier German and foreign films and forbid all films "calculated to endanger important State interests or public order, or to offend National Socialist moral, artistic or religious sentiments, or endanger respect for Germany abroad or her relations with foreign countries."[6] In order to make a film, the producer had to submit the scenario and treatment to the Dramaturg, who eliminated anything repugnant to the state. Then, the film was produced and the completed work was sent to the censor, who made sure it followed the approved scenario. (It might be noted that, in practice, the "advice" of the Dramaturg was ignored, and films were usually shot with a script including sequences which were never submitted for approval.)

The most peculiar part of the law stated that "Presentations which, because of their brutalizing effect are forbidden in Germany, such as bullfights, may be admitted for distribution abroad. Thereby a helping hand will be given to German industry which must lean on exports."[7] This apparently meant that it was possible to make certain films in Germany which could not be shown there; strange as this seems, a few films were designated exclusively for the export market.

Another important part of the new law prohibited the showing of films by private organizations such as film clubs or film societies, which had formerly escaped the general censorship. Presentations by these groups now had to be passed by the censor in the regular fashion. The reason for this article is directly traceable to the continued showings of *All Quiet on the Western Front* by private groups, although the film had been forbidden by government decree since the Weimar Republic.

The only part of the law designed to find favor with the producers was the creation of a state bank for film financing. "Worthy films" could be aided with subsidies of various kinds, a practice which, with some modifications, remains in force today.

There were still some loopholes in film censorship. Foreign films, for the time being, were not as strictly controlled as the domestic product, although the censor was empowered to draw upon an advisory board from the Propaganda Ministry when problems of censorship of foreign films became particularly difficult.

The test case for foreign films was the release of the British film *Catherine the Great,* which was scheduled to have a gala Berlin premiere on March 8, 1934. The title role was played by the popular Jewish actress Elisabeth Bergner, who had emigrated from Germany in 1933 and who had made uncomplimentary remarks about the Nazi regime to the foreign press. Because the film was innocuous in content, it posed a special problem to the censor. Perhaps because Goebbels knew the release of the film would be followed closely by the foreign press, he decided not to take direct action.

But there was plenty of action from another quarter. At the premiere, attended by a fashionable audience, a large crowd of white-collar workers stood outside the cinema shouting anti-Semitic slogans and generally harassing the invited guests. A panic-stricken official of the Propaganda Ministry called Goebbels, who could not be located. The official decided to call Hitler, who personally ordered the crowd broken up by the police. At the second performance, there were threats of another outbreak; in an extraordinary move, the leader of the SA, Ernst Röhm, came on stage before the film and said that his troops would arrest any demonstrators in the audience. The subsequent showings passed without incident, but the film was suppressed on March 10.

In case anyone wondered who was responsible for the demonstrations, Dr. Alfred Rosenberg seemed to fill the bill after his article in the *Völkische Beobachter* of March 10, which read: "The attempt to present in Berlin émigré Jews, especially the warped Elisabeth Bergner, and to make money from them in Germany, represents an inartistic attempt against which we turn, especially because it is not an isolated case."[8]

The same day the Propaganda Ministry announced that all foreign films, after normal censorship, had to obtain certificates from the Ministry clearly stating lack of any further objections. Some writers have come to the conclusion that the Bergner affair was engineered by Goebbels as an excuse to enact new controls; however, he may merely have taken advantage of a situation caused by others.

A similar disturbance was caused by the screening of the film *Früchtchen* featuring the Jewish actress Franziska Gáal, which had run for some time at the Ufa Kurfürstendamm-Theater without trouble. Because this was an Austrian production, it had avoided the strict censorship, but it was also banned after the demonstration.

If British and Austrian films could be censored and banned, American films could also be harassed in several ways. The best example for study is provided by the treatment of the film *The Prizefighter and the Lady* which had been made at MGM in 1933 under the direction of W. S. Van Dyke II.

The star of the film was the Jewish boxer Max Baer. Goebbels was in a sticky position; Max Schmeling had just returned from the United States where he had been remarkably well treated, and he was scheduled to go back. An adverse reaction to Baer's film in Germany would have repercussions in the United States. Goebbels decided the best course was to write an editorial in *Der Angriff* asking his readers to accept the film.

Under the title *Männer um eine Frau*, the film opened in the middle of March at a big Berlin cinema as a benefit for the Winterhelp charity, in a subtitled version with only one small cut. Since titled prints were not popular outside of the big cities, MGM had a dubbed version prepared at the same time for future release. When this version was presented to the censorship board, the board decided to call in a special expert from the Propaganda Ministry. After much debate, the film was still without a licence. At long last the head censor asked the visiting expert if it was the presence of Max Baer in the film which bothered him. When he admitted this was the problem, the censor ordered both versions of the film banned with the official explanation that the film "had slight regard for womanhood."[9]

Unlike some of the other foreign companies, MGM appealed the decision, and the result of the suit was reported by the *Völkischer Beobachter* on September 29:

Metro-Goldwyn-Mayer-Film A.G. has filed an appeal against the decision of the Inspection Office, which forbade the release of the film *Männer um eine Frau* because of the participation of the American boxer Max Baer as a leading player. The Higher Inspection Office [*Oberprüfstelle*] in session today, has denied the appeal and upheld the ban. In agreement with the Inspection Office and with the experts from the Propaganda Ministry heard by the office, the *Oberprüfstelle* confirms that censorship cannot simply pass over the fact that the German people feel the presentation of films with Jewish actors to be a provocation. Therefore, a particularly strict standard must be applied to films of this kind. The relationship of the Jewish leading man—who, in the opinion of the *Oberprüfstelle* is a quite Negroid type in the bargain—with the non-Jewish women in the film, is in particular a violation of the National Socialist sentiment as interpreted by the new film law of February 16. On this legal ground for banning, the further presentation of the film, in either its original or German versions, is not permitted.[10]

Following this, numerous other American films were banned during the year including *The Trial of Mary Dugan, Voices of Spring, My Weakness, The Kid, Roman Scandals, Tarzan and His Mate, Manhattan Melodrama, Stand Up and Cheer, Baby, Take a Bow, Nana,* and *Men in White.*

The presence of Jews in the cast of foreign films was not the only reason for censorship. The last two films just listed fell into different categories, as explained in an article in the *Frankfurter Zeitung,* July 22, 1934:

The *Oberprüfstelle* has forbidden the showing of the films *Nana* and

*Men in White.* The basis of the ban on *Nana*, it is stated, is that the soldier is the main prop of the State, even of a foreign State, and ought not to be presented in a relationship with a prostitute, for thereby the authority of the State might be too readily undermined.

Concerning the ban on *Men in White*, it was announced that the new German State places special emphasis on the training of the new generation of doctors. The doctor should be involved in the science of life; he should be educated to be a human being who understands his fellow men so that he might help them. The film contradicts these high aims since (1) it glorifies the extraordinary position of a doctor who is without this bond with his patients and who lives and works only for his exalted science; (2) it labels the patients in the huge city hospital by number and count, a procedure by which the trust of the public—especially that of sick people—in the doctor is certainly not enhanced; and (3) the private affairs of the doctors are shoved in the foreground, while next door the patients are struggling with death.[11]

Censorship activity of this sort was hardly calculated to endear German films to foreign audiences, particularly when the newspapers in America and elsewhere reported the ban of each film in detail. Goebbels, ignorant as always of foreign attitudes, remarked in a speech before the representatives of the German film industry on March 23 that, "German films enjoy a great vogue abroad and are particularly fit for spreading German mentality and culture to the outside world, thus making propaganda for the new Germany."[12]

Although the banning of films was a major occupation of the Filmkammer in 1934, time was also found to save films, and the first German film archive was founded in March. It was reported by Arnold Raether as follows:

In the Führer's spirit and to express reverence for our Minister of Propaganda Dr. Goebbels, we have founded a film archive. With that, unproductivity should be eliminated as much as possible in the German film system, but, most of all, in the interest of the film economy, creative productiveness should be promoted. The Press section of the Propaganda Ministry is in charge of the archive, and is directly responsible to me.[13]

The archive was dedicated on February 4, 1935, in the presence of Hitler, Goebbels, Secretary of State Funk, Raether, (a high official in the Propaganda Ministry), and various actors and actresses. The new archive was in Harnack House, Berlin-Dahlem, although it would appear that the films were stored at Babelsberg.

One of Goebbels' most brilliant ideas concerned the use of the May Day holiday. This day had been used by the Communists for many years as an excuse for political demonstrations, particularly in the North and East of Berlin. To avoid this, Goebbels secretly planned in 1933 for a gigantic May 1 celebration in honor of the Nazi government, which he carried out with enormous success, completely eclipsing the Communist plans for demonstrations. The first year's celebration was mainly composed of speeches and parades, but for the 1934 event Goebbels decided to add some intellectual appeal by giving prizes in the evening to the outstanding cultural achievements of the year. At a gala celebration at the Berlin State Opera, Goebbels was forced to admit that "the decade of Germany's regeneration has not yet found its final artistic expression."[14]

The grand prize went to a book which almost no one had heard of, let alone read, and the second prize went to the film *Flüchtlinge* (*Refugees*). In the following years, individual first prizes were given for the best film and the best work of literature. It was somewhat ironic that the best film of the year was directed by an Austrian, Gustav Ucicky, and featured Hans Albers, who was not mentioned in the ceremony because he had set up a Lebensgefährtin with a Jewish woman in Switzerland.

Reviewing the film at the time of its December British release, one English critic found it a curious piece of work:

Stated to be based on actual events that happened in Harbin in 1928, the film presents a study of the mass suffering of refugees seeking to escape the horrors of military operation and the particular efforts of a group of German refugees to escape the "gangsterish" pursuit of Soviet agents, whose government is represented as denying to these Germans the status of German citizenship. While flesh and blood endure these agonies and human spirits are broken in anguish, the League of Nations is shown as a place of futile talk, not unmixed with cynicism. Bitter need for present and effective action brings forth a Leader of the German refugees who is portrayed as being alone capable of right judgement, and as having the power to inspire and the will to execute at discretion by revolver shot. The film appears to the re-

The evil Bolsheviks drag the helpless *Wolgadeutsche* to prison,
from Gustav Ucicky's prize-winning film *Flüchtlinge* (1934).

viewers as primarily propaganda—a defense of Germany's withdrawal
from the League of Nations and of the events of June 30th. *Refugees*
is conceived on the grand scale—like *Kameradschaft*, with which
technically and psychologically it has much in common. The tempo
is deliberately slow, allowing the ideas time to sink in: the photography
is first-class both from the view of technics and montage; the acting is
first-class of its kind, though many English people will find it over-
acted. Similarly, many English people will find its psychology crude,
occasionally even absurd and a trifle boring; and those who lived
through 1914–1918 will find the tune of "Pack Up Your Troubles"
something inappropriate in the mouths of Germans and with German
words. Yet those who want to see a self-portrayal of Nazi ideals and
convictions will find *Refugees* very well produced and thoroughly
characteristic. . . . The film is a very good piece of screen work.[15]

*Flüchtlinge* is an uncommonly effective film when viewed today. The
photography of Fritz Arno Wagner is still superlative, and the film's
sound track is extraordinarily sophisticated with off-screen noises often
playing an important part in the narrative. In addition to its propaganda
value, the film was exciting as entertainment, particularly the sequence
in which Albers steals a railroad train and takes his fellow Germans
to safety in Harbin. The supporting players, particularly Käthe von
Nagy and Eugen Klöpfer, perform their roles with conviction and re-
straint unusual for the period.

One tenet of the Nazi educational philosophy was the political in-doctrination of the young. In April 1934, the first steps were taken when the Hitler Youth organization of Cologne demonstrated a model "Film Hour for the Young" (*Jugendfilmstunde*) in which selected propaganda films were screened to members as part of the regular events. This was henceforward mandatory once a month in all Hitler-jugend groups.

However, the most important step was the edict of Dr. Bernard Rust, minister of education, referred to as RK 5020 U-11. This decree ordered the showing of political films within the framework of class-room education. The Weimar Republic's National Institute for School Films was replaced by a new "Office of Educational Films." This eventually blossomed into an enormous organization which was broken down into 30 state offices (*Landesbildstellen*) and 1,007 dis-trict offices. By 1936, 70,000 schools were equipped with 16mm pro-jectors, and 227 films were commissioned for school use and 330 for universities; a total of 10,000 prints were made. Only 60 titles were for vocational training, and 19 for agriculture. The rest were propaganda.

A complex plan for the use of these films in classroom situations was developed during the period. The most common was for a teacher to receive a ten-minute silent film with a printed lecture which he was expected to deliver for forty minutes. Following this, the film illustrat-ing the lecture was projected, and then the students were given a ten-minute quiz to see if they had absorbed the material.

As Dr. Rust remarked, "The leadership of Germany more and more comes to believe that schools have to be open for the dissemina-tion of our ideology. To do this job, we know of no better means than the film. The film is necessary, above all, for the youngest of our citizens—the school children. The film has to bring near to them all political problems of today, knowledge of Germany's great past, and understanding of the development of the Third Reich. The National Socialist State definitely and deliberately makes the film the trans-mitter of its ideology."[16]

In the middle of May, the *Deutsche Allgemeine Zeitung* printed an extraordinary article criticizing the censorship board. It went so far as to say that viewers were tired of films which gave a too rosy view of life, and that perhaps a pessimistic picture might be good for a change. Goebbels immediately saw to it that the author of the article was barred from again publishing his views on films, and forced the newspaper to print an apology, which was done on May 20, 1934.[17]

Criticism of Goebbels' authoritarian methods was openly heard all over Germany, although not in print. The most outstanding denunciation came from Franz von Papen in a speech on June 17 at the University of Marburg, one of the last times anyone spoke up in public against the Propaganda Minister's methods and philosophy. While von Papen escaped with his life, his three writers were later executed, and the speech itself was hushed up.

The Marburg speech was but one indication of a situation of general unrest in Germany, which culminated with the murder of Röhm and many others on June 30. Goebbels was in an ambiguous position until the last minute; it was said that he refused to leave Hitler's side during the period for fear of being assassinated himself.

The Röhm purge also provided the reason for the creation of one of cinema's dubious masterpieces, Leni Riefenstahl's *Triumph des Willens.* Although this film was not released until 1935 (and will be discussed under that year), *Triumph des Willens* was planned as an attempt to show that the Röhm affair had not divided the Party, and to present to the world the spectacle of a unified Germany following the Nazi leadership.

The violent political events continued with the murder of the Austrian chancellor Dollfuss in Vienna in an unsuccessful German attempt to take over the Austrian government on July 25; on August 2 Hindenburg died and Hitler assumed complete power, although Hindenburg had only been a figurehead for some time.

The dire film situation was revealed in the annual report of the industry which was released on August 31, covering films released from June 1933 to June 1934. The figures showed that 117 German films and 104 foreign films had been shown during the period; the respective figures for 1932/33 had been 133 and 72. The reason for the cutback in domestic production could be traced to the uncertainty of the producers when faced with the increasingly complicated film legislation. Even at this early period in the Nazi regime the film companies had started to take refuge from the problems of the present in the production of comedies and period pieces; for the rest of the duration of the Third Reich only few films dealt in any serious way with problems of daily life in Germany.

The Reichsfilmkammer began meetings on September 20 under Dr. Fritz Scheuermann, another of Goebbels' dubious appointments. The purpose of the organization was stated in an article in the *Frankfurter Zeitung* of September 21:

The Reichsfilmkammer met on Thursday in Munich for a working session under the chairmanship of its President, Dr. Scheuermann. Before the private meeting began the President received representatives of the press. The choice of Munich as the meeting place, he explained, was intended to emphasize the significance of Munich as the capital city of art. Fundamentally, Dr. Scheuermann stated, the artistic goal of the Reichsfilmkammer is, following the guidelines of Dr. Goebbels, the absolute film—an artistically, musically, ethnically, and technically independent work of art. We no longer want a film which is an imitation of hackneyed operettas and the like. With regard to the foreign boycott propaganda, it must be stated that assuredly the creation of great National Socialist propaganda films will be furthered, but that these films will be only for domestic consumption, for National Socialism is, in the words of Adolf Hitler, not for export. On the other hand, German films intended for export will be those which, as works of art, have international value and appreciation. In the creation of artistic films, indigenous virtues [*Kräfte*] would receive full attention.[18]

Despite every effort to "improve" German films, Goebbels, in a burst of rare public ill humor, admitted in a speech on November 29 that his efforts to improve the quality of films had been fruitless. He thoroughly frightened the film industry by suppressing two minor comedies which had already been passed by the censor. He said that there was nothing objectionable about these films from a political standpoint, but that he had banned them to warn film companies to cease turning out "merely mechanical productions."[19] He went on to castigate the two offending films as "tasteless, void of any imagination, misusing their cast, musicians, and so forth to turn out dull, stupid, film fare."[20]

The two films in question were *Die Liebe siegt* (*Love Conquers*) (November 22) an operetta film by an obscure director named Georg Zoch, and *Ein Kind, ein Hund, ein Vagabund* (*A Child, a Dog, a Vagabond*), (November 29), by the somewhat more prestigious Arthur Maria Rabenalt.*

The much-abused film industry could not believe that the films had been suppressed on purely artistic grounds; the rumor went round Berlin that the real reason was that British money had financed the Rabenalt film, and that the money was not entirely "Aryan" in origin. The Rabenalt film was heavily cut and rereleased under the title *Vielleicht war's nur ein Traum* (*Perhaps 'Twas But a Dream*), which would indicate that someone involved had a sense of humor. To most of the industry the affair was more like a nightmare; the biggest studios in Germany closed down until the management could figure out the situation.

Despite the example of what had been done to the writer on the *Deutsche Allgemeine Zeitung* who had criticized the film situation in May, the *Berliner Tageblatt* in its Sunday edition of December 2 printed an editorial on the front page pleading for more freedom in the selection of movie subjects. It cited the situation in Russia where, after the creation of *Potemkin* and other major creative films, the government took complete control of the industry and ran it to the ground. It is not recorded what happened to the writer of this editorial.[21]

The rule that a representative of the Propaganda Ministry was required on the set of every film was rescinded on December 13. The reason given was surprisingly honest: no one paid any attention to him. Also, the new system of pre- and post-censorship took care of his function.

On December 21 the Reichsfilmkammer took steps against the problem of foreign newsreel crews which often secured highly uncomplimentary footage of Party functions. In the future, all cameramen would have to be members of a government film organization and would have to produce a special card giving them permission to shoot the event. This, in effect, stopped foreign newsreel photographers.

---

\* The Bauer index lists the date of the official ban on these films as January 12, 1935, although the actual date was apparently somewhat earlier.

The year ended with the most publicized anti-Semitic film demonstration to date. An Austrian film entitled *Ein Mädel aus Wien* (*A Girl from Vienna*) was playing at the Luitpold Cinema in Munich on Saturday evening, December 15, when a group of a hundred Brownshirts forced the management to stop the projection because the leading actor, Arthur Roscoe, was a British Jew.[22] A slightly different version of the incident, minus mention of the organized action of the Brownshirts, was published in the *Fränkische Tageszeitung* of December 18 under the heading "Away with Jewish Films!"

In one of the larger Munich cinemas an uproar broke out last Saturday during the evening performance, as the public energetically rejected the film being shown, *Ein Mädel aus Wien.* An eye witness reports the following:
"The alluring title *Ein Mädel aus Wien* had filled the cinema to the last seat. What was shown in the film had very little to do with our conception of 'German Vienna' but rather it showed, in a trashy and sordid fashion, how a Jew with the power of his purse tries to win a poor German girl [Magda Schneider] and set himself up as her protector. Individual scenes of the film were so repulsive and un-German that the public gave open expression to its indignation: a portion of the audience left the performance well before the end. The remaining public could finally not hold itself back any longer and got up ostentatiously with loud remarks. From the crowd you could hear people call: 'Germans, away from this Jewish film!' 'Show German films!' 'Munich is the city of art and doesn't want to see trash!' and so forth. The performance had to be stopped and the cinema management announced that the admission tickets would be valid for the showing of a better film."[23]

## II

Making one of its occasional attempts to please the Party (or, in this case, Göring), Ufa turned out a comedy entitled *Rivalen der Luft* (*Rivals of the Air*), (January 19). This was not exactly a propaganda film, but contained political elements. It concerned the rivalry of two glider pilots and glorified the excitement of aviation. Well directed by Frank Wysbar, it featured an exceptional cast including Hilde Gebühr, Sybille Schmitz, Wolfgang Liebeneiner, and Claus Clausen.

*Das alte Recht* (*The Old Right*), (January 27, 1934) was a political film of specialized interest. (Films premiered in the first few months of a given year were usually completed the previous year.) It was the first of several productions devoted to the *Erbhofgesetz*, usually referred to as the "Heredity Farm Law," which was passed September 29, 1933. It provided that farm estates over a certain size could not be sold or otherwise disposed of for debts. These estates were to be passed onto the son of the owner, thereby binding the landowner to his property whether he liked it or not. The film was designed for peasant propaganda purposes, and is in everyway the typical propaganda product one might expect for such an audience. It was first shown in the provinces and had no Berlin release until April.

*Stosstrupp 1917* (*Shock Troop 1917*), (February 20) was one of the most successful films glorifying events of World War I. The film was directed by the team of Hans Zöberlein and Ludwig Schmid-Wildy and used an enormous cast in a relatively lavish production. The film was forgotten until it was revived in London during 1963 at the National Film Theatre, where the program note summed up its values as they seemed to a modern reviewer:

This film is a kind of answer to Pabst's *Westfront 1918*. While setting out to be basically an antiwar film, the dialogue continually inserts Nazi militarist and nationalist propaganda, partly to emphasize the treachery of the civilian population in Germany as compared to the heroism and devotion of the common German fighting man at the front. It deals with various battles with the French, in Flanders and the English breakthrough at Cambrai and ends with a Christmas scene in the trenches with an English soldier, captured by the Germans, dying in their arms. The film is extremely well made and presents a remarkable study of trench warfare from the German point of view.[24]

Karl Hartl's *Gold* (March 29) continued the science-fiction trend of the earlier, internationally successful *Der Tunnel*. The story concerns a rich British alchemist who is convinced that it is possible to obtain gold from base metals by means of a giant underwater atomic reactor which he has built off the coast of Scotland. A good German scientist has been working on the same project, but he is killed and his laboratory blown up in a mysterious explosion. His assistant (Hans

The alchemist's underwater laboratory—which frightened allied atomic scientists out of their wits, who were convinced it really *worked*—from Karl Hartl's *Gold* (1934).

Albers) is semi-kidnapped by the British scientist, and sets to work on a new machine. It is a success at first, but when it begins to malfunction, the British scientist attempts to destroy the plant and everyone in it. At the last minute Albers manages to open the sealed gates of the laboratory and escapes with the alchemist's daughter (Brigitte Helm) before the whole operation is obliterated in a spectacular flood.

*Gold* was the Ufa's superproduction of the period, and reportedly took fifteen months to shoot. Albers sued for almost double his usual salary, but lost the case. The film was also made in a French version with Brigitte Helm, Pierre Blanchar, and Roger Karl, which helped to account for the long production period.

When the film was reviewed by an Allied censorship board after the war, the viewers wondered whether German scientists had invented an atomic reactor long before they were supposed to have done so. An effort was made to seize every known print, and the film was put under a restricted category. It is even reported, on reliable authority, that a copy was flown to the United States to be viewed by atomic scientists to see if the machines could actually perform. Of course they were

Willi Schur, Karl Ludwig Diehl, and Hermann Speelmans long for
the Fatherland while incarcerated in a (non-German) concentration
camp in Paul Wegener's *Ein Mann will nach Deutschland* (1934).

simply the product of the set designer's imagination. Because of this
incident, it was difficult to find a copy of this film until recently, and
one film archive kept it "under the counter" for a long time.

Paul Wegener's *Ein Mann will nach Deutschland* (*A Man Must Go
to Germany*) (July 26) was another World War I film, this time concerned with an engineer who returns to his fatherland in order to perform vital military tasks. Produced lavishly at the Ufa, it was well
directed by Wegener (better known as an actor) and played by a fine
cast. However, the script is too heavy with propaganda to be effective
as entertainment despite love interest in the person of the most attractive Brigitte Horney.

Herbert Selpin's *Die Reiter von Deutsch-Ostafrika* (*The Riders of
German East Africa*) (October 19) was one of the first violently anti-
British films, illegally filmed in part on locations in Tanganyika, and
apparently financed in part by the *Reichskolonialbund*. Ranging over
the period 1884–1914, it tells of two friends in Africa, one British
(Peter Voss), one German (Sepp Rist) who, after a series of adventures together (and pursuit of the same girl, who decides on the
German), find themselves on opposite sides when World War I
begins. The British officer is forced to burn the houses of German
settlers but in the end brotherhood is restored, complete with a ride
into the sunset.

The film is exceptionally crude in its script, and Selpin, a relatively sensitive director, was not yet sufficiently experienced to keep his cast under control. The British are usually presented drinking Black-and-White and singing "Tipperary"; there is a musical-comedy native called Mustapha, and a juvenile hero (Rudolf Klicks, the German Mickey Rooney of the period) who saves the heroine from the British at the cost of his life. The film was banned by the Nazi government in December of 1939 as pacifist, and by the Allies after the war as military propaganda.

The most overtly propagandistic of the year's fiction feature films was Carl Froelich's *Ich für dich, du für mich* (*I for You, You for Me*) (November 30) which was produced by Froelich's own production company and distributed by the Propaganda Ministry. Only a few very important political films received this treatment: *Triumph des Willens* and *Friesennot* were two others of the period.

Director Froelich (1875–1953) was one of the most enthusiastic supporters of the Nazi regime and was eventually given the title of

Sepp Rist (center) as the German hero of Herbert Selpin's anti-British
*Reiter von Deutsch-Ostafrika.*

Two city girls
down on
the farm,
from Carl Froelich's
repulsive
propaganda vehicle
*Ich für dich—
du für mich* (1934).

"Professor" after serving as head of the Reichsfilmkammer. His films were largely of the political variety, with heavy love interest added for audience appeal. Actually a good artist, it was unfortunate that he should have become a propagandist; after the war he was forbidden to make films until 1949.

*Ich für dich* concerns the adventures of a group of girls, apparently members of the B.D.M. or "League of German Maidens," who did a year's voluntary service on the farms. This group is shown in its daily tasks, as each girl adjusts to her new environment. One of the girls has a lover who comes from the city to see her. He is presented as a fuzzy idealist and a downright reactionary; when she spurns him, he runs from the camp but is trapped in a quicksand bog and conveniently rescued by some members of the male Labor Service camp which is situated nearby. At the end of the film there is a church baptism of an infant at which both groups of youngsters participate.

This is one of the most objectionable films of the prewar period. The tone is bombastic, the situations and dialogue crudely anti-intellectual. Every possibility is used for propaganda, and there are even some anti-Semitic remarks. On the other hand, the direction, editing, and musical score (Hansom Milde-Meissner) are excellent, and the cast of juveniles (a Froelich specialty) is handled very well. As a piece of well-made political claptrap, the film stands almost in a class by itself.

### III

The nonpolitical films of 1934 do not differ greatly in subject matter from those of 1933, although the trend toward somewhat nationalistic subject matter (even in the most innocuous film) begins to make its mark in a small way. The international market was already diminished, and the type of films which were being made without political content were obviously being aimed at export.

The first important film to be released was a version of Schiller's *Wilhelm Tell* (January 12, 1934) directed by Heinz Paul, usually a specialist in military-action films of the *Douaumont* variety. Somewhat heavy handed, the film boasted a good cast including Conrad Veidt, already in emigration, and a very good performance by Emmy Sonnemann, soon to become Frau Göring. The film was dubbed into English at a later date and was one of the few Nazi-period films which received continued American circulation.

Emmy Sonnemann, soon to become Frau Göring, as the heroine of Heinz Paul's *Wilhelm Tell* (1934).

*Die weisse Majestät* (*The White Majesty*), (January 18), proved a big hit, although the story left much to be desired. The illegitimate son (Gustav Diessl) of a landowner is found squatting on his father's property in the company of a large St. Bernard. Since the father has died, the local law requires that the young man climb a mountain in order to inherit the land. One of the last important "mountain films," although in a debased form, the most that can be said for this film today is that Diessl puts in an excellent performance. The hack direction of Anton Kutter (this was his only German feature) did little to help Hertha Thiele, whose career was on the wane.

The vogue for films set in America (made with an eye for Germans living abroad) resulted in some rather unusual works, although *Der Flüchtling aus Chikago* (*The Fugitive from Chicago*), (January 31) was hardly one of the better examples. It was, however, one of the earliest set in Chicago, the "utopia of gangsters," a setting which greatly appealed to German writers and directors, culminating in the lunatic heights of Selpin's *Sergeant Berry* (1938).

The hero of this Chicago film is a young German trying to make good. He goes to visit a friend named Dux who is in jail, where he learns that the prisoner's father has died in Germany, leaving Dux an industrial empire on the condition that he return immediately. The hard-working friend takes his place, returns to Germany and applies his American know-how to straighten out the company, which has fallen into near-ruin. The real Dux finally arrives, and the usual complications ensue. The film was pleasantly acted by Gustav Fröhlich, Lil Dagover, and Otto Wernicke, but again suffered from indifferent direction by Johannes Meyer, one of the faithful but plodding directors of the period.

The prestige production of the year was *Der schwarze Walfisch* (*The Black Whale*), (March 2), a stylish version of Marcel Pagnol's play *Fanny* with some additional material added from *Marius* by the director, Dr. Fritz Wendhausen. The film marked the return to the screen of Emil Jannings, who had taken two years' leave from the movies, apparently to see which way the wind was blowing. For the remainder of the Third Reich, Jannings was probably the favorite male star, but the quality of his performances steadily declined as he took upon himself the functions of director and editor as well as star.

The story of the film follows the play faithfully. Jannings is touching as the central figure Petersen, Max Gülstorff was a richly drawn Panisse, and Angela Salloker did honors to Fanny. While the film did not have the delightful Provençal flavor of Pagnol's later film adaptions of his own plays, the pace of the German movie is more rapid.

Thea von Harbou's attempt to bring Gerhart Hauptmann's 1893 drama *Hanneles Himmelfahrt* (*Hannele's Ascension*) to the screen (April 13) was hardly in the Wendhausen class. The film probably represents a part of the Nazi attempt to flatter Hauptmann. This apparently worked, because the revered writer was the only literary figure of any importance to remain in the Third Reich. The former Frau Lang's film (her second and last attempt at direction) is murky and properly lugubrious, matching the style of the play.

The light-comedy genre was well represented in the first major film directed by Robert Stemmle, *Charleys Tante* (*Charley's Aunt*), (August 17), with the hoary Brandon Thomas play back on the screen with a good cast including Paul Kemp and Fritz Rasp. Stemmle recalls that he studied the American version of the play, with Sidney Chaplin, before shooting his film, and probably correctly regards his version as superior.

Stemmle is a comedy writer of considerable skill, still much at work in German film. He both wrote and directed numerous films during the Third Reich; these films had relatively little political content, but few of those he directed in the Nazi era were comedies.

Hitler's favorite play was August Hinrichs' comedy *Krach um Iolanthe* (the title might be rendered as *The Pig Scandal*) and it was brought to the screen (August 18) by the ever-faithful Carl Froelich from a script written in part by Stemmle. The Führer's admiration of this inane barnyard romance (it is said he saw it five times) is the only explanation for the type of grade-A production it received. It was even given a prize as an "outstandingly cultural" film. The best actress of the Nazi period, Marianne Hoppe, was enlisted as the star, with first-rate support.

The elegance which had departed from the German screen with the exile of Max Ophüls was carried on in Austria by Willi Forst in his stylish film *Maskerade* (August 21), which deservedly won several awards at the 1935 Venice Film Festival. The film also sent the Germans after the services of the actress Paula Wessely, a rather plain woman who registered excitingly on the screen, no matter what film she was in. It is said that Goebbels couldn't stand her work, but made every effort to sign her for German films because of the prestige attached to her name in artistic circles. *Maskerade* also proved a great success in the United States.

The most interesting film of the year, and one of the best of the entire period, was Luis Trenker's *Der verlorene Sohn* (*The Prodigal Son*), (September 6). Trenker recalls that the idea for the film came to him at two in the morning while waiting in New York for the sailing of the *Bremen*, which was to take him back to Germany after completion of the English version of *Der Rebell* in the United States. Most of the script was written on the boat, and production began almost immediately in the Tyrol when Trenker returned home. Five weeks' work was done in New York City.

The story concerns a young mountain guide with a bad case of wanderlust. He has been living a quiet life in the mountains until the arrival of a rich American and his daughter (played by the Hollywood star Marian Marsh). The young lady is determined to go mountain-climbing, and a trip is arranged, but there is an accident resulting in the death of one of the hero's friends. Disillusioned, the young man decides to accept the invitation of the Americans to visit them.

The mountains blend into skyscrapers in a remarkable montage, and Tonio the Guide is in the United States. (From this point on, the dialogue is in English by all concerned.) He attempts to contact the American girl, but finds that she is away on holiday. Without funds, the boy is thrown out of his lodgings, but eventually finds work building skyscrapers. This job is finished, however, when the foreman discovers he is a foreigner. Things go from bad to worse, and soon the hapless emigrant is forced to steal bread. He ends up in a Salvation Army soup line, a passage which used real derelicts photographed in newsreel style. At last he gets a job as a boxer, and at a fight in Madison Square Garden (the arena was actually used for this sequence) is spotted by the girl and her father, who rescue him.

The third part of the film finds Tonio returned to the Tyrol on the night of a strange neopagan ritual called *Rauhnacht*, somewhat similar

The prodigal son returns to his native village, from Trenker's
*Der verlorene Sohn* (1934).

to Halloween. Peasants in strange masks run through the snow carrying torches; a verse drama about the death of the seasons is performed.
(This sequence combined rituals and costumes from several districts

of the Tyrol.) In the end, Tonio is elected king of the festival and weds
the faithful girl who has been waiting for him.

The film, which has never been seen in the United States, comes
close to being a masterpiece, despite occasional passags of somewhat
dated sentimentality. For the most part, however, it is an uncommonly
tough handling of a romantic theme, touched throughout with a poetry
that is rare in the German cinema.

The scenes of depression New York put similar American efforts to
shame. Rarely has the atmosphere of the period been so utterly con-
vincingly conveyed. We see the United States through the eyes of a
stranger, and the effect is extraordinary. The final pagan scenes re-
mind one of the Russian masters. *Der verlorene Sohn* confirms the
belief that Trenker was one of the most talented directors of the
German-language cinema. Although the film is completely unknown
in the United States, it was awarded the Grand Prize at the Venice
Festival in 1935.

Musical films, the staple of the industry, were in their peak year.
In every way outstanding was Geza von Bolvary's *Abschiedswalzer*
(*Parting Waltz*), (October 4), which was based on the life of Chopin
(Wolfgang Liebeneiner) and his romance with George Sand (superbly played by Sybille Schmitz). The writer of the script, Ernst Marischka, was to have another try at Chopin when his story was used as
the basis of *A Song to Remember* (1944) in the United States.

The American operatic tenor Charles Kullmann began his career in
Germany as a film star, and was a favorite with the public. Karl Heinz
Martin's *La Paloma* (November 14) was better than average for the
genre, with Kullmann getting good support from another Metropolitan
star of an earlier period, Leo Slezak, the father of Walter.

A more German type of musical was represented by Gerhard Lamprecht's Ufa superproduction for the holiday season, *Prinzessin Turandot* (*Princess Turandot*), (November 30). This was based on the
same Gozzi fable which had inspired Puccini's opera, somewhat revised by Thea von Harbou. While the *chinoiserie* was of the *Land of
Smiles* level, the Franz Doelle score was tuneful and the picture as a
whole can be regarded as curiously highbrow for such an escapist
entertainment. The German-language version features Willy Fritsch

and Käthe von Nagy; it was also released in a French print with Pierre Blanchar as the hero.

Another entry for the holiday market was Dr. Fritz Wendhausen's literary version of Ibsen's *Peer Gynt* (December 17) with Hans Albers slightly uncomfortable in the title role. While the film strangely eliminated most of the supernatural elements of the play, the use of real Norwegian settings proved a decided asset. Bavaria, a relatively poor studio, put most of its slender finances into the production, and was rewarded with a genuine box-office hit.

Robert Louis Stevenson, a German favorite, was represented by *Liebe, Tod und Teufel* (*Love, Death, and the Devil*), (December 21), based on *The Bottle Imp*. The director selected for this project was Heinz Hilpert, a recruit from the theatre with a prediliction for the fantastic somewhat in the manner of Frank Wysbar. Hilpert was responsible for two of the last in a long line of fantasy films which had originally brought the Ufa to world prominence during the silent period. Unfortunately, there was to be little room for the supernatural in the cinema of the Nazi era.

# 1935: INTERLUDE

Compared with the turbulence caused by new film legislation in 1933 and 1934, the year 1935 was calm. Goebbels could afford to relax slightly; his worst jobs had almost been done. It was a time for holding the status quo, a time for showing off the new industry to visitors at the International Film Conference in April.

The new year started in a familiar fashion when Goebbels banned a Chaplin film, an almost annual event. This time it was *The Gold Rush* (1925), which had previously been overlooked, probably because it was a silent film. The official reason for the ban was that "the film does not coincide with the world philosophy of the present day in Germany."[1] Another of the familiar "popular demonstrations" resulted in a ban on the Czech-Austrian film *Symphonie der Liebe* (*Symphony of Love*), a work which was also banned in the United States under its alternate title, *Ecstasy*. The reasons, however, were slightly different: in the United States the film's sexual frankness was considered indecent; the Germans objected to Hedy Kiesler, a Jewish actress, in the main role. Miss Kiesler later took leave of Europe to enchant American audiences as Hedy Lamarr.

Goebbels had his hands full when two pet projects backfired within a few days. The first was the failure of a carefully planned film written by his plodding protégé Willi Krause, the new Dramaturg, formerly film reviewer of *Der Angriff*. The second involved his inability to block the career of Pola Negri, who was making an attempt to return to the German screen (she had left for the United States in 1922) in spite of Goebbels' intense objections.

Krause, in addition to his new duties as Dramaturg, had found time to write a novel that was made into a film entitled *Nur nicht weich werden, Susanne!* (*Don't Lose Heart, Suzanne!*). The work was penned under his usual pseudonym of Peter Hagen. The story concerned a young lady (Jessie Vihrog) trying to break into the film industry about 1931 and her battles with two unscrupulous "non-Aryan" producers. The film was directed by the Hungarian Arzen von Cserepy (1881–1946), who had once worked in the United States, and featured a relatively good cast including Veit Harlan.

Befitting the film's official status, an elaborate premiere was arranged, but Goebbels was astounded when the first-night audience on January 24 booed the film when it was over, an unheard-of experience. Making the best of a bad situation, Goebbels attempted to hush up the event and had the film restricted. The weekly fan magazines hardly mentioned it, and director von Cserepy was sent back to Hungary in disgrace, never to make another German film.

In the meantime Pola Negri, after a career in the United States, had returned to Europe, a victim of the sound film. After some work in France, she went to Germany with the idea of producing several films, but ran into the opposition of Goebbels, who apparently simply did not like the lady. Since this was a poor excuse for keeping her off the German screen he invented a story that she had served as a Polish intelligence officer during the Upper Silesian plebicite affair. He also let out a rumor that she was a Jew.

The evening after the Krause fiasco, the actress paid an ill-timed visit to the propaganda minister, who refused to grant her permission to act in Germany, calling her an enemy of the people. Pola Negri had the correct idea that it might pay to go directly to Hitler, who was known to be an admirer of her films. On February 1 she was granted the permission which she had sought, accompanied by an official announcement which amounted to a slap in the face to Goebbels:

Grave accusations were leveled recently against the actress Pola Negri. On orders of the Führer and Reich Chancellor these accusations have been investigated and it has been ascertained that no proof in support of them could be produced. There is, therefore, no reason to oppose Negri's artistic activities in Germany, all the more because the additional assertion that she is of Jewish descent has been proved untrue. She is Polish, and therefore Aryan.[2]

Pola Negri resumed her career, but Goebbels must have taken delight in the fact that her subsequent German films, although produced with lavish care, were poorly received by viewers. At the start of World War II, she returned to the United States.

The most important political event of 1935 was the announcement by Hitler on March 16 that the military was now reestablished—an announcement that in effect ended the restrictions placed on Germany by the Versailles treaty. In line with this, the film industry began to plan military epics on a vast scale, although few could be finished for release until 1936.

Goebbels had long been planning an International Film Conference, which was at last set to open on April 25 at the Kroll Opera in Berlin. Forty nations were represented by 2,000 delegates. At the last minute the 42 British representatives canceled the visit, explaining: "The whole German film business is today so much under the thumb of the government that a strong London representation would have to listen to the opinions of official Nazi Germany instead of cooperating in a free conference. Frankly, we don't regard this Berlin conference as in any way important."[3] The results of the conference were, of course, negligible, but the purpose of the event was not to bring about new agreements. Rather, Goebbels wanted to show Germany in the best possible light to foreign journalists and visitors, using the event much as he was to exploit the meetings of the International Chamber of Commerce and the Olympic Games in 1936.

The guests were wined, dined, and entertained lavishly, and the speeches (which were unusually short by Nazi standards) were translated by earphone into French and English. At the final meeting Goebbels gave an address entitled "Creative Film" which is a small masterpiece of saying one thing while doing exactly the opposite. This winning oration is so interesting that it is worth translating in full here.

It is the most noble task of art to bridge the gap between politics and economics. Art supplies the people with a solid ground on which they can disregard the conflicts of their interests and work constructively together, hand in hand. Art is the most noble cultural expression of a nation. Each nation creates its own specific art and style. Even the greatest artistic genius is in the last analysis a child of his nation and draws his boldest strivings for immortality from the roots of his native soil. International importance belongs to the kind of art which is deeply rooted in its national and folk origin, but whose rooted creativity is so dynamically charged that it goes beyond the boundaries of its native cultural realm and, because of its deep human values, is able to move the hearts of men in all countries and nations.

I realize that I am making high demands on creative movie production and its makers when I apply these age-old laws to it. From this derives for the film art, both in its national and international significance, a number of principles, which I consider essential if this most modern art is to prove and maintain its vital force and take its place of equality among the traditional and historical art forms. These principles form the foundation upon which the film has to prove its strength.

Permit me to develop these sketchy hints:

1. Like any other art form the film has its own laws. Only by obeying these laws can it preserve its own character. These laws differ from those of the stage. The superiority of the stage over the film must be discarded. The stage has its own language and so does the film. Things which are possible in the dim light of the proscenium become utterly unmasked in the harsh klieg lights of the movies. Relying upon its century-old tradition the theatre will try with might and main to maintain a position of condescending sponsorship over the movies. For the film it is a vital artistic necessity to stand on its own feet and to break the hold of the stage.

2. The film must rid itself of the vulgar platitudes of mass entertainment, yet it must not permit itself to lose touch with the people. The taste of the audience is not an unalterable fact that has to be accepted. This taste can be educated both for better or for worse. The artistic quality of the film depends upon the decision to educate the audience in a practical manner even at the cost of financial sacrifices.

3. This does not mean that the movies have to cater to anaemic aestheticism. On the contrary, just because of its wide reach the movies, more than any other form of art, must be an art of the people in the highest sense of the word. Being an art of the people it has to portray the joys and sorrows which move the people. It cannot escape the exigencies of our time and escape into a dreamland of unreality which only exists in the heads of ivory tower directors and scenarists and nowhere else.

4. There is no art which cannot support itself. Material sacrifices which are made for art's sake are being squared by ideal attainments. It is a matter of course that governments support the construction of great state buildings which immortalize the creative expression of a period, governments also support the theatre whose productions reflect the tragic and comic passions of the time, they also extend subsidies to picture galleries which house the people's artistic treasures. It must become equally a matter of course for governments to support the art of the film and to support cultural values, unless it foregoes the chance to place the film on the same footing with other art forms. In that case lamentations about *kitsch* and deterioration of movie standards are merely bigoted attempts to gloss over a sin of omission.

5. Like every other art form the movies must be closely related to the present and its problems. Film subjects, even though they may go back into previous historical eras and draw from foreign countries have to express the spirit of our time in order to speak to our time. In this sense, the film like any other form of art carries, as paradoxical and absurd as this may sound, the tendencies of its epoch to which it speaks and for which it works creatively.

6. Films that are based on these exigencies, while stressing the specific character of a nation, will tend to bring different nations closer together. The film is a cultural bridge between nations and increases international understanding.

7. The movies have the task to create with honesty and naturalness evidence for their very being. Empty pathos should be as foreign to the film as trashy sentimentality, a legacy passed on to it from the stage. An honest and natural film art, which gives our time living and plastic expression, can become an important means for the creation of a better, purer, and more realistic world of artistic potentialities.

If the movies adhere to these basic principles, they will conquer the world as a new form of artistic manifestation.

Germany has the honest intention to erect bridges that will connect all nations, but in back of us the greatness of life is waiting to find artistic expression. There is no other choice: We must lay hold of it and be part of it.

Let us start with the firm determination to be natural the way life is natural! Let us remain truthful so as to accomplish the effect of truth. Let us depict things which fill and move the hearts of men so as to move these men's hearts and to transport them into a better world by revealing to them the eternal.[4]

The delegates might have believed Goebbels if they had not had the experience of seeing a few nights earlier the premiere of a film which went "back into previous historical eras . . . to express the spirit of our time." The special offering was *Das Mädchen Johanna* (*The Maiden Joan*), (April 26), an Ufa extravaganza ostensibly concerning the events of the life of Joan of Arc. Under the dependable direction of Gustav Ucicky, this elaborate charade brought together a cast including Gustaf Gründgens, Heinrich George, René Deltgen, Erich Ponto, Willy Birgel, Theodor Loos, Aribert Wäscher, Veit Harlan, Paul Bildt, Albert Florath and Angela Salloker (as Joan)—a Who's Who of the German legitimate stage.

This would have been quite an event if the Schiller play had been the basis of the film, but Gerhard Menzel's screenplay made it appear that Joan was no more than an earlier edition of Hitler, or, as the program obliquely put it, "a leader who saved her people from despair."[5] To hear Hitler's slogans coming from the mouth of a Saint of the Roman Catholic Church was too much for many of the international audience. Nonetheless, the production was subsequently shown widely abroad as an example of the quality of German film, and the political message passed serenely over most viewers' heads.

Shortly after the delegates left Berlin, it was time for the annual May Day "cultural achievement" awards. The best-film prize went to Leni Riefenstahl for *Triumph des Willens* (*Triumph of the Will*) one of the most important documentary films ever made, taking as its subject the Party Congress held in Nuremberg September 4–10, 1934.

Since so much untruth has been spread about this film, it is necessary to go into the film's genesis in some detail.

In 1933, the director-actress Leni Riefenstahl had been appointed by Hitler to do a film for the Party, which resulted in *Sieg des Glaubens* (*Victory of Faith*), a short which has apparently disappeared despite efforts by the Allied governments, film archives, and the lady herself to locate it after the war.

According to a recent interview with Miss Riefenstahl, *Triumph des Willens* came about in a rather curious fashion.

Interviewer Robert Gardner writes:

So painful was her experience making the shorter film . . . that Riefenstahl left immediately upon its completion for Spain, where she in-

tended to make a new feature. However, once in Spain, she collapsed
and spent two months in a Madrid hospital convinced that all her difficulties could be laid at the door of the German Ministry of Information [i.e. Propaganda Ministry] and her arch enemy, its director,
Dr. Goebbels. . . . The uncompleted Spanish feature was insured by
Lloyds, so Riefenstahl returned to Germany losing no more than a
few months of her valuable time. As soon as she returned, she was
approached again by Hitler to make a film—again concerning the
Party Rally in Nuremberg (1934). At first she would not hear of it
and passed the commission over to Walter Ruttmann. However, Hitler
was not easily put off, and in a series of conversations terms were
agreed upon. Riefenstahl said she would do the film—even though she
had told Hitler she knew nothing about the Party or its organization
—if he would guarantee three conditions: one, that funds be arranged
by her rather than the Party; two, that no one, including Hitler but
especially Goebbels, be allowed to see the film until it was finished;
and three, that Hitler never ask her to do a third film. Hitler agreed
to these conditions, even saying that it was better for the Party not to
have to put up the money, in view of the possibility it might go *kaput*
before the film was finished.[6]

Leni Riefenstahl
and friend
during production
of *Triumph des
Willens* (1936).

Leni Riefenstahl gives direction to her camera crew during filming of *Triumph des Willens* (1936).

An important point to note here, particularly in light of postwar developments, is the fact that the film was entirely financed by Miss Riefenstahl's company, although it was *distributed* by a major company. The Party provided the setting and every facility possible for unimpeded film-recording of the event. The production company supplied the cameramen, under the supervision of Sepp Allgeier, later to become a bitter enemy of the director. The visitors, some 770,000 of them, provided the crowd scenes, helped out by the 350,000 inhabitants of Nuremberg.

The purpose of the film was twofold: to show Germans the solidarity of the Party, particularly following the divisions caused by the Röhm affair; and to introduce the leaders, many of whom spoke a few words, to this pretelevision society. Another, more subtle, purpose was to impress foreign audiences, and at the same time to scare the hell out of them. The film succeeded on all counts.

The finished film ran about two hours, which was probably slightly too long, for after a while the scenes of marching men become tiresome to most audiences. There is also in American circulation a 45-

minute condensed version which was prepared by the Museum of Modern Art during World War II for some kind of military training analysis, and this crudely edited edition, which does no service to the original documentary, has been widely seen. Miss Riefenstahl has taken trouble to disown the truncated version.

A special word should be said about the superb musical score by Herbert Windt (1894–1965), unquestionably the greatest composer of film music in the history of the medium. Windt was a serious classical composer before coming to the films about 1933; his opera *Andromache* was premiered at the Berlin State Opera in 1932 under the baton of Erich Kleiber. Windt, in addition to being skilled in the composition of documentary scores (*Sieg des Glaubens, Feldzug in Polen, Sieg im Westen,* and others) could write excellent music for entertainment films. His work on *Triumph des Willens* takes the "Horst Wessel Song" as its theme. The use of certain excerpts from *Die Meistersinger* was suggested by Miss Riefenstahl herself, however, and these moments are particularly effective.

Contrary to journalistic reports Leni Riefenstahl denied, when interviewed, that she fainted when given the award for her film.

Following the shooting of *Triumph des Willens*, while the film was being edited, the ill-fated General von Blomberg, on behalf of the army, tried to find out what place they would play in the completed epic. When he was informed that the army wouldn't appear at all because the footage which had been shot was of poor quality, von Blomberg went to Hitler and demanded equal time. What he got was a short film *Tag der Freiheit* (*Day of Freedom*), (1935), which was photographed in a single day by six cameramen. This film is also lost.

The reasons why these two short films no longer exist is rather interesting. *Triumph des Willens* was saved because it was sent abroad, but the other films were apparently limited to domestic consumption. Toward the end of the war, Miss Riefenstahl recalls that a representative of the Propaganda Ministry came to her house and demanded her prints and negatives, which were to be stored near Bolzano. She gave all three negatives to him, and they have never been seen since.

Censorship continued, gradually filling in the loopholes of the 1934 laws. On April 2 all members of the Reichsfilmkammer (which now included almost everyone in the film business) had to tell the government their entire holdings of films which were made by "forbidden associations or organizations hostile to the state."[7] Distribution of all German films abroad was ordered centralized in a new office of the Propaganda Ministry on June 8, and all pre-Nazi films with Jewish actors were banned on the same day. A week later, the latter point was reinforced by an article in the *Frankfurter Zeitung*:

> Occasionally it may be observed that films with non-Aryan performers, which were produced before January 30, 1933, and were passed by the Film Inspection Office, have turned up again in movie theatres. It must be pointed out that these films, especially if actors taking part in them are émigrés, are forbidden. Along with their showing, the loan or export of such films is forbidden and will be regarded as an offense to the national consciousness, and as a sign of political unreliability which deserves to be treated as suspicious.[8]

Still, despite threats and legislation, "illegal" films continued to be shown. The same newspaper took up the problem again on July 8:

> The Propaganda Ministry has issued a six-point order for the execution of the film law. It is reported from the proper authorities that, "As a result of the temporary shortage of films, it is necessary for the film industry to fall back on older sound films and even silent films. As a result it often happens that films are secured for projection which were permitted on the basis of the film law which was valid in the Weimar Republic. In several instances even the projection of films with non-Aryan participants has been confirmed; there is no longer any question that these are permitted today. Indeed, a great part of the films not compatible with the aims of the National Socialist régime were rejected in the course of review procedures [*Widerrufsverfahrens*] of the new film law. In order now, however, that all films which are not compatible with the spirit of the new times be absolutely barred from being run in German cinemas, a new basic regulation is needed, to the effect that all permissions granted for silent films and sound films before the National Socialist government be rescinded. The producers of these films are free to have those films which seem suitable for showing submitted to a check by the Censorship Office, for this check will of course be authoritative.[9]

But the shortage of films continued. The German public was not going to pay to see old films again, and demanded American products. On August 6 Hans Hinkel was forced to allow American films that had been written, produced, or acted by Jews to be projected in Germany (the previous ban on such films had stopped the American imports almost completely) on the condition that "films by Jews must be openly and honorably stated . . . anti-Semitism is purely an internal affair which in no case should be connected with the international film business."[10]

Scheuermann, in the course of a speech on August 24 (the same day that new national restrictions on Jews had been announced) stated: "As regards the export of German films, I expect every German producer to make every effort to deal abroad with Aryan firms only and to eliminate non-Aryan employees in case he maintains sales organizations abroad."[11]

The night before, a new method of eliminating Jewish film credits on foreign films was tried at the premiere of the excellent Austrian drama *Episode*. The audience was startled to hear a disembodied voice read the titles of the film over a musical background. When it came time for the name of the Jewish director Walter Reisch, the music was turned up so loudly that the name could hardly be heard.

On September 15, the most severe anti-Semitic legislation was passed, the so-called "Nuremberg Laws," which deprived the Jews of citizenship in the Reich; instead, they became "subjects." Marriages between "Aryans" and "non-Aryans" were forbidden from this date on.

Some months earlier, Goebbels had ordered a hunt for anti-Semitic films made abroad which could be shown in Germany. This considerable effort resulted in one film, an obscure Swedish melodrama entitled *Petterson and Bendel*, which had been made some years before. However, the German rights had already been purchased by the violently anti-Semitic Hamer Verlag (a publishing house). It was premiered in July. But somewhere along the line the dubbed dialogue was purposely garbled in the laboratory, and a full-scale investigation was held in the middle of August on this point. In addition, the crafty Hamer group required theatre owners to lease sixteen other films from them if they wanted to play *Petterson and Bendel*.[12]

The first president of the Reichsfilmkammer, Dr. Fritz Scheuermann, was a capable administrator, but could hardly be called brilliant in his job. In addition, he was the victim of an unusually nasty smear campaign engineered by some disappointed rivals for the post. A grimly amusing letter published by the documentarian Joseph Wulf gives an example of the kind of denunciation which was to become commonplace in the bureaucracy of the Third Reich. Note the writer's careful crescendo of rumors and gossip, building up to the *pièce de resistance* in the seventh paragraph. The letter is addressed to Hans Hinkel by a Dr. Kurt Plischke, otherwise unidentified.

*July 2, 1935*

*Worthy Party Comrade Hinkel!*
Concerning the Scheuermann business, Herr Krazer, who came to Berlin after your communication addressed to him, reported the following to me by word of mouth:

The official father of Scheuermann was Finance Councillor Scheuermann, the factotum and right-hand man of the governor in Strassburg, Graf von Wedel. He was of the Hohenlohe era; Hohenlohe had given him a post. Scheuermann was the fellow one-year volunteer [*Coeinjährige*] of Herr Krazer. Through this circumstance, Krazer once went to the house of the elder Scheuermann and to his great surprise saw there two huge pictures of Kaiser Wilhelm I and Friedrich III in Free-Mason uniforms. Old Scheuermann must have belonged to the same lodge as the two kaisers, otherwise it would not have been possible for him to have those two pictures of them both in their Free Mason uniforms. President Scheuermann is therefore a "Lufton," that is, son of a Free Mason, who may be accepted into a lodge more easily and quickly than kaisers and kings and princes and other highly placed personages.

When Krazer and Scheuermann served as volunteers in Strassburg, a sharp division prevailed between those regarded as socially acceptable and those not fully worthy. To the second class belonged all Jews, all Alsatians with a few exceptions, and, as a special case, Scheuermann, because no one could stand him. To the great surprise of all volunteers, Scheuermann became an officer of the regiment, Field Artillery Regiment No. 51. It was at that time generally asserted that the regiment must have had to stomach him because the governor was behind him. Despite this Scheuermann was cut by all his fellows. In the whole regiment there was not a single officer who would have associated with him.

Since Scheuermann had served shortly before the war broke out, he went into the field with the active regiment, whose commandant was General Flechtner, still living in Schweidnitz in Schlesien. The regiment's adjutant was Major Essig, later associated with General Maercker. One day Scheuermann was discovered with the baggage section. It was rumored that the colonel had sent him to baggage duty because he was of no use in the firing line. For a Prussian officer this was of course an unparalleled degradation and humiliation. The following happened while he was with the baggage:

There was shooting one day. Scheuermann threw himself to the ground and yelled, "I am wounded!" although this was not the case. Sergeant-Major Wurm, who is still living in Munich as a Reichsbank cashier, admonished him to conduct himself in a more manly and brave fashion. Wurm will confirm this episode today. Herr Krazer recently had a talk with him, in the course of which he revealed that Scheuermann is now president of the Reichsfilmkammer. Wurm was greatly astonished that a coward like Scheuermann should hold such a position in an heroic state like that of the National Socialists. He also told Herr Krazer on this occasion that the colonel had sent Scheuermann to the baggage because of his failure at the front.

All the foregoing is confirmed by records and known to the Filmkammer. Scheuermann, however, represented it to the examination committee as malicious slander. It should be added that Scheuermann disappeared suddenly from the horizon of the regiment. Then one day the officers remaining in the front line read that he had been made a commissioner [*Intendanturrat*] in Warsaw and had received the Iron Cross first class, which caused them no slight astonishment. He had no further relations with the regiment from then on (and none after the war).

About six months ago Herr Krazer was with some Party leaders in Munich. As the conversation turned to Scheuermann and Herr Krazer told what has been presented above about Scheuermann as a one-year volunteer, the lawyer Gutmann who was present, said: "It is a well-known story that also circulated at that time in Strassburg as a rumor, that there is dark blood behind Scheuermann through some liason of a Hohenlohe with a Jewess, or something of the sort." Gutmann knew the circumstances quite accurately, because he was a lawyer in Strassburg and was acquainted with the so-called society. It was said in society that Scheuermann had Jewish blood in his veins.

As well informed about Scheuermann as Gutmann is Bank Director Glauer of the Banca Commerciale in Milan. He should have accurate knowledge about Scheuermann's Jewish antecedents, since he went to gymnasium with Scheuermann.

Scheuermann's father was disliked by all civil servants, because he apparently rose pretty quickly from a mere drummer to the top, while the other civil servants had to follow, step by step, the long civil service route in the prescribed time. Krazer is of the opinion that most certainly there are some colleagues of Scheuermann's father who know the exact circumstances. Records concerning him and these colleagues must exist in Spandau among the records about the governorship that were transferred there.

> *Heil Hitler!*
> DR. KURT PLISCHKE.[13]

Since such information could hardly be kept secret in such a gossipy society as that of the Third Reich, Goebbels found it expedient to remove Scheuermann and to replace him with Dr. Oswald Lehnich, a rather sinister little man who had a spotless record as far as the Party was concerned; he had served as a professor at the University of Tübingen and had been one of the first dozen Nazi Party members and SS men at that institution. The switch was reported by the *Berliner Lokal-Anzeiger* (October 29):

The president of the Reichsfilmkammer, Dr. Fritz Scheuermann, has asked the president of the Reichskulturkammer, Dr. Goebbels, to relieve him of his office . . . to give him the opportunity to devote himself to a greater extent than hitherto to economic and legal problems of the film industry. Dr. Goebbels responded to this wish with thanks to Dr. Scheuermann for his honorable and successful work in the rebuilding of the German film. Dr. Scheuermann, who remains a member of the Presidial Council of the Reichsfilmkammer, takes over the directorship of the Film Credit Bank.

Dr. Goebbels has appointed as president of the Reichsfilmkammer Württemburg Staatsminister SS-Opersturmführer Professor Dr. Lehnich. . . and appointed to the office of retiring Oberregierungsrat Raether the head of the Fachschaft Film, Hans Weidemann, to the vice-presidency of the Reichsfilmkammer.[14]

Lehnich was made of far tougher material than his predecessor, as the German film industry soon discovered. With this important position in better hands, Goebbels was able to utilize his own talents in other quarters, and to allow himself some needed relaxation, which, as we will see, had consequences both comic and tragic.

II

The year 1935 will be remembered as the year of *Triumph des Willens*, but the number of political propaganda features was smaller than in any full year of the Third Reich.

Entertainment films and adaptions of literary classics were safer. A good example was Erich Waschneck's elegant *Regine* (January 7), based on Gottfried Keller's famous love story, beautifully played by Luise Ullrich, Adolf Wohlbrück, and Olga Tschechowa. The film was sent to Venice as one of the German entries at the annual film festival.

Another major film in the series of biographical films of Frederick the Great was Hans Steinhoff's lavish *Der alte und der junge König* (*The Old and the Young King*), (January 29), which differed from the others in that it dealt with Frederick's youth and his troubles with his stern father. Jannings played the elder Frederick with all the stops pulled out, ranting and raving, thoroughly out of control. Werner Hinz, as the future king, struck the right combination of fright and dignity. Thea von Harbou's script took full advantage of the more brutal events of the famous father-son clash, with emphasis on the need to obey orders and other virtues suitable to the Nazi system. The execution of the future king's best friend is particularly impressive, but the film as a whole is repulsive.

Benito Mussolini was represented on the German screen when *Hundert Tage* (*Hundred Days*), (March 22), based on his play, was filmed under Franz Wenzler's direction. The screenplay was by Dr. Karl Vollmöller, a writer who should have known better. A German-Italian coproduction, the German version had Werner Krauss as Napoleon with assistance from Gründgens. The play had been performed on German stages with some regularity since 1933, and many famous actors were required to appear in it.

More to the popular taste was Heinz Paul's *Wunder des Fliegens* (*Miracle of Flight*), (April 14), which had the famous stunt-pilot Ernst Udet in a number of his best routines including a scene in which he flew *through* an airplane hangar. The romantic interest, what there was of it, was supplied by the lovely Käthe Haack. The script contained considerable propaganda aimed at getting young people to learn flying, and the film had the blessing of Göring.

One of the few quality directors to remain in the industry (albeit in Austria) was the enigmatic Piel Jutzi, who had turned out two near masterpieces in the immediate pre-Nazi period: *Mutter Krausens Fahrt ins Glück* (*Mother Krausen's Journey to Happiness*), (1929), one of the most pessimistic films ever made despite its ironic title; and *Berlin-Alexanderplatz* (1931), a biting version of the famous Döblin novel with Heinrich George.

*Lockspitzel Asew* (*Double-Agent Asew*), (April 12), was shot in Vienna with a first-rate cast, and proved that Jutzi had lost none of his skill. The story was based on the life of one Neumeier who, in the period before the Russian revolution, staged a number of violent plots for the rebels under the name of Asew, and revealed them to the tsarist secret police under the name of Raskin. When things got too hot in Russia, Neumeier-Asew-Raskin fled to Berlin, where he died.

The film departed from the truth in that Asew ends in Paris, alone and forsaken; actually, he ended his days as a shopkeeper in Berlin. Jannings had long wanted to play the role, but it went instead to Fritz Rasp, who considered it one of his best characterizations. He wrote, "I have not played the part as that of a wicked villain but as a *grand seigneur* with criminal tendencies; as an imposter and actor on both sides of the fence; an anarchist among anarchists, and a ruthless avenger and defender of the ruling power. I have played the man who can soften to the sounds of music like any true Russian. A type of person for whom I have a true affinity."[15]

Asew's wife was played by Olga Tschechowa, and his ruthless enemy by Wolfgang Liebeneiner. *Lockspitzel Asew* has the mood and power of Jutzi's earlier films and deserves to be better known.

Earlier, Jutzi directed another Austrian film, *Der Kosak und die Nachtigall* (*The Cossack and the Nightingale*) (June 28), which was apparently of far lesser quality. Political censorship in Germany held up the film's release for three months. After this experience, Jutzi gave up direction in favor of photography, and shot two minor films before vanishing from the film scene in 1943, another example of the waste of talent during the period.*

* I am informed that a study of Jutzi was published in mimeograph form by the East Berlin Film Archive in 1966. Despite intensive research, it proved impossible to ascertain the date and place of Jutzi's birth, his present whereabouts, or even the correct spelling of his name.

Reinhold Schünzel's *Amphitryon* (July 18) proved the popular hit of the year; it is still occasionally revived in the French version which was made at the same time, although this ran into American opposition when it was released here in 1936. When *Amphitryon* was revived in London in 1964 in its German version, the critic Richard Roud described it as follows:

If it weren't for the fact that *Amphitryon* was made two years after Hitler came to power, I am willing to bet that it would be much more famous than *The Congress Dances*. For *Amphitryon* is a real surprise: from an ever-popular myth (Jupiter disguises himself as Amphitryon in order to make love to his faithful wife), director Reinhold Schünzel has made a delightful operetta. I don't know who the composer Franz Doelle is, but he certainly seems due for rediscovery. He had managed to write a score which is gay, charming and tuneful throughout the film—and there is scarcely a spoken word. *Amphitryon* is also extremely funny—not just the deliberate anachronisms (Mercury on roller-skates etc.) but also the characterizations. The film belongs to the principals: Käthe Gold is deliciously serious as Alkmene and Willy Fritsch in the double role of Jupiter and Amphitryon shows us not only why he reached such fantastic heights of popularity but also how good a performer he could be.[16]

Since even the well-informed Mr. Roud does not know much about Franz Doelle, this is probably a good place to mention this delightful composer. Born in 1888, he studied piano and horn and in 1914 became associated with the Apollo Theatre in Berlin as conductor, later going to the Komische Oper. Most of his film career was spent in the limited genre of the operetta-film and included such works as *Viktor und Viktoria* (1933) previously mentioned; *Die englische Heirat* (1934); *Prinzessin Turandot* (1934); *Königswalzer* (1935); *Boccaccio* (1936); *Und Du, mein Schatz, fährst mit* (1936). However, he was also the house composer for the ill-fated Herbert Selpin on his 1941–1943 films. There is a "Doelle sound" to all his music; it has charm and sparkle.

George Bernard Shaw came to the German screen with *Pygmalion* (September 2), directed by Erich Engel; Jenny Jugo was Eliza Doolittle, Eugen Klöpfer her father, and Gründgens played Professor Higgins.

According to Donald P. Costello's study of Shaw in the film, *The Serpent's Eye*, the playwright signed a contract with Klagemann Films on February 16, 1935, on the condition that a script which Shaw had prepared be followed exactly. But Engel cut some passages and added others including one episode which Mr. Costello feels could have served as the inspiration for the Ascot Gavotte scene in *My Fair Lady*.

Shaw's reaction to the film was thunderous:

There is a German film called "Pygmalion by Bernard Shaw." The makers were bound by their contract and their most solemn promises to follow my scenario exactly. They took the most extraordinary pains, and spent huge sums, in altering it out of all recognition. They spoiled every effect, falsified all the characters, put in everything I left out and took out most of what I had put in. They thought they knew better than I. If they had, they would have been Super-Shaws. As it was, they were in the position of a yokel who buys a hat for the Coronation in Piccadilly and, finding it not to his taste, brushes it the wrong way, jumps on it half a dozen times and then proudly walks down the street to show how well he knows what's what in the way of a gentleman's headgear. So now you know why my plays are still waiting to be filmed.[17]

Despite Shaw's lack of enthusiasm for the film, it is a far more cinematic work than the British versions of his plays done by Pascal. The acting is extremely polished, the direction excellent, and the sets and costumes all one could ask for in such a period piece. Due to legal restrictions the film cannot be revived, but it is worth a trip to an archive lucky enough to hold a print.

It was open season on British playwrights, with Oscar Wilde enjoying considerable cinematic popularity; at least he was not alive to protest any changes made in his dramas. Herbert Selpin's *Ein idealer Gatte (An Ideal Husband)*, (September 6), (also released under the title *Skandal um Gloria*), followed Wilde almost to the letter, which made it unduly static and talky, although Selpin shot some interesting original sequences in London, including scenes at the Paladium and an amusing encounter at the Albert Memorial. The emphasis of the film is on the character of Gloria Cheveley, played by Sybille Schmitz. Unfortunately, Carl Ludwig Diehl and Brigitte Helm are wooden as

Lord and Lady Chiltern, and, since the film was dressed to the teeth and updated to 1935, it shows its age, particularly in some outrageous costumes.

The other Wilde film was *Lady Windemeres Fächer* (*Lady Windemere's Fan*), (October 25), which was more successful than *An Ideal Husband*, mainly due to Lil Dagover as Lady Margaret. But the rest of the cast, apparently drawn from the stage, was not first rate. Heinz Hilpert's sensitive direction showed once again that he was an artist of considerable talent, not limited to the fantastic genre.

Director Herbert Selpin was also represented on German screens with *Der grüne Domino* (*The Green Domino*), (October 4), a complicated mystery drama from a play by Erich Ebermayer featuring Brigitte Horney in a double role as mother and daughter. The full facilities of the Ufa were put at Selpin's disposal in this, his first lavish, big-budget film. The dancing episodes are particularly stylish, and the whole picture has an air of being more choreographed than directed. (Selpin had been a professional ballroom dancer—and also prize-fighter—before entering the film industry as a cutter.)

The important fictional political film of the year was *Friesennot* (*Frisians in Peril*), (November 19) with Willi Krause directing this

In the lavish Ufa tradition, a night ball sequence from *Der grüne Domino* (1935) directed by Herbert Selpin.

time, under the usual Peter Hagen alias. This film falls into the small category of propaganda features distributed directly by the Party.

The story takes up the problems of Volga Germans living in Russia during the revolution. A group of Red Army soldiers, led by the villainous Commissar Tshernoff (played by Inkijinoff, better remembered for his Russian film appearances) invade the town, with the usual pillage and rape. In the end, the long-oppressed Germans revolt, burn their settlement to the ground, pack their bags, and return to the fatherland.

The film is better than most of its kind in the technical department, with fine photography by Sepp Allgeier and a score by Walter Gronostay. Krause, however, was no better at direction than he had been at writing, and he was not helped by a mediocre cast (excepting Inkijinoff).

The aim of the film was to create anti-Russian propaganda, although it was not as successful in this regard as *Flüchtlinge*. However, the film was kept in constant circulation until September 7, 1939, when the Russians suddenly became friends again. It was reissued in 1941 under the title *Dorf im roten Sturm* (*Village in the Red Storm*) when the situation returned to normal.

The rumor had gone round that Goebbels was a prude (which was hardly the case, although his wife Magda was rather straight-laced) and that he censored the type of bawdy remarks which had been so common in earlier German comedy films. To confound this tale, Goebbels gleefully allowed the production of a film called *Der Ammenkönig* (this poses translation problems, but in view of content, it might be called *The Stud King*), (December 5), a wildly bawdy farce well calculated to offend the bourgeoise. It takes place in a small German village about 1835, when the inhabitants refuse to pay the high marriage tax required by the government. Instead, the most virile young man in the town is selected as progenitor of the year. After numerous racy incidents, the tax is annulled, to general regrets. Hans Steinhoff directed in his best *ersatz* Billy Wilder manner, getting the utmost amount of lewdness out of each incident. Although vulgar, the film is also funny and was a big hit of the period.

The great director Arthur Robison (1888–1935) made his farewell to the screen with the third version of Hanns Heinz Ewers' horror story *Der Student von Prag* (*The Student of Prague*), (December 10), which was premiered after Robison's death. Adolf Wohlbrück played the haunted hero with as much elegance as Conrad Veidt had in one of the two silent versions, but without that actor's passionate sense of the macabre. Dorothea Wieck was somewhat miscast as the heroine.

Following Shaw and Wilde, Ibsen was filmed by Detlef Sierck (later Douglas Sirk) in *Stützen der Gesellschaft* (*Pillars of Society*), (December 21), with a stunning performance by Heinrich George as Consul Bernick. Sierck showed a fine feeling for the Scandanavian settings of the original play, and the opening of the film, with its windswept holiday decorations contrasted with the surly attitude of the townspeople, places the viewer immediately in Ibsen's special world. The final shipwreck and storm is well handled, but Sierck's direction of the more intimate passages is even more appealing. The film ranks among the best literary adaptions of the period.

Although it passed without much notice, 1935 marked the first appearance of Veit Harlan as a director. Harlan had long been known as a fine young actor, and had appeared in numerous plays and films. His opportunity for direction occurred on an Austrian film *Die Pompadour* (October 19), which he had helped to script. The first director of the film, a well-known operetta composer, continually showed up at the studio drunk, and Harlan was finally obliged to take his place along with another temporary director.

The film turned out so well that he was immediately put into another project, *Krach im Hinterhaus* (*Quarrel in the Backroom*), (January 2, 1936), which he managed to film in ten days at the small cost of RM 250,000. It starred Germany's favorite film-pioneer Henny Porten in a role she had often played on the stage. With a reputation for fast, cheap direction, Harlan was on the road which eventually found him enthroned in the dubious position of "official director" of the Third Reich.

# 1936: GOEBBELS ABOLISHES THE CRITICS

The days of 1935, characterized by the lack of new film laws and the sometimes lax enforcement of prior Nazi legislation, had put the film colony somewhat off its guard. This was unquestionably part of Goebbels' plan.

However, the long-range designs of the "Little Doctor" had undergone considerable revision since he came to power in 1933. The strong steps of the first two years of the Nazi regime had not had the expected effect: instead of being frightened, the film world had revolted.

By January of 1936, much of the cream of the pre-Nazi film industry had gone into exile, including many non-Jewish members of the community. Austria was the first to benefit, since there was a thriving German-language film market, and studios to absorb the emigrating talent. Austria was but the first stop for many of these exiles; later they would follow a well-trod path to France, England, and the United States.

Goebbels was anxious to keep the best actors in Germany, and went out of his way to offer wavering talent guarantees of unimpeded employment. To their small credit, many of the best-known stars remained in the Third Reich, although there were some notable exceptions. The most spectacular case was that of Conrad Veidt, who,

although not a Jew, scrawled the word "Jude" across a racial ques-
tionaire presented to him, packed his bags and left Germany, never
to return. But Veidt was one of the few to clear out in disgust.      •

The "big four" of the German stage and screen remained: Emil
Jannings (1884–1950), Heinrich George (1893–1946), Werner
Krauss (1884–1959), and Gustaf Gründgens (1899–1963). To those
living outside of Germany, only the names of Jannings and Krauss are
probably familiar, but all four men enjoyed enormous popularity with
Teutonic audiences.

Emil Jannings was the most famous German actor, with a world
following. Shortly before the Nazi takeover he appeared in the ill-
fated *Les aventures du roi Pausole*, a French-German coproduction
directed by the talented but erratic Alexis Granowsky. The production was so bad that even the presence of Jannings couldn't save it;
there is some doubt that the film was ever generally released. As recounted earlier, the actor returned to the theatre and for almost two
years stayed away from the movies. After his return to the screen in
*Der schwarze Walfisch*, he appeared in another ten films during the
Third Reich, confining his work to the stage as much as possible. Each
of these films marks a step in his artistic decline, culminating in bellow-
ing, eye-rolling performances which can only be regarded as embarrassing.

Although Jannings lent his services to films with propaganda content, his loyalty to the regime was hardly more than skin deep; he ex-
ploited the Nazis almost as much as they used him. His post-1934
performances appeared under the names of such directors as Carl
Froelich, Veit Harlan, Hans Steinhoff, and Wolfgang Liebeneiner,
but it was no secret that Jannings' scenes were directed by Jannings,
and his arrogant interference in every stage of production made the
situation a nightmare for his co-workers.

The other "heavy" of the German screen was Heinrich George, a
slightly more restrained actor than Jannings, but much the same in
physique and temperament; his fellow actors nicknamed him "The
Blue Boar," due to his heavy beard and ferocious temper. George had
been an ardent Communist before the Nazis took over, but was able to
switch sides with the greatest of ease. Gossip had it that he set up an

altar to Hitler in his house and forced astonished guests to offer prayers on their knees to the Führer. Some regarded this as a joke he played on his super-Nazi compatriots.

"The Blue Boar" was not an idle nomer. Veit Harlan told me that George had to be treated like a wild animal. There were two Georges: a nice one, and another when he drank. In both states, he was known to express his contempt for the Party hierarchy, particularly Goebbels, whom he detested. For many years George had nursed a hopeless passion for Elisabeth Bergner, and kept an enormous framed portrait of her in his dressing room during the entire Nazi period. Goebbels was not amused.

If Jannings and George belonged to what might be called the "whisper-scream" school of acting, Werner Krauss and Gustaf Gründgens were of a more sophisticated breed, specializing in restrained classic roles. Because they appeared more "intellectual" to postwar investigators, these two actors had a particularly difficult time with the Allied authorities.

Krauss must have presented a difficult problem to the postwar tribunals. It was rumored that the Nazis made his emigration impossible when they discovered that his son had a Jewish wife; it is known that Krauss intervened with Goebbels on the behalf of potential victims of the regime. The reason for his taking the brunt of the postwar attack was his performance in *Jud Süss* although, as we will see presently, he took the role reluctantly.

Gustaf Gründgens, unquestionably the finest actor of the German stage, before, during, and after the war, had the misfortune of having Thomas Mann's son Klaus as his former brother-in-law. At the time of the Nazi take-over, both Gründgens and Mann were members of a theatrical circle with fashionable Communist overtones, and the two were on reasonably good personal terms. Mann left Germany in 1933 and was outraged when Gründgens refused to take the opportunity, despite the fact that Gründgens was at the time in Spain on location and could have remained there with other members of the company.

Gründgens returned to Nazi Germany and obtained the personal patronage of Göring, much to Goebbels' irritation. Klaus Mann wrote a novel entitled *Mephisto* (published in Holland in German and reprinted some thirty years later after Gründgens' suicide) with the actor as an undisguised and thoroughly contemptible opportunist. Smuggled copies of the book were widely read in Germany, and did little to help Gründgens' image, which was never very good in the first place because of his unorthodox private life. In the United States, Mann further criticized Gründgens in his autobiography.

Gründgens realized early that he would have difficulties with Goebbels and decided to cultivate Göring. Göring, always susceptible to flattery, was delighted to add Gründgens to his circle, especially in view of the fact that he knew this would infuriate Goebbels. Although the arts were almost completely under Goebbels' control, a legislative quirk had made Göring responsible for the Prussian State Theatre, and he lost no time in making Gründgens head of this important institution. In this capacity, Gründgens was responsible solely to Göring, and was able to refuse cinema roles he felt unsuitable.

The departure of Elisabeth Bergner, the Queen of the German stage and screen, left the field open for successors. The women, on the whole, stayed out of politics whenever possible, with one or two rather revolting exceptions. The two leading contenders for the Bergner crown were Olga Tschechowa, whose career in films had begun in the silent period, and Marianne Hoppe (later to become Frau Gründgens), a specialist in heavy dramatic roles. Neither actress could be considered sympathetic to the regime.

However, there were other major actresses at work during the period, all popular and capable performers. In alphabetical order, the list would include Maria Andergast, Lil Dagover, Käthe Dorsch, Lucie English, Käthe Haack, Karin Hardt, Lilian Harvey, Hilde Hildebrand, Brigitte Horney, Jenny Jugo, Hilde Körber, Irene von Meyendorff, Renate Müller (a later victim of the Nazi regime), Käthe von Nagy, Pola Negri, Anny Ondra, Marika Rökk, Sybille Schmitz, Magda Schneider, Gisela Uhlen, Luise Ullrich, and Paula Wessely.

By 1936 the film colony of the Third Reich was virtually formed, a stock company which was to continue almost unchanged until 1945. Oddly enough, the new female stars to appear after 1936 for the most part were not Germans, but Scandanavians, including Kirsten Heiberg, Zarah Leander, and Kristina Söderbaum. There was also a rising young Czech actress under contract to the Ufa, Lida Baarova, who was destined to play a curious role in the history of the Third Reich.

## II

Goebbels' technique in bringing the film colony to heel was made up of equal parts of sugar and the whip—a tiny concession followed by another deprivation of alleged privileges. The year 1936 found him in a black mood, a direct result of the generally horrible state of the industry, which was at its lowest general creative peak in many years.

Late in February, he gave a speech on the film situation which greatly astonished the movie colony, timing his oration at a moment when some of the better remaining industry personnel were beginning to extend tentative feelers toward foreign employment. His words were meant to allay some of the general fears, and provided the expected result.

Masking his irritation over the success of American films, he remarked: "The supposed public taste has no rigid standards, but is influenced by the taste of the artist. One only needs to look at such American films as *Lives of a Bengal Lancer* and *It Happened One Night* to be convinced that art in the film is attained through depiction of life in the most natural manner possible."[1] Yet these were but empty words, for the "natural manner" was thoroughly incompatible with official policy.

Most important, as far as the industry was concerned, Goebbels announced that the star system was definitely back in, after an ill-fated try at some semblance of repertoire casting. In line with this, an earlier decree on maximum salaries was rescinded; if the actor was popular, the sky was the limit.

Goebbels also announced that future films would be produced without distributor participation. This was a peculiar decree and needs some explanation. The industry at the period was composed of producer-distributors, who marketed their own product, and independent producers who made films with the hope of getting them distributed by one of the major companies.

To the large distributors the decree was disturbing because it sounded as though they would have to take what was offered to them without any of the normal preselection procedure. The independent producers thought it was a good idea on the whole, but realized that in practice it was impossible unless another body took the place of the distributor, namely the government, which was exactly what was to happen. No distributor was going to take a film he did not like unless forced to do so, which could be done in a variety of ways, most practicably by the government providing a subsidy for good independent ideas, or, on the other hand, subsidizing the distributor to take a film which he did not particularly like. Various methods were tried to get the two groups together until 1942, when Goebbels had all distribution facilities combined under one company called Deutsche Filmvertriebs-Gesellschaft (D. F. V.).

The Ufa organization owned fifteen theatres in Berlin, giving it the best facilities for premieres, as mentioned earlier. On April 2, it purchased both the Marmorhaus and Capitol cinemas, where most American films were given first-run engagements. Since the government had been giving the Ufa a hard time for supposed monopoly techniques, this came as a considerable surprise, although the explanation given for this in 1937 showed it as part of a clever general plan.

If Goebbels was unable to make better movies, the alternative was to silence the critics, which he achieved in several graduated steps. On May 13, he announced that it was now forbidden to write criticisms of music, plays, and films for publication the morning after premieres, although these write-ups could appear after noon on the following day. This idea may be somewhat bizarre, but in our own day one of the leading drama critics of a New York newspaper complained of the undue pressure of deadlines in terms somewhat like those Goebbels used to curb the critics.

In the liberalistic epoch artistic criticism in the German press had begun to run wild to such an extent that it no longer had anything in common with constructive, stimulating, and responsible criticism. The attempt to present to the readers—almost at the conclusion of a performance—a complete criticism of the work concerned became a particular evil.

It is obvious that such criticism had to be written without a proper estimate of the performance and without an opportunity for the critic to collect and digest his impressions. Such criticism, therefore, must be considered highly frivolous. It lacks all reverence for artistic achievement, no matter how great or small.[2]

In practice, this decree made little difference, since the critic, if he did not appreciate the opportunity to work a bit longer on his review, simply filed it at the normal time with his newspaper for publication the following day. Again, what Goebbels had in mind was not immediately obvious to all. The intent was to threaten the critics, to give an example of his power over their profession, and to make them think twice before panning an official project, which was still possible if handled with care.

However, the threats did not work and the ultimate solution was resorted to on November 27, when at a sitting of the Reichskulturkammer it was finally announced that all criticisms of film, drama, literature, painting, sculpture, and other art works was prohibited. Reviews henceforward were to be simply descriptive; neither praise nor blame was to be expressed, nor the expression of any personal opinion. As Goebbels put it:

Because this year has not brought an improvement in criticism of the arts, I forbid once and for all the continuance of criticism in its past form, effective today. From now on, the reporting of art will take the place of criticism which sets itself up as a judge of art—a complete perversion of the concept of "criticism" which dates from the time of Jewish domination of the arts. The critic is to be replaced by the arts editor. The reporting of art should not be concerned with values, but should confine itself to description. Such reporting should give the public a chance to make its own judgments—it should stimulate it to form an opinion about artistic achievements through its own attitudes and feelings.[3]

In a particularly nasty mood, Goebbels continued:

We employed every means to bring the critics to their sole and proper role of art observers, giving them with it the possibility of continued existence. All these efforts have failed. It sometimes looked as if all the scolds who could no longer exercise their faculties in other fields centered in on the arts. We had to call a halt. I therefore found it necessary in the decree announced today to forbid all criticism and replace it with art observation or art description. This does not mean the limitation of free expression of opinion.

We have often experienced in Berlin the experience of 22- or 23-year-old boys taking 40- or 50-year-old artists to task without being able to show a sign of technical knowledge. They will now learn how to describe works of art. That is also difficult and it must be learned. If a critic feels himself capable to do more than that, we are looking for these capacities in many artistic fields and he is welcome to undertake positive work.[4]

The scope of this decree was enormous, not limited to film, but including every kind of artistic expression. In his lengthy remarks, partly excerpted above, Goebbels at one point specifically mentioned films:

German films, once the domain of Jewish and Marxist intellectuals, passed last year their greatest test, providing genuine masterpieces.[5]

Yet during that same year, the industry lost nine million marks!

The following day, Alfred Ingemar Berndt, Goebbels' totally unscrupulous press chief (who held his job until 1938 when his manipulation of news outraged even Goebbels, who replaced him with Fritzsche) told the Kulturkammer:

Judgement of the art work in the National Socialist State can be made only on the basis of the Nationalist Socialist viewpoint of culture. Only the Party and State are in a position to determine artistic values by appeal to the National Socialist artistic standpoint. If judgement has been issued by those who are appointed to pass judgement on art, the reporter may, of course, employ the values thereby established. This situation will arise only rarely, however.[6]

In other words, the reporter must echo the Party, even if he is merely "observing."

The decree also included a section which required every art and cultural worker to obtain a permit from the Reichskulturkammer or Pressekammer. To get this document, the applicant had to be more than thirty years of age and had to show experience in his field.

All-inclusive though this decree seemed, it still left room for mis-interpretation in some quarters. In an embarrassing incident, the Jew-baiting Julius Streicher had made the Nuremberg theatre critics dance on the stage following the performance of a musical variety show. Goebbels tried to hush this up, but Streicher published the full details in his paper, and the item was immediately noticed and printed in the foreign press.

In the middle of February, 1937, the thirty-year minimum age for critics section of the decree was revoked, but only for members of the Nazi party, excluding all others under that age. It seemed that there weren't enough critics above thirty even able to write "descriptions."

In practice, the decree did not have the desired effect. Good writers refused to write the new "criticism" and the public was annoyed at the loss of their favorite reviewers. Goebbels backed down slightly. At the annual meeting of the Central German Press Chamber at Dessau on March 15, 1937, Captain Wilhelm Weiss, head of the Reich Press Association (*Reichsverband der deutschen Presse*) as well as editor of the main Party newspaper, the *Völkischer Beobachter*, stated some changes. In effect, he remarked that all films which were for national socialism were good, and those against it bad, and critics were now allowed to resume their criticism, but on these sole grounds. In part, he commented:

> If a work of art and its presentation contain a National Socialist idea, we favor it. If the opposite is the case, we have not only the right but the duty to be against it. Art criticism is not primarily an aesthetic question, but a political one. Until very recently the majority of theatre critics have neglected this fact.
>
> Only a short time ago emphasis was still placed chiefly on the question of whether a play or film was good from a purely artistic stand-point. The critic must now constantly be aware that what he sees on the stage is politics in the broadest sense of the word . . .
>
> The art of observation does not differ from the former art of criti-cism, in Heaven's name, through the idea that everything is to be accepted as good or exemplary. No indeed! The newspapers make a catastrophic mistake when they believe that they can fulfill the require-ments of the prohibition of criticism by praising everything. This mis-take must be instantly corrected. However, the old idea that there is good art and bad art must be removed.[7]

Since this made almost no sense, Weiss's listeners had to read between the lines, and interpret as best they could. In effect, the cautious newspaper critic was made to understand that he could use some critical faculties, but obviously not on German films since they had to have passed state censorship. But foreign films would now be fair game, which was probably Goebbels' main idea.

The decree on criticism was one of the most extraordinary ever issued under the Third Reich, and brought forth howls of protest in and out of the country. However, the group of "official" artists breathed a sigh of relief, even though the public shortly displayed its own methods of disapproval, as will be discussed shortly.

With the few remaining critics out of the way, Goebbels could sit back and begin his next major film project, the complete nationalization of the industry, a process which began only a few weeks after the criticism decree.

### III

The year 1936 was also notable for the fact that Germany played host to the Olympic Games, an event which was recorded for posterity in Leni Riefenstahl's masterpiece in two parts, *Olympia*. The film took two years to edit and therefore will be discussed under its year of issue, 1938.

Because of the large influx of visitors to Germany, the summer showed the Nazis on their best behavior. Usually austere in spending money on himself, his family, and his friends, Goebbels threw an enormous party at his estate, newly acquired at Schwanenwerder. Actually a precedent had been set in July when he had given the famous Venetian Night on an island in the Wannsee for three thousand guests in connection with the meeting of the International Chamber of Commerce.

But it was only a curtain raiser to what was known later as the Peacock Island scandal. In honor of the Olympics, and to get even with Göring, who had given a few luxurious parties shortly before on the occasion of his wedding, Goebbels went the limit and put on a fête worthy of a Roman emperor.

The entire ensemble of the Berlin State Opera was pressed into service, in addition to three jazz bands (which had been put out of

Lida Baarova
in *Patrioten*

business some time before). Unfortunately, toward the early morning hours, the party turned into a near orgy and Goebbels had to work hard indeed to hush up the scandal.[8]

However, the biggest scandal of Goebbels' career had already started in a deceptively quiet way. In 1934, the Ufa had imported a young Czech actress by the name of Lida Baarova, who made her German film debut in a picture entitled *Barcarolle*.

According to most books, Goebbels first met Lida Baarova in 1936, although he certainly must have seen her earlier since there are photographs extant of Hitler and Goebbels visiting the *Barcarolle* set. In any case, her debut was hardly auspicious. She moved awkwardly, was unfortunately costumed, and had to play the role of a Mexican girl. Her profile was unattractive, and director Lamprecht was apparently forced to shoot numerous scenes of her full-face. She was, in short, exceedingly plain despite efforts to make her into a glamor girl, and decidedly limited as an actress.

Only twenty when she came to Germany, she fell in love with the actor Gustav Fröhlich, and set up housekeeping with him on his luxurious estate on Schwanenwerder, close to Goebbels' new establishment. Goebbels and Lida Baarova met numerous times, but everyone, including Goebbels' wife, Magda, believed that Lida Baarova was going to marry Fröhlich, who had conveniently divorced his Jewish wife some years earlier.

At the Nuremberg Conference in 1936, Hitler, upon being introduced to Lida Baarova, made the mistake of thinking the actress was married to Fröhlich. Goebbels had to explain to the "Führer" that she was not married, and in the process apparently discovered that she had a more than passing interest in him. At which point, as most versions have it, they fell madly in love with one another.

This affair, which was to last until 1938, has been covered in detail in several books.[9] Goebbels enjoyed the favors of numerous actresses anxious to make their careers, but the Baarova business was serious indeed. In 1938 Hitler's discovery of the scandal almost caused Goebbels' resignation from the government, and, indirectly, put Goebbels in such a violent mood that he made several drastic decisions, including the order to begin the production of anti-Semitic films.

## IV

Although 1936 was the second most prolific year in the history of the German sound film, with 143 feature films produced (against 147 in 1934, the peak year), it was startlingly weak in quality. Only a few films approached first rate, and the two best, *Die klugen Frauen*\* and *Fährmann Maria* had been completed in 1935.

Most pictures were comedies or mysteries of little quality; a feeling of coasting enveloped the industry. Despite claims to the contrary, Goebbels had little reason to be proud of the year's films with a very few exceptions.

The best of the lot was Frank Wysbar's unusual *Fährmann Maria* (*Ferry Boat Woman Maria*), (January 7), which is one of the highpoints of the German sound cinema. To all intents and purposes, *Fährmann Maria* closes the series of films of the supernatural which had begun with *Der Student von Prag* in 1914. (However, there was at least one more full-blown tragic fantasy, Heinz Hilpert's *Die unheimlichen Wünsche*, but this was based on a French story and falls outside the classic tradition.)

At the opening of the film, a ferryman of a remote area hears the bell being tolled across the river from his hut. He takes his boat to

---

\* The German-language version of Jacques Feyder's *La Kermesse Heroïque*, directed by Arthur Maria Rabenalt.

the other side, where it is boarded by a strange and silent man. In the middle of the river the ferryman drops dead into the stranger's arms. This story gives rise to a rumor that the river is inhabited by an evil spirit, and the position of ferryman is impossible to fill.

A homeless girl named Maria, seeking work in the village, takes the job. On the first night of her new work she is called to find a wounded young man who is apparently in flight. She takes him across but refuses the summons of his pursuers, whom the young man describes in his delirium as the agents of death himself. The following evening she answers the bell to find the stranger again on the other shore. It becomes obvious that he is searching for the young man, and Maria tries every trick to keep them separated but her simple efforts are in vain, for the stranger has magic powers. Maria's last resort is to sacrifice herself for the man she now loves. She leads the stranger through a swamp filled with quicksand. Then a miracle occurs. The surface of

The legions of Death track their prey in Frank Wysbar's masterpiece of the supernatural, *Fährmann Maria* (1936).

the bog carries the light weight of the girl while the stranger sinks below. The lovers are reunited.

Obviously the film has nothing in common with any films of the National Socialist epoch. It is virtually a silent picture, with small patches of dialogue accompanied by Herbert Windt's luminous score, photographed in an unusual filtered style by Frank Weihmayr. Wysbar and Weihmayr took their actors and crew far from the studio to the remote Lüneburger Heath near Hamburg. This area has a ghostly look, full of watery bogs dotted with sinister poplar trees. (Earlier Wysbar had planned a film called *Der Werwolf* which was apparently started in the same location, but was halted during production in 1934.)

In an era of slapstick comedy and historical pomposities, *Fährmann Maria* strikes a strange note indeed, and it is possible to read a variety of symbolic meanings into the plot, some of them hardly complimentary to the Nazi regime. The horsemen who chase the hero are garbed in black on white horses, looking like the SS. The figure of the Stranger (Peter Voss), who hardly ever speaks, is directly descended from Lang's *Der müde Tod* (*Destiny*); he is obviously the agent of death and evil, but not completely unsympathetic. He is destroyed at the end of the film by faith, pure and simple, much as Wegener's Golem is at last put out of action by a small child, and as Murnau's Nosferatu is destroyed by the girl who offers herself to him.

The film succeeds particularly because of the stunning performance of Sybille Schmitz, in one of her most Garboesque roles. She is the embodiment of womanly virtue and steadfast faith, qualities which endeared the film to Nazi "reviewers" of the era.

But apparently Goebbels loathed the film, probably because the meaning of the story is not clear. It was suggested to him by some alarmed members of the censorship board that the picture was a parable of the defeat of the Nazi ideology, and this would have been enough to ban the film, but Goebbels, unwilling to stir up his "intellectual" advisors, refrained from doing so and even awarded it with the "culturally valuable" subsidy. But it is significant that there were no other films made along the same lines.

Distribution of the film was limited in Germany, and it would seem that it is almost unknown there today. Fortunately, the Museum of

Modern Art in New York obtained a print for its archive before the start of World War II, and *Fährmann Maria* has been screened in New York numerous times. When Wysbar emigrated to the United States, he remade the same story under the title *Strangler of the Swamp* (1945), but this version is a pale shadow of the original.

Detlef Sierck's *Schlussakkord* (*Closing Chord*), (June 27), was a romantic drama done with much the same flair which Sierck (Douglas Sirk) was to evidence in his full-blown remakes of classic tear jerkers for Universal two decades later in the United States. The story, which would have made a fine vehicle for Claudette Colbert, details the trials and tribulations of the widow of a symphony conductor who obtains employment as a nanny in the household where her son has been adopted. To add to her problems, the boy's stepmother is found dead under mysterious circumstances, although a verdict of suicide saves the day. Lil Dagover had a field day as the unhappy stepmother, and the excellent musical sequences saved the film from banality. *Schlussakkord* was named as "Best Musical Film" at the 1936 Venice Biennale.

Lil Dagover was back at work as Madame Pompadour in the historically important *Das Schönheitsfleckchen* (*The Beauty Spot*), (August 4), which was the first German color fiction film. Goebbels had ordered experimentation in color in order to supply the public demand, now deprived of American color films. He was disappointed in the results, although the Opticolor process, developed by Berthon-Siemens, was reportedly better than the Agfacolor system which was officially adopted in 1939.

The film is based on a short story ("La Mouche") by Alfred de Musset, a bit of froth about a plot to introduce Louis XV to a new mistress, and ran only three reels. The direction—somewhat of a major problem here, since it was difficult to match different color takes—was by Rolf Hansen, making his debut under Carl Froelich's supervision.

Willi Krause, now relieved of his Dramaturg position, both scripted and directed (as Peter Hagen) a film called *Nachtwache im Paradies* (*Vigil in Paradise*), (July 16), starring his usual leading lady, Jessie Vihrog, with assistance by Ida Wüst, one of the handful of redhot Nazi supporters in the movie profession. It is worth noting that this one-time power in the film industry could not find a producer among the major companies; he was reduced to working for one of the smallest combines, a good example of how the mighty could fall from the peaks of the Third Reich.

Pola Negri's long awaited return to the German screen was in Paul Wegener's *Moskau-Shanghai* (October 5), a bang-up adventure film influenced by von Sternberg's *Shanghai Express* with elements of *Flüchtlinge* at the end of the picture. Although the film was not bad, audiences found Pola Negri's acting hilarious.

The best comedy of the year was Carl Froelich's *Wenn wir alle Engel wären* (*If We All Were Angels*), (October 9), which contained a number of racy situations that would have curled the hair of an American censor.\* Oddly enough the earlier *Boccaccio* (July 31), directed by Herbert Maisch from the popular operetta, was far less erotic despite the opportunities inherent in the story.

After *Fährmann Maria*, Wysbar made another odd film, *Die Unbekannte* (*The Unknown*), (November 12), which again starred Sybille Schmitz and Aribert Mog, joined by the French actor Jean Gallard. Unfortunately, everything right with the earlier picture went wrong here, for it would seem that the director was far less at home in the drawing rooms of Paris than in his Northern swamps.

*Annemarie* (November 10) was the first major work of the talented Fritz Peter Buch, and a most unusual treatment of the effect of World War I on a young girl, portrayed beautifully by Gisela Uhlen. The story is strangely pacifistic and contains a flow of romantic pessimism quite out of place in the times. The heroine meets a young soldier on his way to the Western Front and falls in love with him. She hears the news of his death while playing the church organ, and instead of the expected uplifting ending, the viewer was left with the image of the despairingly weeping girl playing the hymn "Aus tiefer Not schrei ich zu Dir" ("I Call to Thee in Deepest Agony"). The film was allowed to be made because of its espousal of the doctrine of sacrifice for the state, but the effect on the audience was somewhat contrary to that imagined by its writers.

---

\* The film was revived in one of Berlin's largest cinemas during the summer of 1963, and broke all house records.

## V

If the nonpolitical films of the year were hardly first rate, the political output of 1936 was unusually poor.

A short-lived flirtation with the Polish film industry had a dismal start with the coproduction of *August der Starke* (January 17), a thoroughly overblown biography of the German king of Poland, with the opera singer Michael Bohnen heading a large and distinguished cast under Paul Wegener's somewhat disinterested direction.

Much better was Carl Froelich's *Traumulus* (January 23), which won every sort of prize possible from the Nazi government. Designed as propaganda for new methods of education, it was a sort of poor man's *Blue Angel*, with Jannings again playing a professor with his head in the clouds. But Froelich was no von Sternberg, and let his star ham outrageously. The final scene, in which Jannings gives a speech over the body of the young man he drove to suicide, was considered magnificent at the time, but the passing years have neither been kind to the film nor to Jannings. In addition, the tone of the film, which promotes certain Nazi ideas over those of the past, is thoroughly repulsive. The most that can be said for the film is that it includes some atmospheric photography and the usual good performances from Froelich-trained juveniles.

Luis Trenker's *Der Kaiser von Kalifornien* (*The Kaiser of California*), (July 21), has unusual interest for American audiences, as it was largely filmed in the United States and recounts in considerable detail the curious career of the Swiss printer Johann August Sutter who unwittingly set off the California gold rush. In addition to directing, Trenker was extremely convincing as Sutter, and his script (later expanded into a novel) gave him some fine scenes, including an allegorical finale in which Sutter, dying in poverty, sees the growth of San Francisco.

After their brief fling, Trenker and Goebbels were no longer on good terms. Goebbels was unhappy about the Sutter project, which took Trenker to the United States and out of his control, but allowed it to go ahead because it was financed by Tobis, which at the time received its money from Holland. The film was difficult to make, and Trenker had only $30,000 with which to do his extensive location work in Arizona. Paul Kohner at Universal gave moral support to the project, although he failed to interest his studio in it. The remaining exteriors were shot in Berlin and Italy. While in the United States, Trenker received several offers for Hollywood films, but could not accept because his wife and children were in Germany and Trenker feared consequences for them.

Karl Ritter's annual propaganda extravaganza, *Verräter* (*Traitor*), (September 9), turned out somewhat better than expected, with the real surprise being an excellent performance by Lida Baarova, who was gradually becoming a capable actress. The story was the usual espionage thriller, slickly directed but empty and unconvincing.

The Frederick the Great biographies hit rock bottom with the incredibly bad *Fridericus* (also known as *Der alte Fritz*) (completed in December but not premiered until the following February, a sure sign of trouble). Otto Gebühr again played the king, with good support from Hilde Körber and Lil Dagover, but a bad script and miserable direction by Johannes Meyer doomed the project.

It was a busy year for Veit Harlan, who was continuing to show his particular knack for speedy, cheap production. Four films appeared under his name: *Kater Lampe* (February 19); *Der müde Theodor* (March 12); *Maria die Magd* (November 25); and *Alles für Veronika* (December 12). Harlan regarded all these films as worthless, but admitted to me that he had a certain fondness for *Maria die Magd* because it was based on a play by his father, and gave an excellent role as a nurse to Hilde Körber, his wife at the time.

# 1937: GOEBBELS ABSORBS THE INDUSTRY

With the critics safely out of the way, Goebbels now turned to a new project, an attempt virtually to nationalize the film industry. Even with the carping reviewers silenced, the industry was in bad shape. At a meeting of the Filmkammer, its new president, Dr. Lehnich, stated on March 7 (in case the fact had not been noted before) that film output had dropped in Germany in the past four years. He praised the films which had been made as "nationally characteristic" but still complained that there was too little production. The reasons for this were complex.

The production figures show what happened. Below is shown the number of German language films (including Austrian films) released during a seven-year period. The list is based on January–December figures; the Nazi government normally used July–June totals in statistical analysis.

NUMBER OF FILMS RELEASED

| 1931 | 1932 | 1933 | 1934 | 1935 | 1936 | 1937 |
|------|------|------|------|------|------|------|
| 200  | 156  | 135  | 147  | 123  | 143  | 121  |

There is the initial drop between 1932 and 1933 (—21) largely due to the almost complete halt in production during 1933 described·

above. A slight increase in 1934 (+12), then a big decrease (—24) in 1935, and a big but misleading increase in 1936 (+20). From this point on, production dropped steadily until the demise of the Third Reich.

As observed previously, the 1936 productions were of singularly mediocre quality, with a few exceptions. The increase in production was due to the output of what would be called in the United States "second features," innocuous entertainments which could be made quickly and cheaply with scant fear of government interference. Germany was recovering its economic position following the effect of the depression, and there was more money to spend. But the drop in income, despite apparent gains, of the major film companies was another matter.

For example, here are the figures of the Ufa organization:

| YEAR | GROSS INCOME | EXPORT INCOME |
|------|--------------|---------------|
| 1932–1933 | RM 37.5 million | RM 12.5 million |
| 1935–1936 | RM 44.5 million | RM  5.0 million |

Between 1933 and 1936 cinema attendance rose from 100 million a year to 333 million. But production costs increased greatly, actually doubling in the same period. In 1936, the Ufa made 110 feature films and short subjects, and had a deficit of RM 12–15 million, on the basis of production costs of RM 55 million and sales income of RM 44.5 million.

Government controls, rising expenses, and the gradual but sure elimination of the export market made it virtually impossible for an independent company to make a profit in the film-production business. Goebbels and his economic advisors saw that there was only one solution to this dilemma: to absorb the companies under government control, or find themselves without a film industry.

In 1937 there were three large film producers: the Ufa in Berlin (with its *Alliance Cinématographique* subsidiary in Paris); Tobis in Berlin, although its parent office was in Amsterdam where it had some studios, as well as others in Paris; and the smaller Bavaria company in Munich. The two minor companies in the field were Terra, which released through the majors, and Carl Froelich Productions, which released through the Ufa. All were in serious financial difficulties with the distinct possibility of bankruptcy.

The process by which the Nazi government took complete control of all film-production companies can be said to have begun in December 1936 and to have come to an end in the first months of 1938. The absorption process was devious, and is difficult to disentangle at this date, but the version which is given below would seem to be the most correct possible on the basis of both official reports and newspaper articles of the period.

The first step of the scheme took place shortly before Christmas of 1936 when an anonymous (but actually government-directed) group obtained stock control of the German branch of Tobis. Immediately after this, Goebbels ordered directors and artists to be placed on the board of all film companies, claiming this to be part of an over-all effort to improve the artistic levels of the German film. Tobis, now partly in government hands, agreed immediately, and on January 20, 1937, Willi Forst, Emil Jannings, and Gustaf Gründgens were elected to serve as part of the six-man board of the company, which was at the moment twice as large as the Ufa. The business and financial end of Tobis was handled by three businessmen, Fritz Main, Ernst Scheffler, and Sigmund Jung, the latter representing the government. In a major reorganization, the script division, casting office, and advertising division were put under one head. Production was ordered cut by ten films. In the middle of the year, the board was augmented by two directors, the veteran Hans Zerlett and the fast-rising Veit Harlan, who was on the verge of becoming the "official" director of the Nazi regime.

On December 1, 1937, the government took total control of Tobis, completing a one-year program. The stock was purchased for a reputed RM 8 million, but the Dutch parent company was saddled with the previous debt of RM 2.5 million, which the new owners refused to honor. With the loss of the Berlin studios, the Amsterdam concern was left with only the income from the sound-film patents (widely used through Europe) and some other licence holdings.

The Ufa was still controlled by Alfred Hugenberg, a Nazi sympathizer but no longer in the government. Yet he actually owned less

than half of the stock personally. On March 19, 1937, it was announced that the Deutsche Bank, acting only as an agent for unnamed
buyers, had paid RM 29 million for all the stock on the market, effectively obtaining control of the company.

The showdown was predicted for the annual Ufa stockholders meeting in May. The figures before the group were not pleasant. While
Tobis managed to pay a 4 percent dividend, the Ufa could pay none,
and listed its total 1936 profits as only RM 20,000 and most of this
small sum had been put into color research.

But the Ufa remained a proud organization, refusing Goebbels'
order to add artists to the board of directors. Despite the small profits,
the company had one strong point: a virtual monopoly on key cinemas
all over Germany, owning 111 theatres in 49 cities with a capacity of
120,735 seats. The return from this division of the company was excellent, even if the film production section lost money.

Following the May 5 meeting, all twenty directors of the Ufa were
forced to resign, pressured by the new (government) stockholders.
A new board was set up, comprising the actors Eugen Klöpfer, Paul
Hartmann, and Mathias Wiemann; directors Karl Ritter and Carl
Froelich; and Dr. Hans Weidemann from the Filmkammer. Dr. Emil
Georg von Strauss, third vice president of the Reichsbank, headed
the financial division composed of six bankers. With this new board,
the Ufa could be regarded as being exclusively government controlled,
especially after it was announced that the smaller firms which had
been releasing through the Ufa, and were heavily in debt to the government film bank, would get increased cooperation in the future and
a reduction in their previous liabilities.

At the end of February 1937, Bavaria was virtually bought out by
the New German Cinema Syndicate, which promptly cut down production to the point that by early 1938, the company nearly folded
despite the fact that it had the most modern studio in Germany. At
this point the government stepped in and took over production, making it the last major studio to be absorbed.

The old Terra company, a small concern which released through
the Ufa, was absorbed by that company early in the year. A *new*
Terra, which apparently had no connection with the old company of

the same name, was organized on June 26, with a capital of RM 5 million and a production schedule of 25 films for the year.

At the same time, the Froelich Company, which had been closely tied to the Ufa, was also bought out. Director-Producer Froelich had his own studios, which were geared almost exclusively for color in the Berthon-Siemens process, and Goebbels made much of this acquisition.

Although all these companies were now under government control, the government was not listed as the official owner. The shares were held by such concerns as the Deutsche Bank and the Franz Eher Verlag, the official Nazi publishing house. The latter concern played an important part in the Tobis sale.

In March, the production schedule for the year was announced as 60 films from Tobis, 38 from the Ufa, and 15 from Bavaria. Others from various sources brought the announced production schedule to 157 titles, of which only about 110 were actually made (with an additional 24 from various foreign coproduction schemes).

On March 25, Goebbels ordered a new system of grading films, which would carry with it certain monetary rewards, replacing an older method. The new classifications were, in order of decreasing merit: 1. Politically and artistically especially valuable. 2. Politically and artistically valuable. 3. Politically valuable. 4. Artistically valuable. 5. Culturally valuable. 6. Educationally valuable. At the same time, Goebbels remarked: "The film of present-day Germany must carry in it the ideology of the present-day Germany. But this ideology must never be allowed to become obtrusive bias. Bias which is detected always fails in its purpose."[1]

Now that the previous salary restrictions on actors had been rescinded, it is interesting to state here the income of the upper 1165 "stars" from the list of more than 4,000 registered screen and stage performers. All earned more than RM 400 a year; 215 earned more than RM 6000 a year; 15 earned more than RM 100,000 a year.

With the industry under almost complete control, Goebbels renewed his efforts to cut the importation of American films, which still outdrew German pictures. The limited number of films exported to the United States meant, under the quota system, a corresponding restriction on imports; and in addition the censor began to refuse certificates to large-scale pictures from abroad, admitting only minor films whenever possible. Only 28 American films were seen in Germany in 1936 since this figure represented the number of German films sold in the United States. As a counter to this, the American companies moved their dubbing facilities from Germany to Vienna and Rome.

The four-month report issued on May 10 revealed that until that date, the year had seen the release of fifty films: 28 from Germany, 13 from the United States, 4 from Austria, and one each from France, Italy, Japan, Czechoslovakia, and Hungary. However, the quality of the American films allowed can be judged from the titles released in April: *Maid of Salem* (Paramount); *Bulldog Drummond Escapes* (Paramount); and *Pigskin Parade* (Fox). What the Germans could make of the latter film is anyone's guess.[2]

Yet American films, poor though the selection might be, were vastly preferred by the paying public, and therefore by German cinema managers. The second week of May saw Berlin's largest cinema, the Ufa Palast, playing an American film, and the following week only one major first-run house was playing a German picture.[3]

Earlier in the month Goebbels, who could not understand the situation, told the producers, after the shake-up at the Ufa, that, "the German film has reached the point where it must fulfill its duty to the State, nation and culture. It must exercise international influence. It must become a spiritual world leader. The German film, particularly, has a world mission."[4]

The bickering among various parts of the industry continued. The exhibitors were angry with the producers because they felt the production companies were cutting down the number of films in order to make more profit with less cash outlay. The producers countered with the accusation that exhibitors refused to let a new film play long enough to make a profit.

The kind of films which *were* made were at the root of the problem. One of the prestige productions of the year, Gerhard Lamprecht's *Madame Bovary* (April 23) with Pola Negri in the title role, was being laughed off the screen all over Germany. The simple fact was that the film was ridiculous, with Pola Negri giving a performance which would

The sacking of Florence from Luis Trenker's *Condottieri* (1937), filmed on location.

have been exaggerated in the silent film period. After a particular riotous screening in Essen, the local *National Zeitung* snarled that the reception was due to "the opposition beast of the Kurfürstendamm [referring to the Jews] which, following the prohibition of new film criticism, now prowls about the protective darkness of cinemas."[5] The *Berlin Nachtausgabe* suggested that viewers who didn't like films should simply walk out. This often happened.

The biggest film of the spring season, Luis Trenker's *Condottieri* (March 24) ran exactly one week in Berlin cinemas because of arbitrary censorship imposed by the government due to the religious issue. This lavish German-Italian coproduction had been shot in 1936 in Italy in two different language versions, with Trenker playing the lead, as well as directing. The story concerned the revolt of the Condottieri against Cesare Borgia, and painted some not-very-favorable parables with the German government's treatment of its subjects. The theme of the film was the popular revolt for freedom. In its original state, *Condottieri* was a stunning picture with effective location work in Lombardy and Florence, and boasting magnificently handled renaissance battle scenes.

When presented to the censor (after Hitler previewed the film and told the startled Trenker he hated it), an entire section, crucial to the story, was removed. In it, the rebel leader, who has raised an army and invaded Rome, storms the papal palace with the intention of murdering the pope. But when the two men meet, the rebel falls on his knees before the pontiff. While this was quite orthodox for the Italian audience, it infuriated Hitler because of the pope's recent encyclical ("Mit brennender Sorge"), which was obviously aimed against him. With the mutilation of the film, Trenker lost any vestiges of affection he might have had for the Führer.

Even more scandalous was the case of a comedy film, *Land der Liebe* (*Land of Love*), (June 10). Written and directed by Reinhold Schünzel, this picture (which I have not been able to locate) was from all reports a daring operetta set in a mythical country obsessed with hero worship of a particularly dim-witted sovereign. A few hours before the scheduled premiere late in May, some high officials finally realized that the film was probably a satire on the Nazi regime and called off the showing. It was heavily cut and released the following month. Schünzel, one of the last of the original German film-musical creators, left Germany for the United States, where he was promptly hired by MGM. and successfully pursued a lengthy career in exile as writer, director, and actor.

About the time of the film's scheduled release, *Film Kurier* wrote: "You producers do not get any nearer present realities with heavy-footed tendentiousness. Humor must be coupled with our present attitude and it should not be crushed by ideological phraseology."[6] However, the *Land der Liebe* brand of comedy was never repeated in the Third Reich.

In an effort to break the hold of American films in both Italy and Germany, representatives of the two countries met in Berlin to work out coproduction and import agreements. The Germans agreed to help finance coproduced films, and give them free publicity. The Italians were having a similar problem as far as imported films were concerned: the week of the meetings, every first-run house in Rome was playing an American film. On April 10 Dr. Luigi Freddi and Dr. Lehnich signed a new film treaty. At the same time a similar agreement was worked out for Japanese coproductions, which was to have negligible results as far as the Japanese were concerned—only two such films were made.

The export market was gradually dwindling, and Goebbels was disturbed because foreign capital was important for the film industry and for the country as a whole. The foreign sales figures gave him ample cause for alarm. In 1930 exports brought in RM 22 million, in 1932 DM 12 million, and in 1936 RM 4 million.[7]

Resistance to German films abroad was becoming organized. In New York, the scheduled October 23, 1936, premiere of the French version of *Amphitryon* at the 55th Street Playhouse was postponed by threat of a boycott and picketing by the "Non-Sectarian Anti-Nazi League" and the American Jewish Conference. Despite the fact that the German-language print was not offered, *Amphitryon*'s release was held up for a considerable length of time, but it was at last released to generally good reviews. Goebbels expressed his satisfaction at the failure of the boycott in a speech given on April 6, 1937.

## II

The most important political film of the year was Veit Harlan's *Der Herrscher* (*The Ruler*), (March 17), a free adaptation of Gerhart Hauptmann's play *Vor Sonnenuntergang* (*Before Sunset*) (1932), scripted by Thea von Harbou and Curt Braun. It was awarded the National Film Prize at the annual May Day celebrations, and Jannings was given a special award for "superlative human character impersonation."

*Der Herrscher* was an extremely clever film, and a prime example of the subtle changes which could be made in works of literature to produce political propaganda. An anonymous British critic made a very

Emil Jannings as the Krupp-like industrial baron receives the homage of his family in Veit Harlan's *Der Herrscher* (1937).

perceptive analysis of the film at the time of its English release in July of 1937, and it is worth reprinting here:

Heavy drama . . . of a German steel-master whose wife dies and who thereupon becomes enamoured of his understanding young secretary. His grown-up children and their husbands and wives do their best to upset the proposed marriage, and eventually try to have him certified insane. But he violently refuses to give way; the accusation of insanity is rejected by the courts, and he and his loved one, after much emotional stress, are reunited.

A good-deal of semi-political propaganda is interwoven into the story: from the beginning the steel-master is represented very much in the light of a dictator, and the attitude of his workmen towards him is very reminiscent of that supposed to be shown by the people towards a Fascist leader (at one point they actually call him their Führer). There is also one stretch of rhetoric at a board-meeting where he tells his co-directors that it is their duty to obey him even though it might mean ruin: this is at the end of a harrangue in which he says the firm must carry out experiments, at enormous cost, to assist the State. We are not told *how* the State is being assisted and nothing more is heard of these experiments, which appear to be merely a handle for the introduction of this scene. In the context, the picture of an upright man being wronged by his naughty children is undoubtedly significant:

the symbol is clearly that of the Father of a State. The remark repeatedly addressed to him: "You can't put the clock back" is also an obvious cut at enemies of Naziism who use similar phrases. On the question of the proposed marriage, our sympathies are naturally worked-up in the steel-master's favour, but when he hears of the attempt to certify him insane, he does in fact behave exactly like a dangerous lunatic, and it is therefore impossible to believe that he "has never raised his voice before."

The atmosphere of the film is morbid and tempestuous. Within these bounds, despite several ragged transitions, there are one or two effective technical passages—notably the opening scene at the funeral in the rain, which convey a real enough feeling of mourning and grief, and the scenes in the heart of the steel-works, whose noises and photographic rhythms give the desired impression of Titanic force and violence. In its last stages the film moves with excessively curt steps to its "happy ending," which is purely conventional. The mood throughout is wild and very oppressive, and often on the further side of the rational: the film's moral implications are extraordinarily confused.[8]

*Der Herrscher* was Harlan's first major film, and one of the most successful of his checkered career. Handsomely photographed by Günther Anders and Werner Brandes, the scenes referred to above are still outstanding when viewed today. A good cast was assembled, perhaps helping Jannings to keep his overacting to a minimum.

Harlan told me that the film was made with a minimum of political interference, and gleefully recalled that he and Jannings studied newsreels of the Krupp family in order to duplicate their mannerisms on the screen. However, the film *is* intensely political, and the sections added to the original drama were obviously tied to Dr. Freisler's recently enacted property rights law: at the end of the film, the magnate's immense steel holdings go to his factory workers rather than to his worthless family.

Harlan did not object to the story additions but he refused to show the *swastika* in the film and on the completion of the picture, he said, refused Goebbels' invitation to join the Party. Because of this, he was temporarily suspended from his directorial duties.

If Harlan could handle propaganda themes with some artistry, Director Karl Ritter was solely concerned with getting the message across. Although Ritter made a few nonpolitical comedies, the violent-action military propaganda picture was his specialty. He finished three such films in 1937, all on large budgets with popular stars: *Unternehmen Michael* (*Operation Michael*), (September 7); *Patrioten* (*Patriots*), (September 24); and *Urlaub auf Ehrenwort* (*Holiday on Word of Honor*), (January 11, 1938).

In an article on the Nazi cinema's effect on youth published after the war, Dr. John Altmann takes Ritter to task as the most irresponsible and dangerous of all the film makers of the Third Reich:

> In the person of Karl Ritter, Ufa producer and director, Nazism found an able war propagandist, an uncompromising and unscrupulous personality, just the right man to help mold the Hitler Youth. Acclaimed by the leadership of the *Hitlerjugend*, praised to high heaven by Hitler's Elite Guard, the dreaded SS., as "Our dear friend, a political soldier, a political artist . . . a National Socialist," Karl Ritter created films which became "must" performances in the Schirach organization [the Hitler Youth] and influenced millions of German youngsters.
>
> Karl Ritter's career as a Nazi propagandist began soon after the end of World War I. When national socialism came to power many years later, it started a search for its party members in radio and movies. Ritter was discovered. Between 1934 and 1938 he advanced to become, finally, the leading director of Ufa's war-propaganda series of "pure" Nazi films. A safe estimate of how many young boys—the future soldiers of Adolf Hitler in World War II—had seen Ritter's films between 1936 and 1939 is about 6,000,000.[9]

Altmann's concern about the work of this despicable director is not exaggerated. While his films now seem to be heavy-handed and extremely talky, they were amazingly successful in their aim of making propaganda palatable to the masses, with one or two exceptions.

*Unternehmen Michael* is a particularly nasty piece of work, aimed directly at the youth of Germany. It takes up an episode in World War I when the commander of a German infantry column, hopelessly encircled by a superior British force in France, is overruled in his decision to surrender his unit. Instead, his officers propose *Heldentod* for everyone; they suggest that he give a false cease-fire order, then, when the British storm their position, to order the German artillery to shell their position destroying friend and foe alike. Altmann notes that when some military brass questioned Ritter on the soundness of such a plan, the director replied, "I want to show the German youth that senseless, sacrificial death has its moral value."[10]

*Patrioten* is a more subtle piece of work, with the best screen performance of Lida Baarova, helped along by Mathias Wieman and Hilde Körber. The official synopsis is worth reprinting in full:

A German night bomber flies over enemy territory to deliver its deadly cargo. The bombs are falling on the target but the bomber is brought down by enemy fire.

The only survivor, the German pilot Peter Thomann, bleeding from a wound in his shoulder, is racing through the dawn trying to make his escape from hostile France into Germany. A group of French actors find the exhausted and half-dead man. They don't know who he is or where he came from, since he had exchanged his uniform for the tatters of a scarecrow. The leader of the troupe wants to leave the stranger to his fate, but the female star wants to help him. Therese succeeds in winning over her colleagues and they take the wounded flyer along. Although they cannot converse with each other, both ignorant of the other's language, love binds them together. Peter enjoys Therese's loving care but secretly awaits a chance to escape and regain his freedom in Germany. Therese does not want to lose him. Another actress gives Therese the passport of her dead husband for Peter's use, and later his identity as a Frenchman is established when French troops check the artists. Peter, now Pierre, poses as an artist and entertains French soldiers with his mouth organ. Suddenly the air-raid sirens scream, a German attack is in the offing. Some German flyers are shot down and taken prisoner. Peter establishes contact with them and decides to make his escape.

Charles, the head of the troupe, becomes more and more suspicious. One day he finds a German coin, and he is now convinced that Pierre is a German spy. Therese cannot believe that Pierre is an "enemy." She asks him to reveal his identity to her, and he tells her the truth. Torn between love and patriotism she decides to inform the military commander of Peter's identity. His attempt to escape is thwarted.

He is caught and brought before a soldiers' court, He is vindicated as far as the spy charges are concerned, but is convicted for using a false passport and will be sent off to a war prisoners' camp. The two lovers, each a patriot in his own way, shake hands for the last time and hope for a reunion after the war.[11]

The film was an amazing success in Germany and abroad, some critics misled by what appeared at first to be a pacifist message. Only the Czechs refused to allow it to be shown in their country. The excellence of the acting and the general lack of histrionics make the film seem perhaps the best of Ritter's considerable output, but in common with most of his work the propaganda message is repulsively obvious.

*Urlaub auf Ehrenwort,* which bears a striking similarity to Erich Pommer's British production of the same year, *Farewell Again,** is concerned with the adventures of a group of soldiers who are given an unexpected, and slightly illegal holiday, when their train taking them to the front is delayed in Berlin for the day. The officer in charge gives them permission to leave on their word of honor that they will return before the day is over.

The film then breaks down into a series of stories about each soldier's adventures on this autumn 1918 day. As Dr. Altmann describes it:

> For the third time he [Ritter] used the background of World War I to speak of the war to come and preached self-sacrifice beyond human bounds and the giving-up of all personal happiness. In the film a young composer prefers to die in battle for an already defeated Germany rather than live for the première of his symphony, success and a career; a young, lonely soldier, entangled in his first love affair with an equally lonely girl, gives up fulfillment and a bright future in love to die for this defeated Germany; finally, a "left-wing intellectual" rejects the comradeship of fellow revolutionists and his affair with a "red" girlfriend for the "real comradeship" of fighting men. All these soldiers have a chance to desert defeated Germany while enroute to the Western Front late in October 1918. The men prefer, however, to return to their unit; they choose to renounce happiness, career and political beliefs; they want to die—uselessly—for Germany.[12]

As Ritter himself commented on such themes, "My movies deal with the unimportance of the individual . . . all that is personal must be given up for our cause."[13]

Herbert Maisch was not so lucky as Ritter when he tried his hand at another World War I drama, *Menschen ohne Vaterland* (*Men*

* Directed by Tim Whelan, with Leslie Banks and Flora Robson, original story by Wolfgang Wilhelm.

*Without a Fatherland*), (March 6), which turned into a sort of musical with Willy Fritsch despite the serious subject of the Freikorps in the Baltic during the 1918–1919 period. His second film of the year, *Starke Herzen* (*Strong Hearts*) took as its subject the true story of a Communist revolt during a production of *Tosca* in Hungary. Meant as anti-Communist propaganda, it was produced at the Ufa with a cast of Maria Cebotari (the famous opera singer), Gustav Diessl, and René Deltgen, and an elaborate Herbert Windt score. Despite the 1918 setting, the censor had the idea that the film could be interpreted as anti-Nazi as well as anti-Communist, and banned the picture in November; it was never released.

The effort at coproduction with Japan brought forth two unfortunate feature films, the first and most ridiculous being *Die Tochter des Samurai* (*The Daughter of the Samurai*, sometimes referred to by its Japanese-title translation, *New Earth*), (March 23).* For some obscure reason—perhaps loyalty to the Party—Arnold Fanck was selected as director, despite the fact that he had made almost nothing other than mountain films in his long career. He brought with him from Germany the cameraman Richard Angst (and assistant Walter Riml) and the actress Ruth Eweler. It soon became obvious that Fanck's idea of Japan had little in common with reality, but to the amazement of the Japanese advisors and crew, he insisted on filming the story exactly as it had been scripted in Berlin. The result was a movie which rather resembled a mixture of *Madame Butterfly* and shop-worn Nazi clichés of self-sacrifice for the cause. Viewed today, the picture is of interest only for the performance of Sessue Hayakawa and some beautiful scenery. The film was a great success in Berlin, but the Japanese found it mystifying and ridiculous.

### III

Veit Harlan, the busiest director of the year, found time to make two entertainment films besides the official project *Der Herrscher*. *Die Kreutzersonate* (*The Kreutzer Sonata*), (February

---

* The second was *Das heilige Ziel*, a wintersport film shot in 1937–1938, directed by Kosho Nomura and Shochiku Ofuna, released in a dubbed German print early in 1942. The only Germans involved were the actor Sepp Rist and cameraman Richard Angst.

11), a literate and elegant version of Tolstoy's famous story, with Lil Dagover as Yelaina and superior assistance from Hilde Körber, Peter Petersen, and Albrecht Schoenhals, was in every way a production of high quality. Because the film had a Russian theme, it was one of the few Harlan films to be cleared for screening after World War II. It was followed by a minor comedy, *Mein Sohn, der Herr Minister* (*My Son, the Minister*), (July 6), adapted from a French play and starring the famous actress Françoise Rosay.

The year's masterpiece, indeed one of the finest German sound films ever made, was Herbert Selpin's completely forgotten essay in neo-realism, *Heiratsschwindler* (*The Marriage Swindler*), also known under its alternate title, *Die rote Mütze* (*The Red Cap*), (February 15, 1938). This extraordinary work, which has nothing in common with the period in which it was made nor with any other contemporary film, seems to have met with complete indifference on the part of viewers and critics.

The script was written by Selpin's old friend, Dr. Fritz Wendhausen, for whom Selpin had earlier penned the only script he was not to direct personally, *Der Läufer von Marathon* (*The Runner of Marathon*). Produced by the small A.B.D. Company and released through Tobis, the film seems to have run into trouble and had to wait for several months for showing after its censor certificate was granted. How Selpin could have made this film, following six years of society dramas and one big historical spectacular, is a mystery; it is even

Herbert Selpin's forgotten essay in neorealism, *Heiratsschwindler* (1938). Viktoria von Ballasko (left) and Hilde Körber.

stranger that he received financing for this deeply pessimistic work in an era when positive, cheerful pieces were the order of the day.

Certainly there is little sweetness and light in its story of a professional cad (Harald Paulsen)* who is released from prison only to return to the scene of his previous crimes, the railroad village of Klein-Wustrow, in order to blackmail a former conquest and to pick up a little extra money by robbing young girls of their savings by promises of marriage. After creating a number of tragic situations, the villain is arrested and things are straightened out, but the spectacle of his first victim leaving town at the film's conclusion is anything but uplifting.

Wendhausen's remarkable script was the best Selpin ever had to work with, and although the story is complicated, each character is fully developed and placed solidly in the dismal environment. E. W. Fiedler's photography is harsh, catching the sadness of the tiny railroad stop and its employees, much of the day-to-day routine of the station being shot in semidocumentary style. If Selpin had never made another film, this work would be enough to earn him a place in any history of the German cinema.

The Swedish singer Zarah Leander made a spectacular debut in Detlef Sierck's musical *Zu neuen Ufern* (*Toward New Shores*), (August 31). Goebbels had been looking around for a substitute for the now absent Marlene Dietrich, and found his ideal in the person of Zarah Leander. She had been brought to his attention by the Ufa casting department, which had seen her in a minor Austrian picture and immediately realized her star potential. This unusual actress not only had a voice rather like that of Dietrich (although about an octave lower), but a luminously beautiful face reminiscent of Garbo.

The first of a long series of Leander vehicles, *Zu neuen Ufern* tells the story of a British singer named Gloria Vane who takes the rap for her lover's embezzlement and is deported to Australia, where she is finally "purchased" as the bride of a farmer. The melodramatic plot gave Zarah Leander the chance to sing three of her greatest hits: "*Yes, Sir!*", "*Ich hab' eine tiefe Sehnsucht in mir*," and "*Ich steh' im Regen*," composed by Ralph Benatzky.

*Paulsen was the original "Macheath" in Brecht-Weill's *Die Dreigroschenoper*.

Zarah Leander
in
Detlef Sierck's
*La Habanera*
(1937).

The film commenced shooting in February 1937 and was finished two months later. The Ufa held up the film's release, perhaps fearing that the new star was too exotic for popular taste. These fears were groundless. At the Berlin premiere, there were 78 curtain calls and the astonished studio rushed her into another Sierck film, *La Habanera* (December 18), this picture set in Puerto Rico (although actually photographed in Tenerife). Her male stars in this case were Ferdinand Marian and Karl Martell, and the songs were composed by Lothar Brühe. Sierck's direction of the second film is more assured, without the strained attempts to Sternbergize Zarah Leander which had marred *Zu neuen Ufern.*

Now that Lida Baarova had shown real talent other than having seduced the minister of propaganda, she was given her first musical, an elaborate production of *Die Fledermaus* (October 30) in which she demonstrated a decided flair for light comedy under Paul Verhoeven's direction.

Heinrich George starred in *Der Biberpelz* (*The Beaver Skin*), (December 3), from Hauptmann's comedy, prepared in honor of the poet's birthday, and Emil Jannings chewed the scenery again in *Der zerbrochene Krug* (*The Broken Jug*), (October 19), from Kleist's comedy; this film has the distinction of probably being the first and only screen version of a classical stage play in which the entire text, word for word, was transferred intact. The experiment was not a complete success, but Gustav Ucicky's direction kept the story moving at a lively pace, and the superlative supporting cast helped to counteract Jannings' bombastic performance.

The most entertaining light comedy was an original work, *Der Mann, der Sherlock Holmes war* (*The Man Who Was Sherlock Holmes*), (July 15), a delicious spoof of the famous detective with Hans Albers and Heinz Rühmann as two impossible fumbling private eyes, who manage to hoodwink Scotland Yard into believing they are Sherlock Holmes and Dr. Watson, and go on a search for some stolen postage stamps. In the last scene, Arthur Conan Doyle enters to forgive them for their deception. The film is regarded as the high point of the German comedy film and is still frequently revived. Curiously, the director, Karl Hartl, never repeated the success of this picture.

Still smarting from the *Condottieri* incident, Luis Trenker went to England to obtain financing from Korda for his next film, a remake of the 1928 silent mountain drama, *Der Kampf ums Matterhorn* (*The Battle for the Matterhorn*), under the title *Der Berg ruft* (*The Mountain Calls*), (January 6, 1938). The German version is notable for the debut of the lovely Heidemarie Hatheyer; the English version was called *The Challenge* and starred Robert Douglas and Mary Claire. As usual, Trenker played the lead in both editions. This time there was no censorship problem, for mountain films were always safe—or so Trenker thought until he jinxed the genre with *Der Feuerteufel* in 1940.

# 1938-1939: WAR AND ESCAPISM

By the early part of 1938, the German film industry was virtually under complete government control, the last step being the absorption of the Bavaria studios, discussed in the previous chapter. Little legislation regarding film was passed in the 1938–1939 period.

Looking toward the future, Goebbels laid the cornerstone of the State Academy of Film on February 21, 1938. In his speech, he stated that one of the reasons for the new institution was to train future filmmakers to produce movies which would sell abroad. Not only had foreign film sales shrunk nearly to the vanishing point, but German audiences were also resisting the local product. In order to keep cinemas in business, the quota on imports had to be increased.

The Academy was situated at Ufastadt-Babelsberg, so that the students would be able to use some of the facilities of the giant Ufa physical plant in their work. The importance of this project can be judged by the fact that the first term was scheduled to start on April 15, 1939, and every priority was given to construction of the new Academy.

The catalogue offered thirty-two subjects, broken down into three sections: artistic, technical, and commercial. Yet the curriculum offered such unique courses as "*Weltanschauung*: Nazism as parent of the new German screen art" and "Nazi administration."

Costs were high by German standards. Tuition for the four-term, two-year course was $1000, with an additional $50 for the diploma. A single room for a term was $60 and a double $95. However, meals were cheap, and it was possible to get a good breakfast for twenty cents.

Although it did not work out as planned, Goebbels hoped that a diploma from the Academy would be the only future entry to the film world, replacing the usual path of theatre-to-film which had been the former practice. Foreign students could be admitted, but the catalogue stated that only "Aryans" need apply.

It was obvious that the new Film Academy would not only produce new filmmakers, but good Nazis at the same time. The film colony was far from loyal to the government, especially the actors. On May 14, 1938, it was necessary for Goebbels to enact a decree preventing stars from accepting roles abroad without permission of the Kulturkammer; if they disobeyed, they would be automatically expelled from the organization and hence unable to work in Germany. Furthermore, their passports would be revoked. Exempted from the new law were Germans already working abroad and employed by foreign concerns.

In September 1938, the New York *Times* printed a commissioned piece on the situation of exiled German film personalities, and came up with a list which is startling even today.[1]

Among the directors they reported Eric Charell, Henry Koster (Kosterlitz), Fritz Lang, Joe May, Hans Schwarz, Ernst Lubitsch, Karl Freund, William Dieterle, Wilhelm Thiele, and E. A. Dupont in Hollywood; Kurt Bernhardt, Berthold Viertel, and Robert Wiene in London; G. W. Pabst, Max Ophüls, Léontine Sagan, and Richard Oswald in Paris. Amongst actors, Marlene Dietrich was in the United States along with Fritz Kortner and Mady Christians. Brigitte Helm was in Paris, having been judged guilty of "race defilement" for having married a Jew after 1933; Elisabeth Bergner and her husband were doing well in London.

On the lighter side, a Jewish actor named Leo Reuss fled Germany to Vienna, where he dyed his hair and beard and became a specialist in "Aryan" roles, which were greatly praised by the Nazis. Having had his fun, Reuss revealed he was a Jew, signed a contract with MGM, and departed for the United States.

Among the cameramen, Sepp Algeier, Hans Schneeberger, and Günther Krampf found it more convenient to work elsewhere, at least for the time being. The musical departments of American, British, and French studios were quick to welcome such composers as Hanns Eisler, Friedrich Hollander, Kurt Weill, Franz Waxman, Karol Rathaus, and Mischa Spoliansky. And Germany's three top pre-Nazi producers were also in exile: Erich Pommer, Max Schach, and Seymour Nebenzal.

The list was incomplete, and others were to emigrate at the last minute: Reinhold Schünzel, Frank Wysbar, and Detlef Sierck—all to direct in the United States, and the actor Fritz van Dongen (Philip Dorn), to mention only a few more names. The listed personalities include many not of the Jewish faith, but who resisted the government by going into exile rather than work in Goebbels' studios.

The Civil War in Spain had started on July 16, 1936, and the eventual victory of the Franco forces, aided by the Nazi Condor Legion and Air Force, opened up a new market ready-made for German films. Up to this point, French films had a virtual monopoly on Spanish screens, but early in 1938 a cooperative agreement was set up between Spain and Germany.

Since the Spanish studios were rather primitive, it was decided that Spanish-language films would be shot in Berlin, using the Ufa and Tobis lots. The first project to be completed was a film of *The Barber of Seville* made by the Hispano Company. Ufa then went to Spain to make a musical, *Andalusische Nächte (Andalusian Nights)*, (July 5, 1938), under Herbert Maisch's direction with the great Spanish singer Imperio Argentina as a modern-day Carmen.

Despite the impressive send-off for this program, it was not a success any more than the earlier attempt at Japanese coproduction. Spain was a poor country and could not afford to pay much for the German assistance, and the few Spanish films shown in Berlin were indifferently received. However, the beginning of the Spanish alliance enabled Goebbels to get a foothold in the export of German films to Latin America. Numerous propaganda films were shown in neutral countries during World War II in either dubbed or subtitled versions.

The year 1938 brought about the end of the Baarova affair. Finally fed up with her husband's philandering, Magda Goebbels went to

Hitler with evidence of his love affair with the actress, materials collected for her in secret by Goebbels' trusted undersecretary Karl Hanke.

Hitler was flabbergasted since he had not even heard rumors of the affair, despite the fact that it was common knowledge to almost every German. The Führer ordered Magda to Berchtesgaden to tell her story, then went to Berlin to talk to Goebbels. According to most reports, Goebbels admitted everything and requested to be relieved of his duties and be posted abroad with his mistress. At this point, Hitler lost his temper and told Goebbels that he must break off the liaison at once.

The actress, who had just completed production of her most elaborate vehicle until then, *Preussische Liebesgeschichte (Prussian Love Story)*, directed by Paul Martin and costarring the popular Willy Fritsch, was summoned to the office of the Berlin Police Chief, Count von Helldorf. Fearing to go alone, Baarova brought the actress Hilde Körber (Frau Harlan) with her. Helldorf, who was not an unkind man (and was later executed for his part in the July 20 plot against Hitler), tried to break the news to her gently; Hitler had ordered a separation of six months on the condition that after this period the two could consider the problem of divorce. Baarova was to leave the country immediately and her new film was to be shelved.

At this point, according to the version related by Manvell and Fraenkel, the whole business turned into near farce. Baarova went into hysterics, and her friend cried out for Helldorf to bring some *eau de cologne*. The harassed police chief dashed into his washroom, grabbed the nearest bottle—which happened to hold hair tonic—and poured it on the actress's face.

While Baarova was trying to clean this off, Helldorf warned her that if she disobeyed the Führer's orders, her life would be in danger. Baarova threatened suicide, at which point Helldorf called Hitler and finally obtained permission for her to speak to Goebbels, who was at Göring's house with a witness. Goebbels' last words to her were "*Bleib wie du bist*" ("Stay as you are").[2]

They saw each other once again from a distance, but shortly afterward Baarova returned to her native Czechoslovakia, where she resumed her film career, turning out four films in 1939, some of them

with imported German stars including performers of the calibre of
Ewald Balser. But she was never seen on a German screen again until
after the war. The Martin film was eventually released in March
of 1950.

Goebbels left the Propaganda Ministry to recover at his new estate
at Lanke, where his temper hardly improved. At last Hitler suggested
that he should take a holiday in Greece, and Goebbels shortly afterward departed for Rhodes. In a terrible mood on his departure, he
ordered the immediate production of the first anti-Semitic films, a decision he had avoided making previously.

This order was in some part tied in with the end of the Baarova
affair, but more importantly with the violent Jewish pogrom of November 10, 1938, which had been set off by the murder of Vom Rath
in Paris by a young Polish Jew. An enormous amount of Jewish
property was destroyed by the Nazi mob, yet the Jewish community
was fined RM 5,000 million in "damages."

By the following January, both Goebbels' and Hitler's tempers had
cooled and things were back to normal. Magda moved back with her
husband, and was to bear him his last child, a daughter, in 1940.

At the start of 1939, relations with the United States were steadily
deteriorating. The official attitude toward American films was also
toughened, partly because Hollywood studios were tentatively beginning to turn out anti-Nazi films, the most controversial being
Warner Brothers' *Confessions of a Nazi Spy*.

On January 23, 1939, a "source close to the government" was reported by the New York *Times* as stating:

Incessant agitation against the Third Reich in the United States,
which among other things has hampered the showing of the Olympics
film, otherwise received throughout the world with the greatest applause, and which forced Hollywood film artists to sign an inflam-
matory declaration against Germany, has brought an understandable
reaction in the film industry in Germany.

It is pointed out that the American film industry stands under pre-
dominating Jewish influence and it may be stated that the number of
American films in Germany has declined.[3]

During the week of this statement, not a single American film was playing a first-run German theatre, while two new French pictures received featured release.

In his annual speech before the Reichstag on January 30 at the Kroll Opera, Hitler, near the end of his two-and-one-half-hour oration, made a special point of attacking anti-Nazi films being made in the United States. He ominously announced that if such works were actually produced (apparently seriously doubting such a thing could be possible), Germany would reply with anti-Semitic films which he felt sure "many countries will appreciate."[4] This was, of course, a lie. The first major anti-Semitic film, *Robert und Bertram*, was already in production at Tobis, and only script troubles and internal industry-balking kept *Jud Süss* from being made.

The anti-American campaign was heightened when the influential *Hamburger Tageblatt* announced on March 27 that it would no longer review or advertise American films because of their "offensive character." This was triggered by the impending April release of *Confessions of a Nazi Spy* in the United States—where it might be noted that many in Hollywood wondered whether production of such a film was a good idea.

As the Hamburg writer put it:

The mask has fallen. The State-supervised American film companies [sic] have joined in a chorus of never-ending insult and abuse of Germany. . . . The Reich has been objective enough, but if the policy of hate continues much longer the necessary counter measures will be taken quickly.

The same article mentioned that the motto over the doors of a Hollywood film company which read: "A place for the portrayal of human nature for the enjoyment and enlightenment of mankind," should be rewritten to read "A place for the portrayal of human lies for the consternation and sorrow of mankind."[6]

Research a month before the start of the war showed that perhaps the Germans were not the great film fans Goebbels seemed to think. The average German worker and his family went to the movies once a year. In the wage bracket of RM 960 to RM 2,500 the average yearly expenditure on films amounted to RM 5.21 per family.[7]

With the outbreak of hostilities on September 7, the movie business substantially improved. The Ufa reported that its returns for the week of September 12–18 at one chain showed 1,152,000 paid admissions against 973,000 the previous year. During the last week of September 160,000 Berliners went to the films, contrasted to 126,000 in 1938. As a method of escaping the horrors of approaching total war, nothing could beat the movies.

## II

The films released in 1938 included one masterpiece, Leni Riefenstahl's *Olympia* (April 20) which was given a gala premiere on the occasion of Hitler's forty-ninth birthday with the Führer in the audience.

An unusual amount of publicity had been given to the film, apparently on Hitler's direct orders; Goebbels had a vitriolic dislike of Leni Riefenstahl and her work. But then, trying to sell a documentary to an audience two years after the events depicted had taken place was not an easy task.

Discussing the production of the film with Miss Riefenstahl in 1964, the American critic Gordon Hitchens reported:

She stated that most sports films are dull because the subject is very difficult. She said that she decided from the start to make two films and that "the form must excite the content and give it shape." Most important, she said, "remember that beauty is not names." The editing of *Olympia* was not planned during the shooting but before the shooting. "I had the whole thing in my head" and "I treated the whole thing like a vision" and "I was like an architect building a house." During this period, "I had no private life, only my work."

"The law of film is architecture, balance." If the image is weak, strengthen the sound, and vice-versa; the total impact on the viewer should be 100%, "never more or you tire them . . ." You must alternate tension with relaxation for both sound and picture: "when one is up, then the other must be down . . ." and (gesturing) you move at times "from reality to more and more and more poetry and more unusual camera work." But the beginning "must be quiet, to build . . . to separate the races, each to do a different thing . . . to interest non-sports people in sports." The natural beginning of Part One is "the atmosphere of classic Greece"; Part Two begins with the Olympic

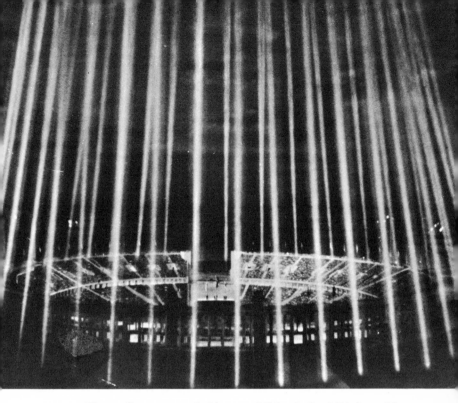

The stadium surrounded by searchlights in Leni Riefenstahl's
*Olympia* (1938).

village, "the only place for it." "I am the visitor to the Olympics . . .
never tire the visitor."

The diving sequence: "a simple idea" and "possible to do it several
ways" and "the same style as the high-jumps." But "the secret" of
*Olympia* is the sound, the three months of mixing. "No general crowd
noises, but like music" and "sound coming in waves" and "no synchronized sound but all made by us in the studio" (demonstrating foot-
steps); even horses breathing and runners panting because "people cry
too much"; and besides, they were using long lenses often from great
distances. "Nonsense" that she had one hundred cameramen, actually
only thirty, of which only six, having feature and newsreel background, were first-rate; 70% of the shooting was useless. Six months
of training with special cameras were needed for shooting the diving.
She showed me photographs of this work and explained the difficult
lighting and focus problems. She stated that one of her cameramen
now lives in Bolivia and has had much feature work in South America.
She plainly was very proud of her *Olympia* crew and of the teamwork
she inspired.[8]

The famous diving sequence from *Olympia* (1938).

(The official program for the film states that the cameramen were Hans Ertl, Walter Frentz, Guzzi Lantschner, Kurt Neubert, and Hans Scheib, with thirty-eight assistants, and with the aid of the newsreel crews of Fox, Paramount, Tobis-Melo, and the Ufa. Special photography for the prologue was shot by Willy Zielke.)

*Olympia* (the title on the film, although its director from time to time has made a point of calling it *Olympiad*) was released in two parts, each running about two hours. The first half, *Fest der Völker* (*Festival of the Nations*) begins with an impressive sequence in ancient Greece, glorifying both architecture and the beauty of the nude body, about fifteen minutes of pure visuals without dialogue, accompanied by a superb Herbert Windt score. This is followed by the carrying of the Olympic torch to Berlin in an impressive montage, culminating in the lighting of a huge brazier high in the stadium. The next major sequence shows the parade of the participants before Hitler and his entourage, some of this cut in the usually circulated prints. The remainder of the first film is devoted to track and field events, and recorded for posterity the great performance of the nineteen year-old Jesse Owens.

The second film, *Fest der Schönheit* (*Festival of Beauty*) starts with the sequences in the Olympic village and continues with most of the other events of the games not covered in the first part. It is difficult to state the exact order of the sequences as originally conceived. The three versions of the film, made in German, English, and French, are slightly different, and subsequent "editors" of the film have rearranged the sports events in such a baffling order that I have yet to see two prints which follow the same pattern. The copy which Miss Riefenstahl prepared for the George Eastman House collection would seem to be definitive, restoring the 88 meters of footage deleted by postwar censors.* The print circulated by the Museum of Modern Art was obtained in 1942 from the American distributor of the film, Excelsior Pictures, but it is so mutilated and reedited (by unknown hands) that it is but a pale shadow of the original.

Verdicts on *Olympia* would seem to depend on the critic's political as well as artistic standards. Leni Riefenstahl has always maintained that the film is apolitical, and cites the fact in her favor that *Olympia* was accepted as the official film of the Olympic Committee, which awarded her a diploma and gold medal for her work in 1948 at Lausanne.

The German leftist critic Ulrich Gregor takes another position which is interesting as representative of the opposition to the director:

> Leni Riefenstahl's films about the Olympic Games . . . are, even in their purified versions that evade mention of Hitler and other Nazi leaders, still outspokenly fascistic in spirit. The films celebrate sport as an heroic, superhuman feat, a kind of ritual. This is especially apparent in the narration, which constantly resounds with words like "fight" and "conquest" and also in shots, for example, of marathon races through the forest that are stylized in Nordic mystery. Even *Tiefland* contains that demagogic contrast between the noble mountain people and the enchained, civilization-sick people of the city or lowlands. Arnold Fanck's "mountain films" are based on this contrast. These few illustrations should suffice to demonstrate the difficulty of separating Leni Riefenstahl's seemingly "unpolitical" films from her blatant propaganda works. Both emanate from a unified mind.[9]

---

* Deleted sections are as follows: In Part One, Hitler's address, spectator shots including prominent Nazis, the awarding of two German victory medals. In Part Two, shots of "Reichssportsführer" von Tschammer und Osten.

Striking a somewhat more objective note, the American filmmaker Robert Gardner wrote:

Neither *Triumph* nor *Olympia* could have been made by a propagandist pure and simple. They are self evidently the work of an artist, even if an artist of an immensely naive political nature. No doubt the rising chorus of Riefenstahl detractors themselves sensed that her success was the result more of genius than of mere luck or of the patronage of everyone's common enemy, Hitler. Clearly, Hitler didn't make the films. In fact, Leni Riefenstahl describes him as a man with absolutely bad taste. He had only the most vulgar values regarding all manner of art.

When finished, the two *Olympia* films, which everyone said could not be made, were an even more brilliant success than *Triumph*. . . . Jim Card, head of the film collection at Eastman House, asserts that *Olympia might* be the best film ever made.[10]

Fortunately for posterity, *Olympia* survived the twin hazards of World War II and nitrate decomposition, and can be viewed at frequent revivals.* The individual spectator must make up his own mind on the political implications of the film, but it is hard to deny that *Olympia*, examined purely as *film*, is one of the most beautiful and exciting works the medium has produced.

For the purposes of this study, the remainder of Miss Riefenstahl's career should be briefly mentioned here, for her next feature film, *Tiefland*, was not released until after the war.

Exactly what happened after the completion of *Olympia* is unclear, some of the confusion caused by the director herself, who had told conflicting versions of events to various interviewers.

As far as can be ascertained, she never mentioned to anyone a mysterious film entitled *Berchtesgaden über Salzburg*, reputedly released in 1938. It runs fifty minutes in black and white, and is apparently without narration or dialogue. James Manilla reviewed it as part of the 1965 *Film Comment* issue devoted to Leni Riefenstahl, and it would seem that this is the sole printed reference to the film. As Mr. Manilla described it:

---

* Most recently, in four parts on American Educational Television shortly before the 1972 Munich Olympics.

Although this is a Leni Riefenstahl effort, it is perhaps her worst picture, and it was obviously done at a client's request; i.e. Hitler wanted a record of his mountain aerie.

The film is typical of Riefenstahl in many respects. It has a big, lush, Wagnerian-type music-track. It opens up with dawn scenes and mountain scenes. In fact, it was a true prototype, for dawn was coming up over the mountains. There are a lot of snow scenes and happy mountain peasant folk. But the picture as a whole is terribly dull. There are some wonderful shots done by several of the many cameramen assigned to the project, and there is some good cutting. But had it been kept to eight minutes or less, it might have been many times more interesting than it turned out to be. Unlike the best of Riefenstahl's work, the music score is undistinguished and the opticals ride.[11]

Riefenstahl went to the United States in 1939, an exceedingly inappropriate time, with the idea of selling the *Olympia* film to an American company. She visited Hollywood where she was roundly snubbed by everyone except Walt Disney, who greeted her publicly. Action against her visit was organized by Budd Schulberg, who was later to defame her in a scurrilous and irresponsible article for the *Saturday Evening Post* in 1946.

On her return to Europe, she organized an elaborate project to film Kleist's epic drama *Penthesilea*, playing the title role of the Queen of the Amazons herself. Special fabrics were woven which would drape in the manner of Greek sculpture; a group of girls were trained to ride bareback for the action sequences. The production was ready to go on location in Libya (with a leading French actor preparing for the male lead) when the war broke out. The project was shelved at an enormous cost.

Her next plan was to film a drama about Voltaire and Frederick the Great, scripted by Jean Cocteau with the author playing both parts. This, too, never went beyond the planning stage.

By now desperate to get to work despite ill health, she decided to make a quick film of Eugene D'Albert's opera *Tiefland*, discarding the music and retaining only the rather creaky story. The strain of this project, which required extensive location work, and which was burdened from the start by her most unfortunate choice of an amateur for the leading male role, seems to have completely broken her health, and

she directed scenes from a stretcher. Both G. W. Pabst and Veit Harlan shot secondary scenes without credit, and the professional actors
gamely put up with the on-and-off shooting schedule. As the costs
mounted up, it became obvious that *Tiefland* was going to be the most
expensive sound film in German history.* In an ambiguous entry in
his diary, dated December 16, 1942, Goebbels wrote:

> Leni Riefenstahl reported to me about her motion picture *Tiefland*.
> It has become involved in innumerable complications. Already more
> than five million marks have been wasted on this film and it will take
> another whole year before it is finished. Frau Riefenstahl has become
> very ill from overwork and worry, and I urged her earnestly to go on
> leave before taking up further work. I am glad I have nothing to do
> with the unfortunate case, and hence bear no responsibility.[12]

The last statement is strange, and probably indicates that the film was
made under Hitler's personal approval, although the director herself
put up a large part of the financing.

*Tiefland* was put on the shelf, and Riefenstahl's activities during the
remainder of World War II are a mystery. It is known that she married
a Major Jacobs, after a long and frustrating liaison with Ernst Udet
who committed suicide after differences with Göring and other top
Nazis in the Air Ministry. She appears to have retired to Austria as
Frau Jacobs, where she was found by Budd Schulberg and criticized in
the article previously mentioned. She was arrested and detained by the
French in 1945 for pro-Nazi activities, and spent many years trying
to clear herself and return to making films.

---

* A director who shall be nameless told me something about her working
methods. As he related, "When my unit was working at the *Tiefland* studio, the
favorite diversion was to go to Mme. Riefenstahl's sound stage to see her at
work. At one point she asked her designer to have a forest recreated tree-by-tree
on the set, à la Fritz Lang. When it was completed, she was effusive in her praise.
The first thing in the morning she asked to be raised on a crane in order to select
shooting angles. When she was high above the artificial forest, she called down,
'Oh, it's just marvelous, but would you mind if we moved that tree there a few
feet.' The crew obliged with difficulty, since the trees were enormous and almost
as heavy as the real thing. To make a long story short, we went to our set, but
when we returned from our production at the end of the day, she was still up
on that crane, moving trees. Almost every one had been shifted a few feet one
way or another."

One of the spectacularly photographed sequences from *Tiefland*, directed by Leni Riefenstahl. (Photo courtesy of Leni Riefenstahl.)

After she was de-Nazified in 1952 and allowed to return to work, she completed *Tiefland*, bringing back the original actors. Thirteen years after the film was started, it at last had a successful release, although Riefenstahl regarded the picture as a failure and withdrew it from circulation as soon as it had made a reasonable profit. For the French version, Jean Cocteau wrote the subtitles, surely one of his grandest bizarre gestures. Since the director controls the rights on the picture, it is unlikely that it will be shown again during her lifetime.

The rest of her activities amount to a record of almost unbroken tough luck. In 1956, she started a film entitled *Schwarze Fracht* (*Black Cargo*), a documentary on African slave trade shot in color. It progressed well until she was seriously injured in a jeep accident which kept her in a hospital for nearly a year. In 1965 she returned to Africa and finished a 16mm color feature on a virtually unrecorded primitive tribe in the Sudan. As of this date, it has not been released. Still beautiful, but bitter over her experiences, Leni Riefenstahl lives today in a Munich apartment.

Objectively, Leni Riefenstahl's films helped the Nazi cause. This does not mean that she was a personal monster, nor that every "moral" aspect of her films is deplorable. For her achievements on this level, she has been widely and no doubt justly condemned—if not always for the reasons stated by her critics—and it seems unlikely that history will reverse the verdict. But it is also necessary to assess her as an artist, accountable only to another kind of history, and it seems possible that on this level, film history will preserve the honors which have been given her.

### III

Karl Ritter, continuing his series of propaganda spectacles, directed one of his most odious concoctions, *Pour le Mérite* (the title refers to a German military decoration), (December 22), just in time for Christmas season release.

The film truly must be seen to be believed. The official program lists 102 speaking roles, although the only "stars" in evidence were Paul Hartmann and Fritz Kampers. The subject matter in this case concerns flyers in Germany from 1918 to 1935, and follows a new pattern which Ritter was to employ in later works, the use of numerous episodes and scenes over a period of years to paint a vast mural of his subject.

Altmann adequately described the film (which, incidentally, is a crushing bore), when he wrote:

Self-sacrifice and useless death being advocated sufficiently, Ritter turned to a new theme and gave his war propaganda series a final, decisive touch: hate and contempt for democratic ideals, praise of Nazi adventurism and ruthlessness. In his film *Pour le Mérite*, Nazi conspirators, Nazi saboteurs, illegal Nazi organizers, and even assassins are the heroes; the Weimar Republic is the defied democratic state, its loyal citizens are the enemies and villains. Treachery, conspiracy, intrigue, and murder are things lauded, and hate is the only emotion extolled. It was the "purest" of all Nazi films.[13]

The Minister of Education, Dr. Rust, ordered a contest in 1939 for school pupils on the theme, "Why is Karl Ritter's *Pour le Mérite* of value to the youth of Germany?" The winner was one Franz Hartwig of Kolberg (an ironic location, in view of later developments) who wrote an essay that took as its central point a scene in which a Nazi, brought to trial before judges of the Weimar Republic's court, screams "I hate this democracy! I hate all democracies like the plague!"[14]

Veit Harlan, back in Goebbels' good graces, made some interesting films which, after Ritter's monumental decalogue of hate, seem uncommonly artistic and sensitive. The most important was *Jugend* (*Youth*), (April 12), which introduced a new actress (again from Sweden), Kristina Söderbaum, who was later to become Frau Harlan after the director's divorce from Hilde Körber.

Frau Söderbaum came from a famous Swedish family; her father had been in charge of awarding the Nobel Prizes. She had wanted an acting career, but her family thought it unsuitable for a girl of her social position. After her father's death she went to Berlin in 1937 to study theatre, and was discovered by a talent scout for Tobis. Following the success of Zarah Leander, there was a great demand for Swedish actresses, and Kristina Söderbaum had the same purring accent of her predecessor. Blonde and rather pleasingly plain in appearance, the actress provided a welcome respite from the glamor girls of the period.

*Jugend* was based on a well-known play by the author Max Halbe; at the playwright's sixtieth birthday celebration in 1926 Harlan had played the role of the youth in the drama, and had wanted to make it

Director
Veit Harlan
during
production of
*Jugend*
(1938).

Kristina
Söderbaum as
the heroine
of Veit Harlan's
*Jugend* (1938),
her debut
on the
German screen.

into a film for some time. The film script was prepared by Thea von Harbou, and Bruno Mondi contributed some exceptional camerawork. To bolster the newcomer in her debut, an unusually fine cast was assembled including Werner Hinz, Eugen Klöpfer, and the magnificent character actress Elisabeth Flickenschildt.

The film made Kristina Söderbaum a star overnight, and within a few years she was the most popular actress on the German screen. The script of *Jugend* provided a scene in which the heroine was drowned; for some reason this went over so well that the unfortunate actress was called on to meet a similar fate in numerous future films, eventually being dubbed with the nickname of *Reichswasserleiche* (Official Drowned Corpse of the Reich)!

Another interesting Harlan film was *Verwehte Spuren* (*Covered Tracks*), (August 26), based on a drama written in 1931 by Hans Rothe, a leading (and rather poor) translator of Shakespeare. Based on a true episode, which has also served as the basis of at least one British film* and numerous television dramas, the Rothe play was put into shape by Thea von Harbou, Felix Lützkendorff, and Harlan.

The story concerns a young girl named Séraphine who comes with her mother from Canada to the Paris Exposition of 1867. They have to stay at separate hotels, and shortly after their arrival the mother disappears without trace. With the help of a young man she has met,

---

* *So Long at the Fair* (1949), with Jean Simmons and Dirk Bogarde. At one time Hitchcock was seriously interested in the story.

Séraphine at last discovers that her mother died of plague and in order to avert a panic, all traces of her existence were covered. Kristina Söderbaum again played the lead, with Fritz van Dongen (later Philip Dorn) as her helper. The film was banned after the war as anti-American propaganda.

One of the curiosities of the year was *Die vier Gesellen* (*The Four Comrades*), (October 1), another piece of Carl Froelich juvenilia which is of interest as the only German screen appearance of Ingrid Bergman, made immediately before her departure for the United States.

The National Film Prize was awarded (in 1939) to *Heimat* (*Home*), (June 25), an unusually effective Zarah Leander film, another Froelich production. Adapted closely from a Hermann Sudermann play, it tells the story of the visit to a small German town of a famous American opera singer (improbably named Maddalena dall'-Orto); actually the lady in question is a former inhabitant of the same town who had to flee many years earlier because of the shame of an illegitimate child. The main problem, now that she is successful, is to win back the affection of her father. In a wonderful scene the two are reconciled, but the father becomes worried about the effect of the affair on his younger daughter, and challenges Maddalena's former lover to a duel. Before this can take place, the villain commits suicide when it is discovered that he has been embezzling from the local bank.

If the previous Leander films had shown the singer's facility in light music, *Heimat* gave her the chance to perform—most creditably— scenes from Gluck's *Orpheus* and excerpts from the Bach St. Matthew Passion for the tear-drenched finale. Theo Mackeben also contributed two popular songs, "*Eine Frau wird est schön durch die Liebe*" and "*Drei Sterne sah ich scheinen.*"

Although the film looks dated, Zarah Leander gave a superb performance, eclipsed only by Heinrich George in one of his best parts. This film was also banned after the war for a period, perhaps because the dialogue contains several anti-American lines.

The year 1938 is also remembered for a series of bizarre adventure films and musical comedies in which the search for exotica hit an unprecedented high.

Not quite up to Busby Berkeley, but a good try: the finale of
Hans Zerlett's *Es leuchten die Sterne* (1938).

Of the musicals, special mention must be made of Hans Zerlett's *Es
leuchten die Sterne* (*The Stars are Shining*), (March 17), which was
a rather mad attempt to do a Busby Berkeley type musical set in a
movie studio, with guest appearances by thirty-six Tobis stars, stage
and sports personalities. The final reel features a number with girls
dressed as signs of the zodiac which is certainly up to the standard of
Warner Brothers' most insane concoctions.

Equally eccentric was Curt Goetz's musical confection *Napoleon
ist an allem schuld* (*It's All Napoleon's Fault*), (November 29), which
takes as its hero an Englishman named Lord Arthur Cavershoot who
seems to be convinced he is the reincarnation of Napoleon, dressing
himself as the emperor. Complications arise when he is invited to the
meeting of an historical conference, and the highlight of the film is a
musical recital given at a garden party in honor of the delegates in
which everything possible goes wrong. Goetz's film is in a direct line
with the pre-1933 musicals, and has a lightness of touch which is
most unusual.

Slightly more serious (but not much more) was Hans Steinhoff's
musical-comedy *Tanz auf dem Vulkan* (*Dance on the Volcano*),

(November 20), which gave an opportunity for Gustaf Gründgens to give what certainly must be the campiest performance by a male star in all of film history. Somewhat oddly directed by Steinhoff, who seemed to have been confused whether he was doing a musical or a historical spectacle, the story deals with the career of the great mime Debureau (later the hero of the French classic *Les Enfants du Paradis*) during the July Revolution against Charles X.

The film is full of delicious touches: the nasty King Charles shooting rabbits inside the palace; the bumbling Louis Philippe shopping for umbrellas. The most outrageous sequence occurs when the king decides to humiliate Louis at a ball. A group of pretty girls perform a dance number which ends with them lifting their skirts to reveal Louis' portrait painted on their panties.

Throughout the film there is a tuneful score by Theo Mackeben including Gründgens' famous mincing production number, "Die Nacht ist nicht allein zum schlafen da." Although pretty much of a one-man show, the film gave Gründgens excellent support by Sybille Schmitz, Theo Lingen, Gisela Uhlen, and Ralph Arthur Roberts.

Hans Albers continued to appear in numerous films in every possible type of role. In Jacques Feyder's only German work, *Fahrendes Volk* (*Traveling People*), (July 1), which was a remake of his French picture *Les gens du voyage*, Albers gave a moving performance as a troubled actor, playing opposite Françoise Rosay (Mrs. Feyder). But comedy was Albers' true *métier*, and one of his most bizarre parts found him cast as a Chicago policeman in Herbert Selpin's *Sergeant Berry* (December 22). Some of the flavor of this madcap work is transmitted in the official synopsis:

Chicago, the Eldorado of gangsters! He who shoots quickest lives longest! This is what the stolid but by no means ambitious Berry discovers when by accident he kills the town's leading gangster. He is promoted to detective-inspector and becomes a public hero. But his superiors expect further miracles and send him to the Mexican border to stop the work of a notorious narcotics smuggler. He is quickly mixed up with the corrupt border police, angry hacienda proprietors and cowboys, legacy hunting caballeros, smuggling farmers and murderous vagrants. At last he captures a beautiful girl named Ramona.[15]

*Sergeant Berry* was the first of several successful collaborations between Albers and Selpin. The director encouraged his star to improvise
while on the set and Albers inserted an amazing number of off-color
lines, most of them uttered in the most innocent manner. Audiences
were delighted to watch Albers stalking through a welter of papier-
mâché cacti, shooting the villains in a bang-up gun battle, and at last
returning home to mother in Chicago, where they are serenaded by the
city police band in a finale of truly staggering vulgarity.

Another exoticum, *Frauen für Golden Hill* (*Wives for Golden
Hill*), (December 30), found Viktor Staal back in Australia, where he
was last seen with Zarah Leander in *Zu neuen Ufern*. The lively story,
by air ace and future director Hans Bertram, was about a group of
Australian miners who advertise for wives from the city. When the
girls arrive it is discovered that they are one short in relation to the
number of prospective husbands, and two bosom friends (Staal and
Karl Martell) have to fight for the favors of the loveliest bride-to-be
(Kirsten Heiberg). The end of the film sinks into melodrama, but most
of it is amusing and moves at a lively pace under Erich Waschneck's
direction. At one point the story gives Miss Heiberg the chance to belt
out a funny song in her best *ersatz* Zarah Leander manner, none too
gently mocking the style of her Scandanavian compatriot.

But the most exotic film of the period was *Kautschuk* (literally the
German word for a rubber plant; the film was released in the United
States under the title *Green Hell*), (November 1), directed by Eduard
von Borsody.

For seventeen years von Borsody had been an officer in the Austrian
army, but the end of World War I found him out of work. His brother
was a set designer for the Ufa and obtained him a job as cameraman,
a position which he held until 1932, when he became an editor. In
1937 von Borsody directed his first film, *Brillianten* (*Diamonds*), about
a jewel swindle, and the picture was a surprise success.

Reviewing von Borsody's varied talents, the company decided to
assign him to a complicated project, which had defeated several other
well-known craftsmen. Two brothers by the name of Eichorn, sons of
a prosperous cigar manufacturer, decided to go into the movie business. They sold their factory and departed to Brazil with the intention

of filming a documentary on the Amazon. Every possible misfortune plagued the expedition, culminating in the death of their cameraman. They returned to Germany in 1936, penniless and in ill health, but in their luggage was 1500 meters of spectacular silent film and a tentative script for a feature film. These items were sold to the Ufa, but the company could not figure out what to do with their purchase, since the footage was far too short for a feature and the script too amateurish.

With the aid of the well-known author Ernst von Salomon and one of the Eichorn brothers, von Borsody fashioned a script which could be fitted around the existing material. The tale concerned the adventures of a young Englishman who went to Brazil in the late nineteenth century, disguised as a butterfly hunter, but with the real aim of smuggling out rubber seeds, which were the monopoly of the Portuguese government. After untold hardships, he managed to get the precious seeds away from the vigilant Portuguese and set up the British rubber industry. Exotic though the story seems, it was based on fact.

Although the script more or less praised British courage at a time when such themes were not pleasing to the German government, the censor passed it. But the Ufa was unwilling to budget much on the film, and the director had to use his wits to save money. From the original Eichorn material he was able to salvage three episodes; some footage of hungry crocodiles; an attack by pirana fish; and a tremendous tropical storm. The popular matinee idol René Deltgen was selected for the role of the adventurous Englishman because he looked rather like Eichorn, easing the problem of matching old and new footage. Eichorn's faithful servant José was brought from Brazil to duplicate his original role.

For the climactic scene in which the hero is rescued by a passing boat, the crew went to Travemünde, near Kiel, and made free use of a German naval training ship which looked appropriate to the period. The interiors were shot in Babelsberg, but only two hundred meters of jungle footage had to be faked, including the famous episode in which the hero is attacked by a giant snake.

In spite of all the difficulties, the film was successful. It would seem to the average viewer that *Kautschuk* was entirely filmed in Brazil. The story is handled in delightful tongue-in-cheek fashion, with elements to charm both juveniles and adults. In particular, the period costumes should be singled out as but one example of von Borsody's loving care on the picture. *Kautschuk* holds up well today and, if revived, might possibly start a whole new series of jungle spoofs.

During the war, impounded prints were purchased in the United States by a group of entrepreneurs who proceeded to write new stories around the stock footage, and produced at least two features and a number of serials from the original materials. A section of one of these pirated films was included in the popular compilation entitled *The Great Chase* (1963) although the origin of the material was kept secret from the viewers.

## IV

With the approach of the war, in September, 1939, the German film industry was already deep in the production of strongly military subjects, aided by a number of specialists who had been busy in this field since 1933.

One of the more curious personalities to make his appearance at this time was the director Max Kimmich. Actually, Kimmich had been around the film world for some time, both in Germany and the United States. In order to support his medical studies he had written scripts, but soon changed his career plans and went to work full time for the Ufa in 1920 as chief dramaturgist for one of its subsidiary groups. He soon had his own small studio in Breslau with three stages running full time, turning out quick, cheap films at a furious rate.

On a trip to Europe Carl Laemmle, the founder of Universal Pictures, saw two of Kimmich's pictures and went to Karlsbad to meet the young man. He immediately signed him to a contract with his new Deutsche-Universal production company, and put Kimmich in charge of finding actors to be shipped to Hollywood, which was then in the midst of raiding the German studios of their best talent for silent films.

Finally Kimmich himself went to the United States, where he made fourteen slapstick comedies, mostly with Arthur Lake. He also found time to write numerous screen treatments for films starring such performers as Laura la Plante and Reginald Denny. Kimmich applied for American citizenship, but five months before this could be completed, Laemmle sent him back to Germany as a director. If Hollywood was going through a German craze with such films as *Sunrise*, the Germans wanted Hollywood-type pictures and the young director's first assignment was a German-language drama set in the exotic area of Lake Michigan. A script which he wrote during these years later served as the basis of the Constance Bennett film *Madame Spy* (1934).

When the Nazis came to power in 1933, Kimmich was put on the industry blacklist because of his collaboration with Laemmle. He was only allowed to write a few scripts of minor pictures and restricted from direction. However, when Paul Wegener, normally an actor, ran into trouble in directing his adventure film *Moskau-Shanghai* (1936) Kimmich was called in to complete it, although he was denied screen credit.

Shortly after this he met one of Goebbels' older sisters, and the two fell in love and were married. (Lest the inference be drawn that this was an opportunistic gesture, it should be reported that the couple are still happily married as this book is being written.) Since he was now Goebbels' brother-in-law, he was allowed to direct under his own name again, and made *Der Vierte kommt nicht* (*The Fourth Will Not Come*), (March 9, 1939), a Tobis melodrama set in Stockholm starring Dorothea Wieck. Nonpolitical in content, it was highly successful.

Kimmich then came to the attention of Emil Jannings, who hired him to direct what must be the most mysterious film of the Third Reich, *Der letzte Appell* (*The Last Roll-Call*). This Jannings-Tobis production boasted a huge cast including, in addition to its producer, Paul Wegener, Werner Krauss, Gisela Uhlen, Jack Trevor, and Paul Richter. The budget was enormous, and Tobis billed it as one of its major productions of the year.

The story was a frankly pacifist tale about a German ship which is converted during World War I into a mine layer. It is captured by the British, but the English boat strays into the minefield and everyone is blown sky-high in what must have been an extremely depressing finale.

With government blessing, the entire German fleet in the Baltic was made available for the battle sequences, and Kimmich reports that the footage was extraordinary. At one point, Jannings, up to his usual meddling, insisted on directing a naval sequence and botched the job so badly that he managed to sink a small military craft.

The film was finished in May. While it was being edited, German-British relations came to such a point that the government ordered all work on the film discontinued. Going to the studio shortly after the ban, Kimmich was astonished to find that every piece of the film had disappeared. It has not been seen since, and even sequences suitable for stock footage seem to have been destroyed. Only a few stills issued for publicity purposes survive from this mysterious film.

A similar end came to Karl Ritter's military extravaganza of the year, *Legion Condor*. During 1939, Göring had invaded Goebbels' domain by giving the incentive to several air films. The first, *D III 88* (October 26), glorified the Luftwaffe in its new role, with a script by the previously mentioned air ace Hans Bertram. The director of this project, rather oddly chosen, was Herbert Maisch, whose earlier work had been confined for the most part to operetta films. Maisch had little love for the Nazis or for warfare, having lost an arm at Verdun, and left the air sequences to Bertram's second unit.

The flying footage was exciting, but on the whole the film was judged as somewhat of a bore, a situation which Göring decided to alleviate with a film on his pet project, the story of deeds of the dreaded Condor Legion during the Spanish Civil War, this group having been responsible for, among other things, the destruction of Guernica.

With the aid of some of the Wilberg generals, Ritter and his Ufa crew started shooting at Babelsberg on August 9. The apparent idea of the film was to combine newsreel footage of the Condor Legion in the 1936–1938 period with some kind of adventure story. However, with the preparations for war underway, and the impossibility of using the German air force as extras in recreated scenes, the film was stopped on September 1. There has been some confusion about the film because another work with the same title was released later; this *Legion Condor* was a documentary prepared from newsreels by Dr. Fritz Hippler, who is discussed in the next chapter.

Actually, the number of propaganda-content films of 1939 is small, 21 out of 118 films produced during the year, at least if one is to follow the list of films prohibited for German showing following the war. (The figures for 1940 were 20 out of 89; in 1941, 29 out of 71.) Most of these banned films fall into the comedy category, a good example of this being *Das Gewehr über* (*Shoulder Arms*), (December 7), a silly farce redeemed only by the camerawork of Piel (for this production "Phil") Jutzi. Another of this genre was *Der Stammbaum des Dr. Pistorius* (*Dr. Pistorius' Family Tree*), (December 12); it is worth mentioning only for the inclusion of a song by Lothar Brühe which was to have some popularity at future propaganda rallies: "Die Herzen gerüstet, die Fäuste bereit, zu den Kämpfen der kommenden Zeit." ("Hearts are ready, fists are clenched, ready for the battles ahead.")

## V

Dr. Todt's new *Autobahn* received its cinematic tribute in Robert Stemmle's *Mann für Mann* (July 21). The first part of the film is semidocumentary, and was shot during the second and third years of construction. Stemmle's source material came from the stories of workers, particularly an episode in which some caissons collapsed, killing many people. Armed with a lavish budget and the best crew at the Ufa, Stemmle took more than nine months to shoot the film.

Following the reception after the Berlin premiere, Stemmle recalls that he was driving back to his apartment and decided to pass the theatre where the film had been shown earlier in the evening. To his horror, he saw workmen busily taking down all the advertising. After a sleepless night he called the studio to see what had happened. It seems that the sequence of the caissons collapsing was considered almost subversive by some first-night viewers, since obviously caissons didn't even shake on German-built roads. Stemmle was called back to the studio and worked for another six months to reshoot the whole section of the film, changing building faults to the influence of an earthquake.

With or without the earthquake, the film was hardly good entertainment, with long, rather dull documentary sequences uneasily mixed with a banal romantic plot. The only point of interest is the final catastrophe, which is excitingly photographed and edited.

The nonpolitical films were of greater interest. Working at his usual break-neck speed, Veit Harlan managed to direct two creditable melo-dramas: *Das unsterbliche Herz* (*The Immortal Heart*), (January 31), and *Die Reise nach Tilsit* (*The Journey to Tilsit*), (November 2).

The former film, beautifully acted though it is, seems in retrospect one of Harlan's heaviest and most vulgar films. Based on a 1913 play by Walter Harlan (1867–1931), the director's father, it takes the curious subject of the life of Peter Henlein, the inventor of the pocket watch.

The scenario begins with the shipwreck of the geographer Martin Behaim (1459–1506), caused by poor weight clocks which were then in use. Behaim is brought to trial by his angry backers, but he is freed with the help of his friend Henlein. The inventor becomes obsessed with the idea of creating a truly workable small watch, and neglects his wife, who is pursued by an apprentice. By accident, Henlein is shot by the apprentice with a pistol loaded with a new double bullet

The spectacular funeral of the inventor Peter Henlein, from Veit Harlan's *Das unsterbliche Herz* (1939).

he has designed. An operation is apparently successful, but Henlein later finds out that half of the bullet is in his body, gradually moving toward his heart. He keeps this secret from his wife, who cannot understand why he is neglecting her in favor of his work. After numerous complications, the spring-propelled clock is at last invented; Henlein dies but gives his blessing to his wife and apprentice.

The brilliant cast included Heinrich George as Henlein, Kristina Söderbaum as his wife, Michael Bohnen as Behaim, and Paul Wegener as the doctor. The lavish sets were designed by Hermann Warm (who had done *Caligari* and Dreyer's *Passion of Joan of Arc*) and the music was largely drawn from the works of J. S. Bach. In an era of absolutely sexless films, there is an astonishing scene in which Kristina Söderbaum, naked under a fur robe, tries to arouse the passions of her inventor-husband. The scene is also ridiculous and borders on the vulgar because Harlan had no idea of how to film such an episode and his wife looks extremely uncomfortable.

The film is also of some historical interest because many exterior scenes were photographed in Nuremberg, later to be destroyed. Harlan went on the radio to ask the cooperation of the citizens, who put on their own medieval costumes, usually reserved for special local festivals, and performed free of charge. The film received excellent reviews both in Germany and abroad, and a rave from the New York *Times* when it opened at the 86th Street Playhouse on October 20. It was perhaps the last German film to be so praised until after the war.

*Die Reise nach Tilsit* suffers from the fact that it is based on the same story which had been used by F. W. Murnau as the basis of his American masterpiece, *Sunrise*. This is unfortunate, for Harlan's film is uncommonly well made and differently presented.

As Harlan told me in 1963: "I was a friend of Murnau when he was in Germany, and of course saw *Sunrise* later when it came out. But I didn't see it again before I made my film. Murnau made his whole film into a piece of scenery, all in the studio. I did my version in Memel, where the story takes place. Murnau's *Sunrise* was a poem, but if you'll excuse me, mine was a real *film*."[16]

He was right. Although *Sunrise* is one of the great films of all time (and one of my favorite pictures), the Harlan version is no pale shadow. Despite its small budget (about $140,000), it is a beautifully produced work, stunningly photographed by Bruno Mondi, scored sensitively by Hans Otto Borgmann; the two leading actors, Fritz van Dongen (Philip Dorn) and Kristina Söderbaum, bear comparison with George O'Brien and Janet Gaynor with van Dongen actually a considerable improvement. The ludicrous passages in the Murnau film involving the vamp from the city (Margaret Livingston) are much better handled in the Harlan film, perhaps because Anna Dammann was a better actress. Unfortunately, *Die Reise nach Tilsit* is an almost unknown film and hardly likely to be revived.

At the Berlin premiere on November 15, there was a scandal when Frau Goebbels ostentatiously got up and walked out of the cinema; the story of the film was too close to the Baarova affair to please her sensibilities.

Following completion of the film, the Dutch-born van Dongen accepted an invitation from Henry Koster to come to Hollywood, changed his name to Philip Dorn and made his American debut in a film appropriately entitled *Escape* (1940).

Eduard von Borsody followed up the success of *Kautschuk* with two more popular films, *Sensationsprozess Casilla* (*The Sensational Casilla Trial*), (August 8), and *Kongo-Express* (December 15).

The story of the former film had appeared in the *Münchner Illustrierte*, and the director bought it after the first installment had appeared. The soap-opera plot deals with the kidnapping of an American child film star and a trial ten years later. It was crisply directed and boasted an unusual surprise ending.

*Kongo-Express* was an attempt to cash in on the amazing popularity of *Kautschuk*, but suffered from a talky script which, curiously, bears a strong resemblance to Alfred Hitchcock's first film, *The Pleasure Garden* (1925). Again, the African backgrounds look convincing, but in this case the whole film was photographed in Germany. The exteriors were shot on a small railway line between Hannover and Celle, with some 200 meters of track side planted with African foliage; and an ancient cow-catcher locomotive drove back and forth to simulate the train trip which is the nucleus of the story. The romantic triangle was composed of Marianne Hoppe, Willy Birgel, and René Deltgen.

Hans Schweikart's *Befreite Hände* (*Freed Hands*), (November 28), was another tear jerker worthy of mention for the fact that it proved to be an enormous public hit and has been revived more or less constantly since its original release. Schweikart, whose second film this was, showed his excellent control of actors, most of whom had worked with him on the stage. Brigitte Horney gave one of the best performances of her career as a wood carver, and managed to make the most implausible passages convincing.

The horror cycle came to an absolute but brilliant close with Heinz Hilpert's *Die unheimlichen Wünsche* (*The Unholy Wishes*), (October 6), based on Balzac's tale "The Wild Ass's Skin," already filmed in the United States by Goldwyn in the silent period. Hilpert was one of the three leading Berlin stage directors, and did little work in the film medium. For this remarkable movie he gathered six of the best actors in Germany (Tschechowa, Käthe Gold, Flickenschildt, Hans Holt, Balser, and Dahlke), obtained the services of the great cameraman Richard Angst and the composer Wolfgang Zeller. The sinister atmosphere of black magic runs strongly through the picture, and *Die unheimlichen Wünsche* was a fitting finale to its genre. Apparently the film was not appreciated in high places, for it had to wait eight months after provincial release before it had a Berlin showing.

The former actor Wolfgang Liebeneiner directed a charming remake of *The Italian Straw Hat* under the title *Der Florentiner Hut* (*The Florentine Hat*), (April 4), with Heinz Rühmann as the harassed bridegroom. However, Olga Tschechowa, who had starred in the René Clair silent version, did not repeat her earlier role.

Eduard Mörike's virtually perfect novella, *Mozart auf der Reise nach Prag* (*Mozart on the Way to Prague*), regrettably almost unknown outside of German-speaking countries, was strikingly filmed under the title *Eine kleine Nachtmusik* (December 18, premiere in Prague). The rather obscure Viennese director Leopold Hainisch showed himself capable of transfering Mörike's gentle, but doom-laden story to the screen, and Hannes Stelzer was a convincing Mozart.

One of the best remembered films of the period was Willi Forst's elegant *Bel Ami* (February 21) from the Guy de Maupassant story, with the director as the caddish hero, a film superior to the later

American version of the same story by Albert Lewin with George Sanders. Criticism of Forst's film in French histories of the cinema tends to be harsh, for the movie was released there during the occupation and seems to have unfortunate connotations to many who lived through the period. While Forst's Paris seems Viennese, the film is still charming and one of the best examples of its type.

A number of near feature-length documentaries were released during 1939 (including one on the subject of touring the United States), the most interesting from an historical standpoint being *Westwall* (August 10). The subject was, of course, the building of the so-called "West Wall," which surrounded Germany from the Netherlands to the Swiss border, having been built in eighteen months. In an extraordinary step, Hitler ordered the film to be shown in every movie house only two days after the last stone was in place.

The idea of the film was not only to impress the local audience, but to frighten foreign observers by demonstrating Germany's military preparations. The theme is announced in the titles: "1914—encirclement but undefended boundaries—today—encirclement but invincible borders!" Viewed today, the film is a hodgepodge of documentary shots backed up by a grandiose pseudo-Bruckner score. A moment of unintended hilarity is provided by a sequence of shots in which workers carry logs up an enormous pile, backed up by a carefully synchronized score which puts the viewer in mind of Busby Berkeley. To sum up the Nazi military might, there are long, dull tracking shots of endless rows of artillery and shells. The direction of this slap-dash short was credited to Fritz Hippler, whose work in the anti-Semitic film will be discussed in the next chapter. *Westwall* can be regarded as the director's warm-up for *Feldzug in Polen* (*Campaign in Poland*), a far more impressive piece of work ready for showing in Berlin in February 1940.

# 1939-1940: THE ANTISEMITIC FILM

One of the least understood facets of the Nazi cinema is the production of anti-Semitic films. Much of what has been written is confused with respect to titles, directors, actors, and plot lines. The subject is difficult to analyze objectively, but it is possible to get the basic facts on the whole repulsive matter.

For all intents and purposes, there were four major anti-Semitic films:* *Robert und Bertram* (July 7, 1939); *Die Rothschilds Aktien von Waterloo* (*The Rothschilds' Shares in Waterloo*), (August 17, 1940); *Jud Süss* (*Jew Süss*) (September 24, 1940); and *Der ewige Jude* (*The Eternal Jew*), (November 28, 1940). The first three are fiction features, the fourth a "documentary." Care should be taken to avoid confusing *Jud Süss* with *Der ewige Jude*; even some standard histories of world cinema make this error.

In addition to these four films, scenes were randomly inserted in motion pictures made during the remaining years of the Third Reich which contained anti-Semitic slurs. As an example, a nonpolitical biography, *Rembrandt* (1942), contains a sequence of Jewish money lenders depicted in a scurrilous manner. Almost all of Karl Ritter's films include passages of Jewish stereotypes.

* *Die Degenhardts* (1944) is reported to be virulently anti-Semitic in passages. I have been unable to locate a copy of this film for evaluation.

In an article on the Nazi cinema, the Austrian writers Helmut Blobner and Herbert Holba state that anti-Semitic themes were used un-
officially for Party films not shown to the general public. No record
of such pictures seems to exist, but this might be a reference to the
imported Swedish picture *Petterson and Bendel*; in any event, the first
known German anti-Semitic picture was *Robert und Bertram*, which
was reported in production at Terra on December 29, 1935, with a
cast including Ludwig Manfred Lommel and Kurt Vespermann in the
title roles, assisted by Leo Paukert and Ursula Herking, although no
such film seems to have been actually made. The book was credited
to Gustav Raeder, whose same story served as the basis of the 1939
*Robert und Bertram* as well as a postwar film of the same title which
apparently eliminated the Jewish characters.

The director selected for the project was Hans Heinz Zerlett, a prolific specialist in both musicals and action pictures. Zerlett was highly
regarded by Goebbels as an "actors director" and was maried to Olga
Tschechowa, one of the reigning queens of the German screen. Zerlett's work until then was mostly unpolitical, and he is particularly
remembered for his remake of Duvivier's *Le Carnet du Bal* under the
title *Reise in die Vergangenheit* (*Journey into the Past*), (1944) which
starred his wife. In any case, *Robert und Bertram* was skillfully put
together, however repugnant the subject matter.

The story, set in 1839, can be briefly summarized:

Robert (Rudi Godden) and Bertram (Kurt Seifert) are two vagabonds lately escaped from jail. They learn that the daughter of the
local inn keeper is being forced into marriage with the Jew Bieder-
meier, a friend of another Jew, Ipelmeyer, who owns a mortgage on
the inn. They gain access to the betrothal reception by offering to wash
glasses, and after hearing the girl's plight, decide to set things straight.
They steal the horses of the local police and rush to Berlin.

Once there, they succeed in installing themselves in the house of
Ipelmeyer (Herbert Hübner). During a costume ball, Bertram entertains the guests with a song while Robert tries to steal jewelry and at
the same time pay court to the grotesque Frau Ipelmeyer (Inge
Straaten). Ipelmeyer is drugged by mistake, and the two manage to
frisk him and his guests of jewels and money before making a getaway.
They send the loot to the inn keeper's daughter, enabling her to pay

off the mortgage and also marry the man of her choice—a loyal soldier in the army of the local prince. Robert and Bertram continue on their journey, and at the end of the film are welcomed into heaven by an angelic choir.

These goings-on are accompanied by an elaborate musical score arranged by Leo Lux from the works of Flotow, Mozart, and others.

It is reported that when the film was reissued in 1942, a new ending was substituted which showed the two vagabonds joining the army, marching under the girl's new husband.

Viewed almost thirty years after the film was made, and compared with the evil, smirking *Rothschilds*, *Jud Süss*, and *Der ewige Jude* in all their oily professionalism, the anti-Semitism of *Robert und Bertram* seems simple-minded, with roots in the eighteenth- and nineteenth-century vulgar comedies popular in Germany, featuring distorted Jewish characters. But this type of primitive satire hardly fitted into Goebbels' plans for hard-hitting anti-Semitic films, and the next effort, *Die Rothschilds*, released more than a year later, was a far more vicious concoction. As *Film-Woche* put it, the film had as a target "the advancing of the ideals of the time by means of the film art medium."[1]

This time, the director selected was a major name, Erich Waschneck, whose career was already established in the silent-film era. Waschneck, who refused to be interviewed by me, had a pre-Nazi reputation for quality pictures, and at least two of his early sound films seem assured of a firm place in German film history: *8 Mädels im Boot* (*Eight Girls in a Boat*), (1932), and the charming *Abel mit der Mundharmonika* (*Abel and the Mouth Organ*), (1933).

Waschneck's films, as a general rule, were well scripted and cast but heavily directed, lacking lightness and grace. *Die Rothschilds* is no exception, and the dull film played to empty houses across Germany.

The plot, suggested by the Austrian Mirko Jelusich, traces the history of the Rothschilds family, distorting the facts, and taking as its finale the celebrated incident of the pigeons that flew from Waterloo with the news of Wellington's victory; the Rothschilds reported that Napoleon had won, and in the ensuing panic on the bourse, managed to make millions.

The film concluded with the following lines printed over a back-

A religious ceremony is interrupted by bad news in Erich Waschneck's *Die Rothschilds* (1940).

ground of a flaming Star of David and a map of England: "As this film is completed, the last members of the Rothschild family are leaving Europe as refugees and escaping to their allies in England, where the British plutocrats are carrying on."

*Die Rothschilds* was not only anti-Semitic, but violently anti-British, falling into another group of films which were to become increasingly common. Some critics have read into the film a message to intellectuals to toe the line, but this is hard to substantiate. *Die Rothschilds* is a failure as art, entertainment, and even as propaganda.

Unquestionably the most notorious film of the Third Reich was *Jud Süss*. It brought disgrace and worse on almost everyone connected with it, and was in the public limelight when it became the central exhibit in Veit Harlan's postwar trial for crimes against humanity. A great deal has been written about the film, much of it incorrect as to plot and performers; hardly anyone outside of Europe seems to have seen the film, although some cinema historians have discussed it in inaccurate detail.*

* The scholarship of some historians regarding this film can be evidenced by the fact that three books credit Krauss with the role of Süss, and another devotes a lengthy footnote to explaining why Stefan Zweig's [*sic*] novel was used as the basis of the film.

In October or November of 1938, about the time of the Baarova scandal, the Propaganda Ministry sent to all German film companies a request to produce anti-Semitic films. No titles were mentioned, but Goebbels had suggested several times the possibilities of screen versions of *Die siebente Grossmacht** (*The Seventh Power*), Marlowe's *The Jew of Malta*, or Shakespeare's *The Merchant of Venice*.

The idea of bringing the story of *Jud Süss* to the screen had apparently originated with the writer Ludwig Metzger, who had unsuccessfully tried as early as 1921 to interest a film company in the subject. Metzger was from Württemberg, where the events of the tale had taken place in the eighteenth century, and seems to have been obsessed with the gruesome subject.

In 1925, Lion Feuchtwanger wrote his novel on the subject under the title *Jud Süss*, translated into English as *Power* the following year. This was filmed in England in 1932 by the Jewish director Lothar Mendes and a large cast including Conrad Veidt and Frank Vosper. The film followed Feuchtwanger's novel with some fidelity, and Veidt played the title role of Josef Süss Oppenheimer with satanic brilliance. Indeed, with a little editing, the British movie could have been released in Germany as Goebbels' desired project, and he toyed with the idea; he had the film screened many times.

It is important at this point to separate the three Süss Oppenheimers: the historical original; Feuchtwanger's fictional character; and the Nazi-interpreted monster.

The real Süss was born in 1692 in Heidelberg. As a young man he went to Frankfurt where he rapidly became a power in the financial world, one of the few areas open to Jews at the time. In 1732 he made his way to the court of the genial Duke Karl Alexander of Württemberg as a financial advisor to the sovereign, loaning him a large amount of money. In return, he was gradually given financial control of the duchy, with authority to collect taxes and tolls, hardly a position to endear him to the duke's subjects. His solution to the court's continuing need for money was to debase the coinage. Apparently, Süss terrorized the duchy for a number of years, creating general mayhem

* An obscure novel by Alfred Schirokauer which had reached its fourth edition in 1914.

under the protection of the profligate duke. When Karl Alexander died, the duchy revolted, and Süss was hanged on February 4, 1738.

From this obscure incident, Feuchtwanger wrote a lengthy novel which tried to probe the psychological reasons for Süss's path to self-destruction. The plot is complicated, and introduces secondary characters, the most notable of whom is Rabbi Gabriel, reputed to be the Wandering Jew of legend. Feuchtwanger also gave Süss an illegitimate daughter, Naemi, who is eventually killed in an attempt to escape the duke's amorous advances. Midway through the novel, Süss discovers that he is half-Christian, which sets up a new series of problems; he eventually decides that he would rather be the most powerful Jew in Germany than just another Christian near the top. In bitterness following his daughter's death, he plans the destruction of the duke and himself. Duke Karl is killed in a foolish war, which Süss has set up. His protection gone, Süss is imprisoned but refuses to admit his Christian blood, which would save his life. He is executed, but before his death comes to accept and take consolation in the teachings of Judaism.

The book had an enormous sale in Germany until it was banned by the Nazis along with the rest of Feuchtwanger's books in 1933. It is interesting to contemplate whether the film would ever have been made if the book had not been written, for the life of the real Süss was such an obscure footnote in German history that the practical Goebbels would probably have dismissed it as being of too little appeal to the general public.

Metzger was irritated by the success of the book on a subject which he had been nursing long before Feuchtwanger got hold of it. When he suggested the theme to his usual collaborator Wolfgang Ebbecke during their work on the film *Central Rio*, a number of objections were raised, especially the fact that the subject of Süss had already been done in England, and also that the public might confuse the proposed film with Feuchtwanger's novel which was, after all, not anti-Semitic.

Undaunted, Metzger went to one Herr Teich, the story editor of Terra, who also turned him down. In a final effort Metzger approached the Ministry of Propaganda where the subject was received "like a

Werner Krauss (Rabbi Loew) and Ferdinand Marian (Süss Oppenheimer) plot mischief in Veit Harlan's viciously anti-Semitic spectacle *Jud Süss* (1940).

bomb hitting its target," according to Ebbecke's postwar testimony.[2]

Teich received word that Terra should make the film, and reluctantly put the project before the head of the studio, who refused to do it. Goebbels had him fired and replaced by Peter Paul Brauer, a minor director with no experience as producer.

After a meeting with Goebbels, Brauer put the subject on a priority basis and named himself director of the project. In July of 1939, Metzger signed a contract with Terra to write the picture in collaboration with Eberhard Wolfgang Möller, highly regarded as a loyal propagandist for the Nazi regime.* In a remarkably short time the first version of the script was prepared, and the sets were constructed on the Terra lot.

The major problem was the casting of the picture. Candidates for

---

* Möller, dubbed the "Clifford Odets of Germany," was a successful playwright, author of such popular works as *The Panama Scandal, Rothschild Wins at Waterloo,* and *The Grey Eminence.*

the title role included Gustaf Gründgens, Ferdinand Marian, René
Deltgen, Rudolf Fernau, Richard Häusler, Siegfried Breuer, and Paul
Dahlke. Gründgens was approached first, but his post of director of
the Prussian State Theatre left him no free time. Teich was sent to
recruit Marian, but without success. Displeased with the delay, Goebbels told Dr. Hippler, his film chief, to fire Director Brauer from the
job and put Veit Harlan on it.

At this point, about November 1939, Harlan was in difficulty with
his ambitious film *Pedro soll hängen*, which will be discussed later.
Harlan's contract with Tobis obliged him to direct three films a year
and also to write three shooting scripts for an annual income of RM
200,000, but his current project was running overtime because of
Goebbels' interference. In a postwar interview with me, Harlan said
that since *Jud Süss* was to be made at Terra, he never considered himself a candidate for the direction, having overlooked a clause in his
contract which allowed him to be loaned out to another company.

Harlan believed that his next film was to be a version of Hebbel's
*Agnes Bernauer* and was working on the script when Brauer called
him to inform him that he would be the new director of *Jud Süss*.
After the war Harlan claimed that no director of any repute wanted
to have anything to do with the project, and that he objected. A few
days later he received the Metzger-Möller script with considerable re-
visions penned in green ink by Goebbels himself. Harlan said he went
to Goebbels and argued that he had a picture in production and another in preparation. He asserted that he called the script "dramatized
*Stürmer*" (referring to Streicher's anti-Semitic newspaper) and that
he had stated that such a piece of bad writing would not result in
"picturing a despicable Jew but rather in making a despicable picture."

According to Harlan's postwar testimony (the meeting with Goebbels, unfortunately, had no witnesses) he further objected to the script
because all characters were negative. Goebbels shot back that he
didn't think Harlan would turn down playing the role of Richard III
just because he was a negative character. Goebbels went into a temper
tantrum, shouting that he knew well enough that all his directors were
dreaming of going to Hollywood (which was probably quite true),
but that as far as he was concerned all persons employed in the film
industry were soldiers and must obey orders without question.

Harlan later said that, "on the verge of a nervous breakdown" brought on by this scene and the *Pedro* catastrophe, he sent a letter to Goebbels requesting to be sent to the front as a soldier rather than direct *Jud Süss*. Goebbels answered, still according to Harlan, that "If you don't make the film, you are a deserter, and will be shot, for all film workers are soldiers." A few days later Goebbels put out an order that any further employees of the movie industry who volunteered for the front in lieu of accepting assignments would indeed be shot, and obtained Hitler's signature on the document.

Taking on the project, Harlan viewed the English picture and then journeyed to Lublin to see the ghetto, where some sequences were to be filmed. (In the end, these passages were shot in Prague.)

The casting problems continued. Goebbels now wanted Willi Forst for the title role, but Harlan successfully argued that Forst was too much of an operetta specialist to be considered for such a heavy part. Emil Jannings was Goebbels' next suggestion, and he hinted darkly that Jannings could not turn the part down because Goebbels had some evidence of Jewish blood in Jannings' family tree. Jannings might have accepted the part without the threats, but Harlan helpfully argued against this casting on the grounds that "one can't have an opera with three basses" referring to Eugen Klöpfer and Heinrich George, who had already been signed for secondary roles.

The final choice was Ferdinand Marian,* a rather oily matinee idol with a marked resemblance to the late American comic Ernie Kovacs. Marian had a small following, but was no major star, although he was later to prove his genuine talents in several remarkable performances.

Marian was ordered to Goebbels' office for a 2 P.M. meeting, and the night before "begged Harlan," as Harlan later claimed, to help him get out of the part. Harlan said that he told Marian to stand up for his rights as an artist (this ploy sometimes worked on Goebbels) and warned him "don't look at Goebbels' feet or you're lost." At the Propaganda Ministry, Goebbels apparently played one of his best scenes. Marian had to appear in make-up from a murder mystery entitled *Morgen werde ich verhaftet* (*Tomorrow I'll be arrested*), since the appointment with the propaganda minister fell between

---

* In a first marriage Marian had a Jewish wife, by whom he had a daughter (Wulf, p. 10).

takes at the Tobis lot. According to Harlan, the interview began with Goebbels remarking, "You ham, you look like a clown"; after several minutes of complaints about Marian's acting, Goebbels moved nose-to-nose with the actor, smiled in his most winning manner, and asked, "Why don't you play Jud Süss?"

As Harlan reported it, the following dialogue ensued. Marian: "I can't play that kind of role, I'm a *bon vivant*." Goebbels: "Who gives you your parts—the public or me? I know you want to go to Hollywood, but here you get more money than scientists, and yet you refuse to play the part the Führer wants you to play. Don't tell me you won't play it, tell my aide." With this, Goebbels stomped out of the room. Marian, cowed, then cried after the departing Goebbels, "I'll do it!" (This scene was recorded for posterity by a secretary, according to Harlan, who said that it was revealed after the war. I have not been able to locate the document.) Marian, said Harlan, was so miserable that he went home, got drunk, and wrecked his apartment with an ax.

Harlan maintained that Werner Krauss, an actor with a world reputation, was unhappy when he learned that Goebbels had cast him as Rabbi Loew (the Rabbi Gabriel of the novel, rather sinisterly rewritten). But he had a reason to worry, for his son had married a Jewish woman, and even before the Gottschalk affair (described at the end of this chapter) he must have suspected what Goebbels would do if he refused the part. As Harlan told the story, Krauss went to his doctor, trying to find a medical reason for begging off, but was unfortunately in excellent health. The doctor suggested a curious possible escape: he told Krauss to play the "great actor" routine with Goebbels and say that the role was too small, agreeing to do it only if he could play *all* the other major Jewish roles as well. Whether this preposterous idea was in fact proposed, or was a later explanation, is unknown; at any rate, if it was proposed, Goebbels must have accepted it, for Krauss did play the multiple roles.*

The only role remaining to be cast was that of the heroine Dorothea

---

* Krauss later played Shylock in a particularly evil production of *The Merchant of Venice* in Vienna in 1943.

Sturm, the victim of one of Süss's amatory adventures, a character found neither in history nor in Feuchtwanger's book. Goebbels insisted that Harlan's wife Kristina Söderbaum play the part, which Harlan claimed she was unwilling to do; he said that he argued she had just had a baby and was too weak to act. Goebbels said that could be solved with a special dressing-room and a wet nurse for the child. He also offered to halt shooting if Frau Harlan should become ill. The actress was so alarmed that, by Harlan's later report, she considered flight to her native Sweden.

From November 1939 to March 1940, Harlan worked on the script. On March 15 the shooting began, under highly charged circumstances. Harlan claimed that "virtually every actor was performing under duress" (including a very young Wolfgang Staudte in a small role) and the set was said to be filled with representatives of the Propaganda Ministry and the Gestapo to insure cooperation. After a few days, the tension eased, and one of Goebbels' press photographers shot a still photo of Marian and Krauss in their Jewish costumes. Harlan claimed he destroyed the positive print when it was shown to him, but "forgot" the negative, and the photograph was used in the film's publicity campaign "against his wishes."

When the studio work was finished, the shooting moved to Prague for the sequence of the entrance of the Jews from Stuttgart and the scenes in a synagogue. By August 1940 the elaborate and expensive film was completed and ready for Goebbels' preview of the rough-cut. Harlan claimed that he and his actors "did everything possible to minimize the more vicious scenes in the story." He even asserted that he gave Süss a final speech before his execution which "he hoped would escape Goebbels' eye and give the whole film a somewhat ambiguous finale." Süss, bound in an iron cage, cursed his judges in a remarkable passage:

You madmen, servants of Baal, judges of Sodom! May your limbs wither as the willows of dry Kidron! May your bodies rot during your lifetime, may the bones of your children and grandchildren be filled with pus. Every day shall bring you wretchedness, misery and pain. No sleep shall soothe your eyes; wicked neighbors shall destroy your peace. May your first-born son bring you shame, may your memory

be cursed, and may your cities be destroyed by fires from heaven . . .
No bread shall diminish your hunger, your thirst shall go unquenched
with drink. No ear shall hear your pleas, your harvest shall benefit
foreigners, all your efforts shall yield no wages, the work of your hands
shall not benefit your inheritors, and you shall be forced to deny your
own God with your own tongue![3]

When this defiant scene, in which Süss curses the enemies of the
Jews, was shown to Goebbels, he went into a rage, said Harlan, and
berated the director for his "political insensitivity," especially because
of the line "may your cities be destroyed by fires from heaven." Goebbels, who wanted the death of a cringing Jew, not a proud martyr, had
the scene extensively reshot and edited, by other hands, and ended the
film with a written proclamation.

As released, the action of the film can be synopsized as follows:

Süss Oppenheimer of Frankfurt arrives at the Duchy of Württemberg, and swiftly ingratiates himself into the favor of the Duke Karl
Alexander (Heinrich George). The Duke confides his money problems to Süss, who offers to loan him the money needed for his diso-
lute life in return for the tax revenues of the Duchy. Against the advice
of the old Rabbi Loew (Werner Krauss), he overextends his power.
With the help of his hysterical secretary Levy (also Krauss), he abducts the beautiful Dorothea Sturm (Kristina Söderbaum), daughter
of the powerful Counsilor Sturm (Eugen Klöpfer) and brutally rapes
her while her lover (Malte Jaeger) who is planning a revolt against
Süss, is tortured in a cellar. Dorothea manages to escape and drowns
herself. The story is made known and the Duchy revolts as the Duke
dies. Süss is condemned to death. He is placed in an iron cage and
hauled to the top of the scaffold before being executed in the presence
of his grim jury. As the Jews leave the city, a bystander comments,
"May the citizens of other states never forget this lesson."

To an unconcerned viewer today the film may seem more tedious
than vicious; although it runs only eighty-five minutes, it seems longer
because of the leaden direction, bombastic acting, and dark-toned
photography. Yet the effect of the movie at its own time is undeniable,
and the German movie industry has to accept the historical charge that
it contributed its full share to the martyrdom of the Jews during the

The execution of Jud Süss, the gruesome finale of Veit Harlan's film.

Nazi period. *Jud Süss* was banned for viewers under fourteen. Teenagers who saw the film beat up Jews after seeing it. The effect of the film on adolescents is described as follows by Blobner and Holba:

> The impact of the film on adolescents was enormous and devastating. For example, in Vienna an old Jewish man was trampled to death on a public street by a Hitler Youth band which had just seen the film. Special mention must be made of the refined tactics of the authorities who looked the other way when such a film was officially classified "unsuitable for young people." The lowest instincts of mankind were appealed to. This is seen in a rape sequence, intercut with a torture scene, which was cleverly built up to a climax. Ferdinand Marian acted superbly and made of Jew Süss a personified Satan.
>
> Without doubt, this film was the best propaganda film of the Third Reich due to the high-level film technique. Well-known players . . . portrayed their roles so convincingly that even the unbiased spectator was captured by their acting. The fascination exercised by this film was twice as dangerous, since the insidious intention of this work was fully attained—the film was a great box-office hit.[4]

Goebbels drummed up an unprecedented publicity campaign for this film, which was first shown in Berlin in late September of 1940; by Christmas it was playing in sixty-six theaters in Berlin alone.

Himmler declared *Jud Süss* compulsory viewing for all military troops at home and on the front, as well as for the SS and the police. The film was widely exported to occupied Europe against a background described by Wulf thus:

> It is no coincidence that the three anti-Semitic movies *Die Roths-childs, Jud Süss,* and *Der ewige Jude* were premiered precisely in 1940. Unquestionably Goebbels had those three films made and shown because of the planned and later actually executed "Final Solution of the Jewish Problem," even though the actual date when that "final solution" was decided by the mighty of the Third Reich has not been established with complete accuracy. All historians base their view generally on three documents: the urgent circular by Reinhard Heydrich to the chiefs of all "special troops" (Einsatzgruppen) of the security police of September 21, 1939, in which he already talks about the "final goal of the Jewish problem in the occupied territories"; then, Hermann Göring's letter to Heydrich of July 1941, in which he orders Heydrich "to submit the organizational, factual, and material premises to carry out the desired final solution of the Jewish problem"; and, finally, the notorious conference report of the representatives of all the top authorities in the Third Reich in Berlin, Grosser Wannsee 56–58, of January 20, 1942—known today as the Wannsee Protocol.
>
> At any rate, the movie *Jud Süss* was always shown to the "Aryan" population, especially in the East, when "resettlements" for the death camps were imminent. This can be verified by many eye witnesses from their own experience—so far as Poland is concerned, it can be testified to by the writer of these lines himself. It is certain that the film was shown in order to incense in this way the "Aryan" population against Jews in the respective countries, and thus to choke off in the bud any possible help to them on the part of the people. . . .
>
> All this was at a time, alas, when the ashes and the blood of the millions of the gassed and murdered still made an impression on the world at large.[5]

In France, partisans threw bombs into cinemas that screened the picture. But the French fascists Bardèche and Brasillach loved it. Even in their 1948 revised *Histoire du Cinéma* they lauded the film's "almost joyous crescendo."[6] It is noteworthy that one of the authors of this "histoire" was executed after the war for his activities. (The third edition of the volume dropped the quoted statement.)

The tragic finale to the affair is the fact that the greatest success of the film was in the Middle East, where Arabic-dubbed prints were still circulating during the 1960's.

Although Harlan destroyed the negative in April of 1954, which he claimed was missing until then, it was reported shortly afterward that a print was sold to Beirut and Cairo, dubbed in Arabic. Terra, the original production company, requested a cut on the profits on the basis of fifty-year rights. A long investigation followed, and the embarrassed Bonn government claimed the film was being distributed openly in the Arab states through Sovexport, via East Germany, where a second negative was known to exist. In 1959, another negative was seized in Lübeck from a dealer who planned to sell it to the brother of King Ibn Saud for $100,000. As recently as May 1968, *Variety* reported further intrigues involving a print smuggled from Basel to Karlsruhe by a smalltime film promoter who was arrested, jailed, and given a fine.[7]

Apparently the ghost of the unfortunate Süss has not found rest yet. As this book was completed, another movie on the subject was announced by a West German company with Hans Oppenheimer directing from a script by Hans Habe.

Although what happened to the film personalities of the Third Reich is discussed in the epilogue of this study, the effects of *Jud Süss* on its participants might be mentioned briefly here. Harlan was tried twice for crimes against humanity. He was freed for lack of conclusive proof but was unable, as was his wife, to make films for a number of years. Ferdinand Marian, one of the first actors to be de-Nazified after the war, apparently committed suicide in an automobile crash as a result of his feelings of guilt over having appeared in the picture; shortly after Harlan's 1950 trial, Marian's widow was found drowned in Hamburg. Werner Krauss was blacklisted and an attempted postwar stage comeback in Switzerland was greeted by street riots. Heinrich George died in 1946 in the Russian-controlled Sachsenhausen concentration camp. Wolfgang Staudte, who became an important film director after the war, was criticized from many quarters when it was discovered he had played a small part in the picture.

Horrible though *Jud Süss* was, some of its reputation may be based on confusion with an even more hideous film, *Der ewige Jude* (*The Eternal Jew*), a four-reel "documentary" on the "Jewish problem" put together with diabolical skill by Dr. Fritz Hippler and a special detail of the Propaganda Ministry.

Hippler is an enigmatic figure, working today as a travel agent in Berchtesgaden where I interviewed him in 1963. Through the help of Veit Harlan a meeting was arranged, an unusual occurrence as Hippler has taken pains to stay out of the limelight since his exit from the film world of the Third Reich in 1943. In the opinion of many, Hippler was the evil genius behind a number of projects.

Hippler was cooperative in talking to me about his life and work. (It might be added here that several well-known directors were amazed to hear that Hippler was still alive, so carefully had he divorced himself from the film scene.) His career was so curious that it deserves some space here.

Hippler studied sociology and law in Heidelberg. In 1935 he became a power in the newsreel division of the Propaganda Ministry and a confidant of Goebbels, but fell into disgrace with his supervisor over the conduct of the Baarova affair. After making the *Westwall* picture discussed earlier, he became a military member of the government film unit and was sent to the Western front, returning in 1939 to become head of the film division of the Propaganda Ministry, a position he held until 1943. His first major project was *Feldzug in Polen* (*Campaign in Poland*), a "documentary" he put together in time for release in February of 1940. Rumors that both Leni Riefenstahl and G. W. Pabst worked on this picture have never been substantiated, and Hippler refuses to discuss the matter. This film was a major success and has gone down in film history as a propaganda "classic." Hippler apparently also supervised its companion piece, *Sieg im Westen* (*Victory in the West*), which purported to document the French campaign.[8] This was released on January 29, 1941, as part of the annual celebration of the anniversary of the Nazi seizure of power.

Goebbels, before departing for Greece after the Baarova scandal, had directed that an anti-Semitic documentary be made but left no explicit directions on how this was to be carried out. During the war in Poland, Hippler had supervised some documentary footage on life in the ghetto, intended for archive purposes. When Hippler was put in charge of the Jewish project, this footage was reprinted, and he went back to shoot additional scenes in Warsaw and Lodz. Besides, the archives were combed for suitable newsreel and feature film footage, but when this was at last assembled, the film still lacked a script. This was, according to Hippler, apparently provided by the mysterious Dr. Eberhard Taubert, a red-hot Nazi behind several odious projects of this nature.

The film is scurrilous. It compares the Jews with rats, then charges that they dominate the world economy. An excerpt from the American film *House of Rothschild* (1934) is inserted to show the alleged dishonest tricks of Jewish bankers: members of the Rothschild family hide an elaborate dinner and dress in old clothes when the local tax collector pays a surprise visit. (The excerpt is used in the original English-language version, with German subtitles—and of course with no hint of its original comic intent.) Scenes of Passover celebrations and Talmud classes are used to illustrate the supposedly disgusting nature of Jewish cultural life. In the final scenes, a brutally repulsive treatment is given to ritual butchering practices—a particularly vile misrepresentation, since in fact Jewish slaughtering methods are no more inhumane than those used in nonritual establishments. The film ends with contrasted scenes of "German men and German order," as the official synopsis puts it, "which fill the spectator with a feeling of deepseated gratification for belonging to a people whose leader has absolutely solved the Jewish problem."[9]

The film is shown in less than forty-five minutes, perhaps the most hideous three-quarters-of-an-hour in film history. At times it is as hard to watch the action as to view the postwar newsreel footage of concentration camps. The slaughterhouse passage is so terrible that it is prefaced by a remark from the narrator that the squeamish should shut their eyes. *Der ewige Jude* is certainly the "hate" picture of all time, and one of the great examples of the way in which the film medium can be used as a propaganda tool far greater than the printed or spoken word alone. Fortunately, the film is inaccessible beyond a few film archives where it is kept in the restricted division usually reserved for pornography, which is exactly the genre to which this film belongs.

The film was also made in a slightly different version for Czech audiences; why this was done remains a mystery. Hippler's filmography ends with his direction of the documentary *Legion Condor*.

In 1943, Hippler requested permission to be transferred back to the military film unit, which Goebbels granted readily, as relations between the two men were strained. Hippler was captured by the British and spent three years as a prisoner of war. He was de-Nazified in 1951, and employed by the United States Army as a translator in the Transportation corps.

Evidently the plan of the prosecution at the war-crimes trials was to bring action against Harlan first, and then follow with lesser film personalities—although anyone who has seen *Der ewige Jude* might wonder why Hippler was not first on the list. In the end, the failure to convict Harlan put a stop to further prosecutions, though many men from the *Filmwelt* were at least as guilty of crimes against humanity as Harlan. (Some were not available for trial, such as Karl Ritter.)

To sum up, the four major anti-Semitic films constitute the most odious part of the record of the film industry under the Nazis, however we interpret the situations and motives of their makers. But even a vile chapter of history needs to be written accurately.

### II

This chapter on the anti-Semitic film is an appropriate place to record briefly the tragic story of Joachim Gottschalk, one victim of Goebbels' insane race policies. He was not alone, but the case was so spectacular that it deserves special attention.

Although Goebbels generally left members of the film colony alone despite their known resistance to his policies, he found it necessary from time to time to make a public example of someone who had "gone too far." As described elsewhere, the director Herbert Selpin was murdered (although suicide was the announced cause of death) for remarks against the state. A prominent member of the Ufa management was executed under incredible circumstances which are fully documented; unfortunately these papers are still classified, although available for the researcher in Washington, so neither the victim's name nor the details of his trial and execution can be recounted here.

The beautiful actress Renate Müller was hounded by the Gestapo to the point that she committed suicide in Berlin in October of 1937 at the age of only thirty rather than put up with Goebbels' sadistic harassment. This case aroused the film colony, but nothing equaled the reaction throughout Germany to the fate of Joachim Gottschalk, one of the most popular actors of the period.

There are two slightly different accounts of what happened. Annedore Leber's book *Das Gewissen steht auf* (*The Conscience Rises*), published in 1956, has the advantage of some information unearthed after the war when the case was investigated. But the most moving description of the 1941 Gottschalk affair is found in Howard K. Smith's *Last Train from Berlin* (1942). Smith was the correspondent for CBS in Berlin at the time, and records the tragedy with deep and personal involvement.

Gottschalk, a sort of German Fredric March, was a born picture-stealer, and made his way to fame strictly against the will of the Propaganda Ministry, which deprived him of all publicity in film magazines and newspapers. The reason this handsome young actor was disliked by the authorities was the fact that he was married, and happily married, to a full-blooded Jewess, and repeatedly refused suggestions from the Nazis to divorce his wife and enjoy a smoother rise to fame. As the war proceeded, Gottschalk's popularity grew in Germany, for he seemed to have a knack of getting good roles in strictly non-propaganda films, which irked the Nazis all the more. With Paula Wessely he made the biggest box-office hit of the first year of the war, *Ein Leben lang*. The film was truly excellent and with it, Gottschalk first won fame in countries outside the German sphere of influence to which the film was exported. With Brigitte Horney he made another truly good film, *Das Mädchen von Fanö*, then played the role of Hans Christian Andersen in *Die schwedische Nachtigall*, which made him perhaps the most popular actor in Germany. When the anti-Jewish campaign was begun, Goebbels presented Gottschalk with an

ultimatum; he was becoming a German institution, he had qualified
inadvertently as good propaganda, and he must divorce his wife, or
he would be banned from his profession for evermore. Gottschalk
promptly refused to leave his wife, and the half-Jewish child she had
borne him. So he was informed that, regardless of his decision, he
could no longer live with his polluted family; the Gestapo gave his
wife and child one day to pack and join the Jewish exodus to the East.
Gottschalk was not permitted to go with them.

On the appointed evening,* the Gestapo invaded the Gottschalk
home to put an end to this unbearable *Rassenschande*. They found the
family there waiting, but it was dead. Ten minutes before they came,
Gottschalk had killed his child, his wife and himself. The incident was
a hideous one, and the story spread over Berlin like wildfire. The
*Artistenwelt* was incensed and it was said that there was nearly a revolt in the film studios. German women who, in legions of millions,
had cried their eyes dry at Gottschalk playing a war-cripple in *Ein
Leben lang*, were horrified. Dr. Goebbels and Herr Himmler had
under-estimated the fibre of their film-hero, if they had not under-
estimated the breadth of his popularity.[10]

The Leber book adds a few details that Smith could not have known
at the time. Apparently Goebbels was willing to ignore Gottschalk's
mixed marriage (the fact that he was allowed major film roles backs
up this belief) unless it was thrown in his face. The actor, who had
great courage or else a streak of great foolishness, made the mistake
of taking his wife to the reception following the premiere of the Andersen film, where she was met by many high-ranking Nazis unaware of
the fact that she was a Jew. When Goebbels learned of this, he was
reported to have merely said, "I can bear this face no longer," and
Gottschalk was immediately banned from the stage and screen. As
Ernest K. Bramsted summed it up:

> In a farewell letter [to a friend] Gottschalk quoted the melancholy
> words of the playwright Heinrich von Kleist, who had also put an
> end to his life over a century earlier: "The truth is that nothing on
> earth could help me." When Goebbels heard of the tragedy, he com-
> mented on it in terms "of diabolical cynicism." Small wonder, for the

* November 6, 1941.

life of an individual meant little to him, especially when it did not conform to the official line.[11]

Bramsted footnotes the quote of Goebbels' reaction as coming from Werner Stephan's *Joseph Goebbels: Dämon einer Diktatur* (1949), a somewhat unreliable, sensationalist source. According to Hippler, who is not reliable either, something to the contrary was true. He claims that Goebbels was aghast at the news, realizing that it was terrible propaganda, and tried to switch the blame on Himmler later. In any case, it was at this point that Goebbels lost any loyalty that the film colony might have had for his policies and himself. "Mickey Mouse," as he had been referred to by almost everyone in conversation, had turned into a rat.

*Ein Leben lang.* "The actor Joachim Gottschalk shall not be mentioned henceforth, in word or picture."
(See page 176.)

—*Kulturpolitische Information* No. 17, 1941
(Archive of the Institut für Kulturforschung,
Munich)

# 1940-1941: FILMS OF THE EARLY WAR PERIOD

The start of World War II in September 1939 found the German film studios prepared for the new military conditions. Members of the Filmwelt, as long as they toed the line, were deferred from military front service on Goebbels' and Hitler's dictum that film workers were soldiers of the Reich on special duty. A request to be transferred to the battle lines was tantamount to treason and the petitioner could be shot for disobeying orders. The number of such applications was small and the dubious privilege of being shot on the Eastern front was granted only to those in official disfavor.

Still, many lesser technical workers were conscripted, causing a cut-back in the number of films produced. In 1940, 89 feature films were made, twenty of which with a heavy propaganda line; in 1941, 71 pictures were completed, twenty-nine banned after the war. With the decrease in the number of productions, more money and time could be spent on making more ambitious projects with greater care than had been possible previously.

Foreign films were rapidly on the way out, excepting those from occupied countries. On August 14, 1940, Metro-Goldwyn-Mayer was ordered to close its German offices, and on September 7, 1941, Paramount, the last major American company with German distribution facilities, was shut by government decree.

178

This did not prevent Goebbels from keeping close track on the latest American pictures, which were provided for him by the embassies of neutral countries, especially Spain and Portugal. As his hardworking aid Semmler reported in his diary:

> Goebbels always has his adjutant and press officer with him at lunch and supper, even if his family are there too. The adjutants have very menial jobs. They have no political functions; they are just superior domestics. . . . It is their job to see that after supper there is a new film available—preferably a foreign one—and they are held responsible if the Minister's collars and cuffs have been overstarched at the laundry. A thankless job.[1]

These film sessions were particularly dreaded by his staff because a good foreign picture could send Goebbels into a monumental rage. One director recalled that a screening of *Gone With the Wind* was good for a full week of jealous tantrums. To make the situation worse, Goebbels never learned English, and the translation had to be whispered to him line by line, out of earshot of the other viewers equally ignorant of the language. After one of the propaganda minister's extremely frugal dinners, it was often torture to suffer the pangs of hunger and total boredom as film after film unreeled in the private projection room. As Semmler recalls one unfortunate evening:

> When the Zarah Leander film *Das Herz der Königin* was finished, she and her leading man [Willy Birgel] were invited to supper with Goebbels. Afterwards the film was given its first private showing. While the performance was going on the adjutant fell asleep and soon began to snore. He was tactfully woken up by a servant, but Goebbels took the incident so much to heart that he at once begged Zarah Leander's pardon for what she must regard as an unpardonable insult. Admittedly the film was not very good, but Goebbels was so annoyed with his sleepy adjutant that he dismissed him soon afterwards.[2]

The film in question, *Das Herz der Königin* (*The Heart of the Queen*), (November 1, 1940), was one of a series of anti-British pictures timed to coincide with the campaign against England. Its subject concerned Mary, Queen of Scotts, and her conflict with Queen Elizabeth I. But instead of using the Schiller play on the same subject (*Maria Stuart*), the Carl Froelich Ufa superproduction turned the tragedy into a sort of musical tailored to Zarah Leander's special talents. The cast, using many stage performers, was good, and the Walter Haag sets were elaborate. Theo Mackeben composed a properly gloomy score, one lullaby, "*Um das Fenster weht der Wind,*" achieving considerable popularity. But the unfortunate adjutant was probably not alone in falling asleep: the film was an overproduced bore.

At about the same time, Goebbels hit on the idea of making two propaganda features with Irish settings, featuring the revolt against England. It is doubtful whether these pictures were ever screened in that neutral country—indeed, if they were they must have convulsed audiences. But they are not without interest today because of their peculiar subject matter, and the direction of Max Kimmich.

The first, and less successful, was *Der Fuchs von Glenarvon* (*The Fox of Glenarvon*), (April 24, 1940). Kimmich in talking with me claimed that the films with Irish settings were his idea, not Goebbels', and that his aim was to make the pictures more pro-Irish than anti-British. He had heard the story of the *Fox* when he was in the United States, and wanted to do it there with Joe Pasternak. However, the finished script, by Hans Bertram and others, stressed the perfidy of the English during the 1921 rebellion. The rather curious theme of the protection of the minority against the majority appears from time to time, but it must have escaped Goebbels' attention. For this major Tobis production, Kimmich had Fritz Arno Wagner as his cameraman, and a fine cast including Olga Tschechowa and Ferdinand Marian.

The film had considerable success and was followed by *Mein Leben für Irland* (*My Life for Ireland*), (February 17, 1941), a far more ambitious picture with a definite slant toward the youth market. The leading character is an eighteen-year-old Irish boy named Michael O'Brien (Werner Hinz) who is put in an English boarding school for the children of political prisoners. The excitement occurs during the revolt in Dublin. The hero and his Irish-American friend Patrick (Claus Clausen) help to save the day for the nationalists, performing sabotage against the British invaders.

Torture by water sequence from Max Kimmich's *Mein Leben für Irland*
Heinz Ohlsen (in water); Will Quadflieg (behind) (1941).

Although the actors are a bit overage (and oversize) for short pants,
and the continuity and editing betray a limited budget, the battle scene
at the end of the picture, brilliantly photographed by Richard Angst,
was successful. In an apparent effort to equal Harlan's sadism in *Jud
Süss*, Kimmich's screenplay inserts a scene in which Patrick is tortured
by his school chums on the presumption that he is a traitor; there is
also a well-directed scene in which the unruly students refuse to sing
the national anthem and burn the Union Jack amid great jubilation.

Interviewed in 1963, Angst recalled the film with considerable horror. A munitions expert had been brought to Tobis to lay the mines
for the final battle sequence. Before the scene could be shot, he was
called suddenly to the front, and left an incomplete plan of his charges.
When the scene went before the camera with hundreds of extras,
several were killed and a number wounded when they stepped on the
expert's handiwork. Unaware of the fact, the cameras kept turning
and the all too realistic footage was used in the picture. The incident
was hushed up, and Kimmich, he says, never heard of it until after
the war, as the sequence had been supervised by a second-unit director,
Kimmich being elsewhere for the day.

The two Irish films were small fish compared with the Hans Stein-hoff epic *Ohm Krüger* (*Uncle Krüger*), (April 4, 1941), Goebbels' first attempt to make a domestic (albeit black-and-white) equal to *Gone With the Wind.* Several years of preparation went into this gigantic spectacle, which ran 132 minutes in completed form. One can praise the film's enormous scope, but that is about all that can be said in its favor, outside of some excellent photography by Fritz Arno Wagner.

The subject is the life of the great Boer hero Ohm Krüger (Emil Jannings), who tells his life story in flashbacks as he lies dying in a Swiss hospital. His sons, Jan (Werner Hinz) and Adrian (Ernst Schröder) have opposite views on the validity of their father's struggle during the Boer War, and this ideological confusion is presented with considerable (if long-winded) skill. However, the purpose of the film was to provide anti-British propaganda, and it is not long before the juggernaut begins to roll. The English are terrible villains one and all. They incite the colored natives by handing out guns during a mission service to the tune of "Onward Christian Soldiers." They feed rotten meat to the Boer women and children in the giant concentration camps they have invented in South Africa, and bayonet the prisoners without regard to age or sex; the viewer is told that 26,000 women and

A slightly tipsy Queen Victoria (Hedwig Wangel) takes Ohm Krüger (Emil Jannings) on a tour of Buckingham Palace in Hans Steinhoff's *Ohm Krüger* (1941).

children were murdered. (The unbelievable gall of blaming the invention of concentration camps on the British—whether true or not—showed Goebbels at the height of his cynicism.) Rarely has any film presented blacker villains than Kitchener (Franz Schafheitlin), Cecil Rhodes (Ferdinand Marian), and even Chamberlain (Gustaf Gründgens).

Some lead-footed, if genuinely grotesque humor, is provided in the famous scene in which, following the war, the old Krüger is invited to Buckingham Palace to meet the whisky-swilling Queen Victoria (Hedwig Wangel), who reels through the corridors with alcoholic refreshment provided by John Brown. While breathless crowds wait outside the palace for news of the momentous meeting, the two old people discuss their rheumatism.

*Ohm Krüger* moves with agonizing slowness, and the interior sequences are singularly uninteresting. Theo Mackeben's music is introduced whenever things threaten to grind to a complete halt; a particularly notable example is the scene in which the Prince of Wales (Alfred Bernau) learns of the death of his mother while watching a ribald Parisian cabaret entertainment—an original invention of the screenwriters.

Although Hans Steinhoff was credited as director, and Emil Jannings was listed as producer, most of the direction was actually the work of Jannings, who despised Steinhoff. When the film started to run behind schedule, Jannings hired Herbert Maisch and Karl Anton, two established directors, to shoot secondary scenes. Maisch's contributions include a speech by Jannings on a balcony, the Swiss sequences in Lausanne (actually photographed in Geneva), and the musical passage in Pretoria. Steinhoff was unaware that the scenes had been filmed until the work was completed, and was justifiably outraged.

This hardly bothered Jannings, who was allowed to do what he wanted by the indulgent Goebbels. *Ohm Krüger* was selected as the best foreign film of the year at the Venice Festival, and was designated at home as the first "Film of the Nation." In an impressive ceremony, Goebbels gave Jannings something called the "Ring of Honor of the German Cinema."

There is little question that the role of Krüger gave Jannings one of his best German-language parts. Even Louis Marcorelles in his largely uncomplimentary article on the Nazi cinema praised his performance, noting especially "in the final images, Jannings, staggering blinded in his tent, only the whiteness of his eyes showing, becomes the symbol of a powerless humanity in the grip of fate."[3]

Herbert Maisch's film *Friedrich Schiller* (November 13, 1940) was a far better biography, despite some Nazi emphasis on certain parts of his life. As the postwar report of the Control Commission for Germany described it:

The film shows Schiller's early youth when a Cadet at the military academy and court of Karl Eugen, Duke of Württemberg, at Stuttgart. He is fundamentally opposed to military discipline and philosophical ideas of his times and the interplay of these conflicting ideas in his relationship with the Duke forms the main part of the film. The Duke considers him a rebel, forces him to concentrate on obtaining his medical diploma, then transfers him to one of his regiments. Schiller, however, secretly continues writing, completes *The Robbers*, and it is published and performed in the theatre. The enraged Duke orders his immediate arrest, but with the help of friends from the court and academy, he escapes from Württemberg.

This is an excellent production with outstanding acting, excellent photography and editing. It suffers from an excess of Prussian "barking of orders and Schiller's pan-German nationalist ideas are given prominence.[4]

Maisch, a theatrical director, was given the project although he was known to be cool to the Nazis. In one of the final scenes, which shows an excerpt from *Die Räuber*, the actors playing Pastor Moser and Franz Moor (Albert Florath and Bernhard Minetti) play their roles with such conviction that the lines would seem almost directed against the Nazi regime. As originally shot, the movie's last word was Schiller's whispered "Freiheit!" as he escaped the duke's domains, but Goebbels' censors caught the line and cut it.

Indeed, Schiller proved difficult to fit into the pattern of the standard pre-Hitler proto-Nazi which the regime demanded. In a long article on the picture, the producer, Paul Joseph Cremers, was hard put to make a propaganda example of his life. The closest he could come was in the following paragraph:

His heart beat with the unrestrained passion for the ideal of a coming age. The vision that Schiller sensed with a prophetic certainty was of something greater than the politically corrupt circumstances of his time, greater and more lofty than the egocentric will of small principalities and their mortal rulers. And the greater idea in which he believed and for which he fought was *Ein Deutschland, ein Volk, ein Vaterland!*[5]

Again photographed by the busy Fritz Arno Wagner, *Friedrich Schiller* featured the popular juvenile Horst Caspar in the title role, assisted by Heinrich George as the duke, with Lil Dagover and Eugen Klöpfer in supporting roles.

The subject of the life of Bismarck was another tempting project, which was eventually filmed in two parts: *Bismarck* (December 6, 1940) and *Die Entlassung* (*The Dismissal*), (October 6, 1942), both directed in dull style by Wolfgang Liebeneiner. The first picture was the weaker, with a second-rate cast for the most part, but the second episode found Jannings as Bismarck and Werner Krauss as the Geheimrat von Holstein. Despite these two actors, the camerawork of Fritz Arno Wagner and a very good score by Herbert Windt, the second film is almost as dull as the first. The oddest episode of *Die Entlassung* occurs during Bismarck's dismissal, in which Wilhelm II (Werner Hinz) is shown as a homosexual making coy advances toward a piano-playing friend, oblivious to the fall of his father's greatest statesman.

As a dramatic hero of nationalist culture, one of the most peculiar choices was J. S. Bach's eldest son Friedemann. Although Traugott Müller's film played fast and loose with the story of the unhappy young man, *Friedemann Bach* (June 25, 1941) was a biographical film of unusual taste.

On first glance, the Bach family seemed cultural film material, but, unfortunately for Goebbels and his writers, most of their lives were dull and largely concerned with the composition of religious music, something which was to be avoided if possible. Friedemann, the black sheep of the family, fitted better than the others in most respects. Generally acknowledged to be the most talented pianist, organist, and composer of the elder Bach's many children, he rebelled against the stuffiness of his family and became court composer to the debauched August III, elector of Saxony and king of Poland, outraging his family by composing scores for somewhat naughty ballets. His brother Emanuel is sent to save him from the jaws of vice, but it is too late: Friedemann has become a court fop. When his father dies, he resolves to reform and applies for Johann Sebastian's former position of organist and composer. But his advanced music and past reputation cost him the job. Returning to his old way he falls into ruin, working as a violinist with a vagabond troupe. His relatives and former court friends try to bring him to his senses, but he refuses to hear them. Finally, in need of money, he attempts to sell some of his father's manuscripts in a music store. A customer derides his name, Friedemann attacks him and is stabbed. Emanuel takes him home to die.

*Friedemann Bach* was the only feature film directed by Traugott Müller,* which leads one to suspect that much of the picture's success is due to Gustaf Gründgens in another capacity than that of leading man. (Almost all of his sequences are photographed in soft focus, worthy of a fading Hollywood starlet.) Eugen Klöpfer and Wolfgang Liebeneiner performed capably as other members of the Bach family.

One of the few examples of a biography of a non-German can be found in Peter Paul Brauer's *Die schwedische Nachtigall* (*The Swedish Nightingale*), (April 9, 1941), which is actually a dual biography, more concerned with Hans Christian Andersen than with Jenny Lind. With Joachim Gottschalk and Ilse Werner in the leading parts, this Terra production reaches moments of almost unbearable pathos, especially because it was Gottschalk's last film before his suicide. His performance as the hopelessly-in-love Andersen is one of the milestones of German screen art. The final sequence of the picture is an elaborate pantomime of "The Emperor's Nightingale" which is introduced as a tale told by Andersen to some youngsters after the end of his romance with Jenny Lind. Unfortunately, the film was banned for children's viewing for reasons that escape me.

---

* Müller, who died in 1944, was Gründgens' usual set designer for his stage and opera productions.

## II

The war brought its quota of military epics, with the indefatigable Karl Ritter hard at work on his films of hate and violence, after a brief respite with the nonpolitical *Bal paré* (May 22, 1940).

His three contributions to the war effort, all released in 1941, were *Über Alles in der Welt* (March 19); *Stukas* (June 27), and *Kadetten* (*Cadets*), (December 2). It is hard to select the most objectionable.

By far the most elaborate was *Über Alles in der Welt*, an Ufa super-production differing from most Ritter pictures in that a few stars—at least minor ones—were in evidence. The official synopsis is worth translation:

On September 2, 1939, England and France declare war on Germany. In England, France, and on the high seas, Germans are hunted down, persecuted, and imprisoned. The Colombes Stadium in Paris has been turned into a concentration camp where Germans and Jews are confined. Two of the prisoners are Fritz Möbius (Fritz Kampers) of the Siemens-Schuckert factory and Dr. Karl Wiegand (Carl Raddatz), a German correspondent in Paris. Escape seems impossible, but Wiegand is freed and attempts are made to enlist him in anti-German propaganda activities. Wiegand pretends to be interested in the proposition and vouches for Möbius. This is their only possible way to regain freedom and return to Germany.

Both men flee, Möbius during an air attack. Wiegand goes to the front, accompanied by Leo Samek (Oscar Sima) of the League for Human Rights, and a girl, Madeleine Laroche (Maria Bard). The three observe the battle of an Austrian battalion. In the heat of battle, Samek and Madeleine loose their heads and run away, but Wiegand remains steadfast and makes his way across the battlefield to join the German ranks.

At the same time, the members of a Tyrolean musical group are dragged from a London stage into a concentration camp. Samek and Captain Stanley of the Secret Service (Andrews Engelmann) try to free them and enlist their services. Three members of the band pretend to be interested. They are taken to France, watch the same attack which made it possible for Wiegand to escape, and also make it across the lines to Germany.

At the outbreak of the war, the German tanker *Elmshorn* is on the high seas in the Atlantic. The ship is pursued by an English destroyer. The captain of the tanker directs his crew to sink and abandon the ship so that it will not fall into British hands. The crew is picked up by the British destroyer *Arethusa*. Soon afterward an explosion on the destroyer causes cries of "German submarines!" And indeed, a German submarine emerges from the sea, takes the Germans off the British destroyer, and deposits them at Vigo, Spain, from where they make their way through friendly Italy to Germany.

On a Pommeranian airfield, German planes are ready to go into action. They attack the Polish hinterland. One of the planes does not return, but has to make a forced landing in enemy territory. A German plane flies to the rescue. Braving enemy fire, the plane lands on Polish soil, picks up the German crew and brings them back to their home base. But the rescue plane is hit and the crew tries to save itself by parachute. Among them is Hans Wiegand (Hannes Stelzer), Karl's brother. The group flees across the forests and mountain passes of France and reaches the Italian border.

On board a German minesweeper stands the captain and one of his officers. They scan the air with their field glasses. The Germans down 37 of 45 enemy planes. The radio announces: "This is our answer!"

The film closes with a symbolic apotheosis of Germany's invincible strength. The five unconnected episodes, all showing Germans overtaken by war in foreign lands or on hostile seas, prove the great sacrificial love Germans hold for their fatherland which they will rejoin regardless of danger.[6]

By using the episode structure again, and cutting the story line of everything save violent action and pure hatred, Ritter kept this film moving along at a much faster pace than his usual work. The British propagandists are shown as Jews, and in one sequence there is a nightclub act with girls clad in Union Jack bikinis. So much for Dr. Ritter's views on England.

*Stukas*, his next picture, has all his worst vices: blatant propaganda, slapdash production values, crude editing, and a terrible script. As Howard K. Smith recorded his stupefied impressions after having viewed it in Berlin:

It was a monotonous film about a bunch of obstreperous adolescents who dive-bombed things and people. They bombed everything and everybody. That was all the whole film was—one bombing after another. Finally the hero got bored with bombing and lost interest in life. So they took him off to the Bayreuth music festival, where he listened to a few lines of Wagnerian music; his soul began to breathe again, he got visions of the Führer and of guns blazing away, so he impolitely left right in the middle of the first act and dashed back and started bombing things again, with the old gusto.[7]

This final reel of the film is one of the silliest pieces of misguided propaganda ever conceived by the human mind, and must have sent even the most stalwart Nazi out of the cinema with a snicker. After the lofty strains of *Siegfrieds Rheinfahrt* die away over a montage of the bomber reunited with his comrades, Ritter cuts to some incredibly faked shots of individual pilots singing (with considerable embarrassment) the strains of the "Stukalied."

*Kadetten* was an even worse film, and morally more objectionable, if such a thing can be possible. As Blobner and Holba describe it:

Taking a story from the year 1760, a readiness for self-denial which many young people possess was appealed to and stimulated. The film's thesis "who dies young dies well" was only too quickly understood and led many young people directly to a mass grave. The film relates an episode out of the Seven Years' War and deals with the fate of Prussian cadets who do honor to their military training and to Prussianism. The soldierly spirit had just about established roots in the hearts of the youngsters (the cadets' ages ranged from 9–12 years) and it resulted in many heroic deeds. A group of very young cadets are captured by the Russians, but they succeed in escaping. Entrenched in a crumbling fortress, they bravely fight back the waves of attacks launched by the enemy with heroic courage, until reinforcements arrive. Friedrich von Tzülow, the German *Rittmeister* is one of the main figures. Formerly a Prussian officer, he later deserts to the Russians after being unjustly criticized by the king. However, he realizes that deep in his heart he is still a Prussian, and so he gives up his life in order to save several cadets.[8]

*Kadetten* was actually finished in 1939, but, because of the change in the Nazi-Soviet line, was shelved and not released until December of 1941, when the anti-Russian tone was again acceptable. It made little difference, for the film is a crushing bore and Ritter lacked Carl Froelich's skill in the direction of children.

Actually, bearing in mind the original production date of *Kadetten*, it was one of the first military films aimed at the youth market, and set a sinister precedent. Young people found the theme all too appealing, and Goebbels was ready to oblige with further essays in this direction.

*Kopf hoch, Johannes!* (*Chin Up, Johannes!*), (March 11, 1941), directed by the actor Viktor de Kowa, is even more unappetizing than

Ritter's work because it had a present-day setting. The theme here is the superiority of National Socialist teaching methods and the conversion of an independent thinking youth into a follower of the fascist party line.

The hero, Johannes, is a young man from an aristocratic family previously stationed abroad. His nationalist ideals have become corrupted by foreign influence, which deeply disturbs his parents. When he attempts to put out a flaming haystack which others have ignited on the family estate, he is unjustly blamed for arson and shipped off to a Nazi-supervised boarding school. A nice farm boy from the estate goes along and soon sets a good example. Johannes is sensitive and artistically talented, but weak; the director of the school first deprives him of a medallion of his mother, and discourages his playing of the accordion, both of these steps taken to bring him into line with his fellow-students as part of the conformist process. Naturally, in time he becomes a good little Nazi and a joy to his parents and comrades.

Outside of some schmaltz involving the farm boy's near-fatal illness, the film has a neo-documentary flavor. The scenes of the young boys wallow in a sort of pagan joy in the body which is divorced by miles from Leni Riefenstahl's exaltation of physical beauty in *Olympia*. The routine of the school is thoroughly terrifying when viewed today—the boys even gargle in unison! Yet from all reports, the picture proved enormously appealing to youth and confirmed Goebbels' belief in the merits of this type of production.

It was followed shortly by *Jakko* (October 12, 1941), directed by Fritz Peter Buch, a film considerably less offensive. The book was by Alfred Weidenmann, a specialist in children's films who had already directed some short works in this genre. Rather than attempting a documentary approach, a melodramatic story line was used about a young man who has trouble adjusting to life with the Nazi Navy-Youth group. If the director is to be believed, the film was at least *started* as a serious study of adolescent problems, and the picture contains the barest minimum of propaganda. Instead, something along the lines of *Emil and the Detectives* was attempted with the hero, Jakko, foiling a crime engineered by the chauffeur he believes to be his father. Goebbels was displeased with the picture's lack of politics and interfered with production so that the film took almost a year to complete. Because of this, Buch was required to direct a government propaganda feature, *Menschen im Sturm* (December 19, 1941) about the problems of Germans living in Yugoslavia at the start of World War II.

Two other juvenile features are worthy of note: *Jungens* (*Guys*), (May 2, 1941) and *Himmelhunde* (*Hounds of the Sky*), (February 20, 1942). The former film, directed by Robert Stemmle, was a small picture about youth problems set on an island in East Prussia, and dealing with the efforts of the "guys" to break up a smuggling ring. To make this rather innocent film, Stemmle had to add some materials about a Hitler Youth leader organizing the project, and it is intimated during one passage that denunciation of family and friends is not a bad thing if done for the good of the state. Otherwise the film is light on propaganda, and gives an appealing and unusual view of everyday life in 1941. It must be emphasized that this type of treatment of reality was rare, as contemporary problems and real-life situations were frowned upon as screen entertainment. The half dozen pictures which tried to show life as it was, albeit in a favorable light, let a welcome breath of fresh air into the stuffy artificial film matter of the era.

*Himmelhunde*, directed by the uninspired Roger von Norman for Terra, again takes the theme of obedience and the necessity of obeying orders, following a juvenile distortion of the plot line of *The Prince of Homburg*. A young man in the Hitler Youth Glider Group wins a race with a plane he was told not to use. Despite his victory he is punished, for obeying orders without question is more important than winning prizes. It takes a while to bring the hero around to the fact, but he at last emerges as another obedient Nazi.

Looking at these films today, one begins to get the idea that the wholehearted cooperation of youth with the Nazi regime was not all it should have been as far as the Party was concerned. Film after film features a recalcitrant hero (but never a heroine) who has to be brought around to believing ideas which he does not initially support. American juvenile pictures with such themes are usually set in reformatories or prisons. This comparison would be an interesting subject for extended treatment.

Alfred Weidenmann, mentioned previously as the author of *Jakko*, was the best-known name in films for and about children. He began his career with three such short pictures: *Kriegseinsatz der Jugend* (*War Effort of Youth*), (1940); *Soldaten von Morgen* (*Soldiers of Tomorrow*), (1941); and *Ausser Gefahr* (*Out of Danger*), (1942). Unfortunately, these titles do not seem to be available for analysis, but Weidenmann's two features, *Hände hoch!* (*Hands Up!*), (October 25, 1942), and *Junge Adler* (*Young Eagles*), (May 24, 1944), still exist. They are out of the chronological order of this chapter, but they are part of the story of the Nazi juvenile film and should therefore be discussed here.*

*Hände hoch!* was an adventure comedy about children evacuated from the cities and sent to a recreation camp in Slovakia. The film, although slight on story, was well made and has considerable charm. It belongs to the small group of films distributed by the Party and was shown in almost every German cinema. It won numerous prizes and awards was was well received.[9]

More important was *Junge Adler*, an Ufa production concerning the rehabilitation of the delinquent son of a rich airplane manufacturer through his work as a Hitler Youth laborer in his father's factory. The daily life of the boys was recorded with great skill, helped by the fine photography of Klaus von Rautenfeld. A particularly brilliant montage occurs as the boys go for a sport holiday on the beach, and the sequence ends with a beautifully designed tracking shot of the hero pulling his bicycle through the rising tide. The budget for this *Staatsauftragsfilm* (officially commissioned movie) was apparently large, an unusual condescension for juvenilia, and two such well-known actors as Willy Fritsch and Herbert Hübner were featured in the cast, as well as a very young Hardy Krüger.

The weakness of the film is its secondary story of a boy composer who has his work played by an orchestra in the airplane factory at the film's climax. However, Hans Otto Borgmann's music was catchy enough, particularly the boys' marching song. And unlike some of the

---

* A two-part film entitled *General Stift und seine Bande* (1937) and *Drops wird Flieger* (1938) makes the list more or less complete, but these pictures were not of feature length, and their contents and directors are unknown to me.

A lesson in airplane building from Alfred Weidenmann's *Junge Adler* (1944).

other juvenile films of the period, there is no sadism, no violence, and no histrionics. Although *Junge Adler* appeared too late to be of much practical propaganda value, it can be considered successful in its theoretical aim of providing stimulus for youth to work in war plants—assuming there was any choice in the matter.

Oddly enough, these films made for children and young people did not prove as popular with their intended audience as one might think. The standard study of films for youth published during the period, A. U. Sander's pedantic *Jugend und Film* (1944), has buried in the middle of its turgid text a remarkable section on film likes and dislikes of the junior audience. Inasmuch as criticism of Nazi films was out of the question for general publication, it comes as a shock to discover a list of the ten films most favored by students and the ten *least* liked, in addition to an extraordinary list of the reasons why some pictures were disliked.

Although it can be suspected that the candidates for consideration were rigged to some extent, the only film made for youth which can be found on the favored list is *Kadetten,* in tenth place! (The most popular were *Der grosse König, Bismarck, Die Entlassung, Friedrich Schiller, Heimkehr,* and *Ohm Krüger*—in that order.) Many fewer votes were tabulated on disliked films, but the headliner was the Heinz Rühmann air-propaganda comedy *Quax der Bruchpilot,* which will be discussed later. The other titles were mainly light comedies or musicals with little appeal to this age group, although it is surprising to find two Harry Piel (the "Douglas Fairbanks of Germany") features high on the hate list.

The reasons for disapproval are worth listing here:

      The film made no sense: 915 votes;

      The film was stupid: 768 votes;

      Implausible, unnatural: 591 votes;

      Dislike of title, without

        viewing the picture (!): 192 votes;

      Boring: 165 votes.[10]

The author does a great deal of pussyfooting in his text about how to explain his findings, but the numerical listings were there for the edification of anyone willing to read his book.

### III

The remaining political films of 1940–1941 contain some interesting examples of specialized propaganda.

Goebbels had a somewhat lunatic, if well-justified, obsession with the activities of fifth columnists, and pounded the message of spies on the homefront. One of the more successful essays on this theme was Arthur Maria Rabenalt's *Achtung! Feind hört mit! (Beware! The Enemy is Listening!)* (September 2, 1940). As the official program described the action:

After the critical September days of 1938, foreign espionage in Germany is picking up. Twice as many spies as in previous years are at work gathering data about the Kettwig factory which lies not far from the border. Old man Kettwig and his "Edison," Dr. Hellmers, are aware of the dangers of espionage and try to keep out foreign agents who pose as workers, engineers etc., to gain entrance to the factory. Hellmers has a young assistant, Inge Neuhaus, who seems to be much taken with the boss's son. But one day she meets a man who means more to her than Bernd Kettwig. He is an adventurer by the name of Faerber. She goes with him to Baden-Baden, accompanied by young Kettwig, who is soon having an affair with a girl named Lily, one of Faerber's friends. As it turns out, Faerber and Lily are foreign agents who try to get the secrets of the Kettwig factory. When Inge and Bernd realize what is happening they decide to turn their two lovers over to the German authorities. Faerber is forewarned and tries to escape in a plane but he is shot down and buried beneath the wreckage. Germany has proved its alertness toward foreign agents.[11]

Rabenalt was hardly at home in this kind of film, but obtained some good acting from Kirsten Heiberg as the spy Lily and René Deltgen as her accomplice.

The same director was far more suited to . . . *reitet für Deutschland* ( . . . *Riding for Germany*), (April 2, 1941), based on the biography of the famous horseman Freiherr von Langen. Injured on the Eastern front during World War I, von Langen is shown returning to a defeated Germany as an almost certain cripple. His estate is in ruins, and he stakes everything he has to take his horse to the Geneva International Steeple-Chase Competition. After months of vigorous training to overcome his disability, he becomes a great rider again and wins a surprise victory for Germany. (So much of a surprise that the band at the historic occasion didn't have the sheet music for the German national anthem.) The production values on the picture were first-rate throughout, with some unusually arty shots of the Russian countryside at the opening of the picture; the final racetrack sequence provided a foolproof climax. The picture is loaded with militarist and nationalist propaganda, but Rabenalt knew how to keep a story moving.

The film *Wunschkonzert* (*Request Concert*), (December 30, 1940), took its title from Germany's most popular radio show, which was broadcast every Sunday afternoon from 4 to 6 P.M. Numerous individual episodes provided an excuse for musical numbers by such favorite stars as Marika Rökk and Heinz Rühmann, and the rather messy story was held together by Eduard von Borsody, who was responsible for his own script. Made on a moderate budget without many name stars in the dramatic sections of the film, *Wunschkonzert* was an astonishing public success and was screened constantly throughout the war years. Unfortunately the picture contains a large dose of military propaganda of a peculiarly simple-minded variety.

The Gründgens-Göring association had gradually cooled to the point that the actor-director's protector allowed Goebbels to cast his highly valued personal star in a bit part in *Ohm Krüger*, over Gründgens' violent objections. What Göring and Goebbels must have thought of Gründgens' last directorial effort (until after World War II) has been variously recorded, but they were certainly not prepared for *Zwei Welten* (*Two Worlds*), (January 5, 1940). The script by Felix Lützkendorff showed the adventure of two boys and two girls working on a farm for the summer, and the conflict-of-generations theme. Under Gründgens' direction, the romantic quartet became peculiarly paired, with the two boys making eyes at one another throughout the film. To put it bluntly, the film was a clever homosexual charade designed to amuse those viewers who were tuned-in to the subliminal message. Since the director's proclivities were public knowledge, the cognoscenti included almost everyone who saw the picture. The girls were exceptionally homely, and cameraman Walter Pindter was obviously directed to give the two unknown male stars the full soft-focus treatment. Washing his hands of the film world, Gründgens requested permission for duty at the front, which was granted. *Zwei Welten* can not be revived (it contained a good deal of Nazi stomping and shouting), but it is certainly one of the strangest pictures made during the Third Reich.

Luis Trenker was also having trouble with Goebbels. *Der Feuerteufel* (*The Fire Devil*), (March 5, 1940), was his last film made during the Third Reich as a director in Germany. Another of Trenker's blood-and-thunder mountain adventure pictures, concerned with a popular revolt against Napoleon, *Der Feuerteufel* contained some material which Goebbels considered subversive. A scene showing an allegorical representation of the "Spirit of Freedom" was censored, but it was hard to know what to do with the passages involving Napoleon (Erich Ponto) in which some none-too-subtle parables were drawn with Hitler. After a short run, Goebbels banned the picture for domestic release but allowed it to be shown to soldiers at the front. Trenker was put on the blacklist and only allowed to act in inferior films, by other directors.

In Hans Bertram (b. 1906), Göring at last found a director capable of glorifying his Luftwaffe, previous efforts in this direction having failed for one reason or another. The rivalry between Goebbels and Göring may have had something to do with the situation, for the air-propaganda films before the start of the war were mainly low-budget adventure pieces using second- and third-rate technical talent. Goebbels was undoubtedly aware of the excellence of the American air spectacles and the inherent cinematic qualities of the genre. Only with the advent of the war and the need for propaganda in this direction did he allow major air films, both fictional and documentary, to be made.

Bertram was an ideal choice for the assignment. From 1927 to 1933 he was the advisor and organizer of the Chinese Naval Airforce in Amoy (Fukien). He made numerous world flights, and his first book, *Flug in die Hölle* (*Flight into Hell*), (1933), had sold 870,000 copies by 1951 and was translated into English in 1938. This was an account of his 1932–1933 Australian flight, which nearly ended in disaster. Thirteen of his books and screenplays were filmed, including the previously mentioned *Frauen für Golden Hill* (1938), *D III 88* (1939), and *Der Fuchs von Glenarvon* (1940).

Göring was particularly annoyed that *D III 88* had failed, and justly complained that the wrong director had been put on the project. He insisted that Bertram, who had already done second-unit direction on other pictures, be put in charge of the documentary *Feuertaufe* (*Baptism of Fire*), (1940), which recorded the role of the air force in the Polish campaign, much as Fritz Hippler's *Feldzug in Polen* (1940) concentrated on the role of the army. Both films were effective propaganda and widely shown abroad. Bertram's film is lighter in tone, and almost treats the air war as a game. The film is marred by Göring's insistence on a personal appearance to thank his air force at the end of the picture, but outside of this unfortunate sequence, *Feuertaufe* is a documentary almost in the Riefenstahl class.

The success of the documentary caused Goebbels to have second thoughts about Bertram, and allowed him a gigantic Tobis production entitled *Kampfgeschwader Lützow* (*Bomber Wing Lützow*), (February 28, 1941), which was a fictional treatment of the Polish campaign. Bertram's book was not particularly good, and the cast could hardly boast a major name, yet the film is one of the best directed, photographed, and scored propaganda pictures of the Third Reich. Norbert Schultze's music was particularly outstanding.

Whatever the faults of the book, there was plenty of action. The most famous episode is the rescue of a group of Volksdeutcher from their Polish captors, who are marching them down the road. The German airforce flies down and expertly machineguns the Poles while saving the prisoners. At the conclusion of the film, pilots were shown taking off to "future victories in England" as the text optimistically put it.

Yet even at this early date, the public was actively resisting war films. As Howard K. Smith described the reaction of the 1941 audiences:

Cinemas are not popular, principally for the reason that they do not take people's minds off war. Once the Nazi film dictators made the mistake of affording a very visible measure of what the public thinks of their propaganda films by opening a second rate comedy called the "Gas Man" [a Carl Froelich farce with Heinz Rühmann] at the Gloria-Palast on the Kurfürstendamm, while fifty yards away at the Ufa-Palast an extra, super-colossal one hundred and fifty per-cent war film, "Bomber Wing Lützow" was playing. The mediocre comedy played to packed houses at every presentation while the war film showed to a half-empty theatre. Unfortunately, even mediocre comedies have become rarities as war and propaganda films increase in number. The latter can be exhaustively described by a five letter word. They're lousy.[12]

If hard-core propaganda films on the air force were not selling tickets (and certainly not because of the technicians of *Lützow*), Goebbels tried the soft-sell approach. A fairly innocent comedy, *Quax, der Bruchpilot* (*Quax, the Crash Pilot*), (December 16, 1941), scripted by Robert Stemmle as a vehicle for Heinz Rühmann, concerned a silly young man who wanted to take up flying to impress his girl friend.

There are no uniforms in the private flying school, but the message to youth was clear—get out and learn to fly for your country on your own. As noted earlier, this picture, according to Sander's study, was the most disliked film among juvenile audiences. Nevertheless, it had a certain bumptuous charm, and was well directed by Kurt Hoffmann. Slightly cut, it is still being shown in Germany today.

From the first Nazi pictures in 1933, the story of Germans living abroad seeking to return to the fatherland proved a popular theme. Busy screenwriters recorded the plight of exiles stranded in China, Manchuria, Russia, Yugoslavia, Poland, and even by inference, in the United States. The earlier examples of this genre were usually set during World War I or in local revolutions of one kind or another, but with the outbreak of World War II the situation could be put across more strongly.

Of the new cycle, *Menschen im Sturm* (*Men in Struggle*), (December 12, 1941) has already been mentioned as the project concerning Yugoslavian Volksdeutsche forced on Fritz Peter Buch when one of his other films ran over budget. Despite an outstanding cast for this kind of picture and first-rate technical credits, the story of nice Germans and nasty Yugoslavs hardly drew crowds to the box office. The same could be said about *Wetterleuchten um Barbara* (*Summer Lightning on Barbara*), (October 17, 1941), directed by Werner Klingler as a Sybille Schmitz vehicle. The subject here was slightly different from the standard Volksdeutsche epic; the problem attacked was that of the annexation of Austria in 1938.

The definitive essay in the Germans-abroad direction was the Austrian epic *Heimkehr* (*Homecoming*), (October 10, 1941, premiere in Vienna) directed by Gustav Ucicky with Paula Wessely. As a wildly irresponsible propaganda vehicle, *Heimkehr* was rightly recognized as being in a class by itself, and was awarded the much-coveted "Film of the Nation" designation.

The story is set in Poland in the spring of 1939. The Poles are (understandably) suspicious and hostile of the German-speaking minority in their midst, particularly since this group continually spouts pro-German slogans. The trouble starts when the heroine and her friends go to see Jeanette MacDonald in *Maytime* at the local cinema, but arrive too early and are forced to endure a Polish newsreel which lauds the army. When the Polish national anthem is played on the sound track, something like mass hysteria grips the audience. Being good Germans at heart, the heroine and her companions refuse to stand up. Her husband, who has joined them, is murdered. On the way back from the cemetery, a small child puts out the eye of another German with a slingshot. As spring passes into summer, the hostility of the Poles increases, and with the outbreak of the war in September, the whole German colony is thrown into jail, which, in any rational analysis of their nationalist behavior, is exactly where they belong. They are locked in a cellar, where the Poles plan to kill them all by firing a machine gun at a blank wall and having the bullets ricochet into the group of men, women, and, of course, small children. But a brave German grabs the gun, and the bullets harmlessly strike elsewhere. Suddenly German planes bomb the town, and the prisoners escape.

The finale of the film has Paula Wessely give the following speech: "The time will one day come, when we shall live among Germans, and when one enters a store, no word of Yiddish or Polish will be spoken, but only the German tongue. We do not only live a German life, we also die a German death. And dead, we remain German." As Blobner and Holba observed, the full oration includes thirty-six compounds of the word "German."[13]

It is somewhat confusing that this anti-Polish, pro-German picture was made in Austria. In retrospect, the intention was probably to help justify the Anschluss to those recalcitrant Austrians who were unhappy over the event, and using the most famous of all Viennese actresses to state the message. Whatever the actual intent, the film is without doubt a classic of its type and has been excerpted in several postwar documentaries on Nazi Germany as a typical example of the Nazi film.

The discussion of the propaganda films of the 1940–1941 period would be incomplete without mention of a confusing picture, Wolfgang Liebeneiner's *Ich klage an!* (*I Accuse!*), (August 29, 1941), a feature on the subject of euthanasia.

The word "confusing" is used for the reason that, separated from the time and circumstances which produced the film, *Ich klage an!* takes on another aspect, and one must be careful here to separate the

Paul Hartman attempts to comfort his dying wife (Heidemarie Hatheyer) in Wolfgang Liebeneiner's euthanasia propaganda picture *Ich klage an!* (1941).

original intention behind the picture from the idea one gets from viewing it today.

The story is simple and well told. A doctor performs a mercy killing of his wife, a talented pianist, who is suffering from multiple sclerosis. He confides his crime to a friend, who betrays him to the police. During a lengthy court trial, which takes up a major part of the film, the views both for and against euthanasia are quite honestly examined. We have sympathy for the doctor in his plight, but at the end of the picture, the verdict is left to the spectator.

All of this sounds innocent enough today—indeed, there have been several Hollywood pictures along similar lines which stacked the deck far more in favor of euthanasia without anyone getting unduly excited —but the background to the picture is truly sinister.

Gerald Reitlinger in his study *The Final Solution* (1953) writes:

Himmler, who did not always try to avoid being a commonplace man, and who, as Count Ciano observed, "felt the pulse of the German people," had never been happy about it [the project of exterminating the mentally ill and physically incurable persons in special institutions set up for this purpose]. In December 1940 he had recommended Brack to suppress the Graefeneck Institute, writing that it was better to educate the public to euthanasia through films. Taking the hint, Viktor Brack persuaded the Tobis company in the summer of 1941 to produce the film, the sentimental story of a professor who is put on trial for hastening the death of his young wife, an incurable invalid.[14]

Further comment on the film can be found in François Bayle's horrifying *Croix gamée ou caducée* which reported in detail the February 1947 trials of "doctors" and others engaged in "medical research" of the most revolting variety:

> The population was made to approve of euthanasia through films such as *Ich klage an!* [15]. . . . Viktor Brack, the friend of Himmler, was the administrator of the project of euthanasia, claiming pity for invalids, but not unaware of the indignation of Vonyi and Martin Bormann. They resisted the exterminations, saying, "There is no merit in the name of euthanasia." [At his trial] Brack . . . interrupted [the prosecution] and said without modesty that the propaganda film *Ich klage an!* was a fine cinematic work and that they [the court] should view it in order to comprehend the mentality of himself and his kind. It tells of a doctor who hastens by a few hours the death of his wife who is doomed. There is a complete absence of mention of the reports of the extermination of the mentally ill, the mentally deficient children, and the other victims of euthanasia. The film does not line up with the actual facts. However, the film is not pure propaganda . . . . When the projection of the film was completed I asked the Judge [Sebring] what he thought. He told me in no uncertain words of the coarseness of Brack's group.[16]

The writing credits on the film do not shed much light on the matter. It is credited to one Eberhard Frowein and Harald Bratt ( a prolific writer of screenplays) on themes from the novel *Sendung und Gewissen* (*Mission and Conscience*) by Helmuth Unger and an "idea" by Herr Bratt. The director, Wolfgang Liebeneiner, was obviously selected for his skill in romantic drama rather than for any talents in the political film sphere; the leading actress was Heidemarie Hatheyer, a big name on the stage but known for only one film, and the rest of the cast, though of a generally high level, could not be considered of great box-office appeal. The film was far from a failure with audiences, but its appeal was limited to more intellectual viewers willing to sit through 126 minutes of almost constant dialogue. As propaganda for euthanasia it must be considered a failure, and as entertainment it was dubious at best.

### IV

If propaganda and cinematic artistry made strange bed-fellows, the nonpolitical films—which all too often had to resort to the costume-picture milieu—were more successful on the whole. As Louis Marcorelles remarked, "When the war came in 1939, the German cinema had attained a polish, a technical finesse and mastery capable of conquering the European and eventually the world market, and was at least assured of a struggle on equal terms with its rival across the Atlantic."[17]

Taking a break from political claptrap, Gustav Ucicky directed a splendid version of Alexander Pushkin's *Der Postmeister* (*The Postmaster*), (April 25, 1940), which is almost a model of literary adaptation. Favored with a sensitive script by Gerhard Menzel, and superb performances by Heinrich George, Hilde Krahl, and Siegfried Breuer, romantic camerawork by the veteran Hans Schneeberger, and a period score by Willy Schmidt-Gentner, the film has been in almost constant issue in Germany during and after the war.

The curious *Die Geierwally* (August 13, 1940) was an almost too-artistic effort by Hans Steinhoff to bring about a revival of the mystical mountain film. The simple story depended more on Richard Angst's camerawork than the talents of its large cast, but as an almost lone example of *l'art pour l'art* it fully deserves the good reputation it has gained in postwar German film histories.

Hans Schweikart's *Das Fräulein von Barnhelm* (*The Girl from Barnhelm*), (October 18, 1940), represented an exceptionally happy attempt to adapt a literary classic, in this case Lessing's comedy *Minna von Barnhelm*, to the screen. It is an attractive and sympathetic film, with a young cast full of enthusiasm for their roles. Despite the opportunities for propaganda inherent in the setting of the Seven Years' War, the battle scenes are effective and simple, and the sequences of returning troops pacifistic.

Equally delightful was Josef von Baky's *Annalie* (September 9, 1941), an affectionate comedy about a young girl who is always late, beginning with her birth. Luise Ullrich had a virtuoso assignment in playing the heroine in a period spanning more than fifty years, and did the job most capably except in the adolescent scenes where she is too old to convince.

After six minor films, von Baky at last had a subject worthy of his considerable talents, and the enormous success of the picture prompted Goebbels to select him to direct the biggest entertainment project of the Third Reich, *Münchhausen*. Although the final episode of *Annalie* was set in 1941 and contained a bit of propaganda (this was cut for later, postwar release of the film, and its absence passes unnoticed), the film avoided some obvious clichés, while adding a new one which is perhaps worthy of mention. In a tear-jerking sequence, the heroine (again too late) has reached her husband on the battlefield of World War I, only to have him die in her arms. She is unable to express her grief and is abruptly brought back to reality when a wounded soldier, unaware of the situation, asks her to light his cigarette for him. She does this in a moment worthy of Wyler at his best, and it still can bring an audience to instant tears.

Of the usual, semi-idiotic musical comedies, only one stands out, Geza von Bolvary's *Dreimal Hochzeit* (*Thrice Wed*), (June 24, 1941), which because of a Russian theme was banned almost immediately after release. The director made a creditable attempt to recreate the Hollywood musical, aided by Marte Harell and Willy Fritsch, experts in this genre. For a change the plot—about a Russian prince who tries to marry a commoner three times—had some witty and unusual touches, and a number of funny bits of dialogue.

Goebbels had ordered top priority given to research in color film, and by 1941, having abandoned the Siemens process for a number of reasons, had settled on the new Agfacolor. This type of film was far from perfect by the time the first feature was photographed, but the basic problem with Agfacolor remained constant: the difficulty of obtaining enough light to shoot indoor sequences properly and to match separate "takes" of the same scene, in which the colors varied with maddening lack of logic. Outdoors, Agfacolor could achieve remarkable results in bright sunlight. Unfortunately, it was not realized that the color dye system used would prove unstable; within a very few years the blues and yellows would begin to fade, and most existing prints of Nazi-period Agfacolor films are now in what looks like sepia.

The initial project was an Ufa production, *Frauen sind doch bessere Diplomaten*, (*Women are the Best Diplomats*) a dreadful 1848–period musical directed by Georg Jacoby with the popular singers Marika Rökk and Willy Fritsch in the leads. Veit Harlan was present at the preview for Goebbels, and gleefully recounted to me the propaganda minister's reaction—most of the comments unprintable here—culminating in a near apoplectic order to "take this shitty mess out of my screening room and burn it." The picture was premiered on Halloween of 1941 but almost immediately withdrawn when audiences expressed their disapproval in equally blunt terms. The Agfacolor researchers went back to the laboratory with Harlan in tow, the director having promised Goebbels that the next color film would be better or he could "have his head." Harlan was quick to learn the limitations of the new color process, and his *Die goldene Stadt* (*The Golden City*), (1942), showed that under proper conditions Agfacolor could be quite pleasing.

To close this chapter, mention should be made of the German-Swiss coproduction *Michelangelo* (March 15, 1940), a superb documentary on the life and works of the artist, directed by Curt Oertel. This picture was released in the United States in 1950 as *The Titan* by Robert Flaherty, who reedited the footage and prepared an English commentary, while being vague about the original source of his materials. For this reason the film is usually referred to as a Flaherty film, which it is not. Credit is long overdue to Oertel, whose techniques have had an enormous effect on subsequent films of this type made for both the commercial cinema and television.

# 1942-1945: FILMS IN TWILIGHT

The final period of the Nazi film industry reflected the increasing seriousness of war conditions. Although the doctrine of "total war" was not put forward until 1943, by 1942 the general situation already demanded cutbacks in production, changes in subject matter, increased censorship of completed pictures—all manifestations of the beginning of the end.

In February of 1942, Goebbels completed the last major section of his over-all plan to reorganize the film industry. Distribution, previously handled by the individual companies, was put under a central agency, the *Deutsche Filmvertriebs-Gesellschaft m.b.H.*, usually referred to by its abbreviation DFV.

It is worth noting that feature film production figures for the period, breaking the product down, roughly, into categories:

|  | 1942 | 1943 | 1944 | 1945 |
|---|---|---|---|---|
| Drama | 31 | 31 | 34 | 32 |
| Comedy | 15 | 39 | 29 | 29 |
| Musical | 7 | 10 | 9 | 10 |
| Documentary | 3 | 2 | 1 | 1 |
| Biographical | 8 | 2 | 2 | 0 |
| TOTAL | 64 | 83 | 75 | 72 |

The figures cited for 1945 include pictures completed after the end of the war as well as films which were started and abandoned at some stage of production.

The number of propaganda vehicles, based on postwar censorship bans was: 1942:19; 1943:13; 1944:8; 1945:6. This is interesting in that it indicates the increasing number of entertainment films that the public demanded and the decrease in propaganda pictures which Goebbels was willing to budget. However, this interpretation is somewhat misleading, because the newsreels, which were strongly propagandistic, continued their political message, as did the many short features.

The first DFV release catalogue for 1942–1943[1] (again using, apparently, the July–June figures, rather than January–December count cited above) breaks down the full release schedule by company:

| | |
|---|---|
| Bavaria | 8 films |
| Berlin-Film | 8 films |
| Prague-Film | 3 films |
| Terra | 11 films |
| Tobis | 12 films |
| Ufa | 12 films |
| Wien-Film (Vienna) | 6 films |
| TOTAL | 60 films |

Of the announced films, all but two were completed, although several were finished and not released because of censorship.

In addition, the catalogue listed 72 *Kulturfilme* (short subjects), nine of which made in color by Ufa, on various themes ranging from propaganda to travelogues. Twelve foreign pictures were also released in German versions, three from Italy (including Rossellini's *The White Ship*), and nine from the Nazi-controlled Continental-Film Studios in Paris.

These French pictures were a constant annoyance to Goebbels, mainly because their quality was so much higher than the German product made at the same time. He recorded in his diaries for May of 1942 some thoughts on the matter:

I took a look at another French movie, *Annette et la Dame Blonde* [directed by Henri Decoin]. It is of the same levity and elegance as the Darrieux movie, *Caprices* [directed by Leo Joanon, 1941]. We shall

have to be careful about the French so that they won't build up a new
moving-picture art under our leadership which will give us too serious
competition in the European market. I shall see to it that especially
trained French film actors are gradually engaged for the German
movie (May 13, 1942).[2]

In the evening we viewed a new motion picture produced by our
Continental Gesellschaft in Paris after a scenario written around the
life and activity of Hector Berlioz. The film is of excellent quality and
amounts to first-class national fanfare. I shall unfortunately not be
able to release it for public showing. I am very angry that our own
offices in Paris are teaching the French how to represent nationalism
in pictures. This lack of political insight can hardly be beaten. . . . I
ordered Greven [Paris representative of the Propaganda Ministry] to
come to Berlin from Paris, to give him absolutely clear and unmis-
takable directives to the effect that for the moment, as far as the
French are concerned, only light, frothy, and, if possible, corny pictures are desired. No doubt the French people will be satisfied with
that too. There is no reason why we should cultivate their nationalism
(May 15, 1942).[3]

In the afternoon I had a long argument with Hippler and with
Greven about the aims to be pursued in our French film production.
Greven has an entirely wrong technique in that he has regarded as
his task to raise the level of the French movie. That is wrong. It isn't
our job to supply the Frenchmen with good pictures and it is especially
not our task to give them movies that are beyond reproach in their
nationalistic tendency. If the French people are on the whole satisfied
with light, corny stuff, we ought to make it our business to produce
such trash. It would be a case of lunacy for us to promote competition
against ourselves. We must proceed in our movie policies as the Americans do in their policies towards the North and South American con-
tinents. We must become the dominating movie power on the
European continent. Insofar as pictures are produced in other countries, they must be only of a local or limited character. It must be our
aim to prevent so far as possible the founding of any new national
film industry, and if necessary to hire for Berlin, Vienna, or Munich
such stars and technicians as might be in a position to help in this.
After I talked to him for a long time Greven realized the wisdom of
this course and will pursue it in the future (May 19, 1942).[4]

To an extent, Goebbels managed to cut the quality of French pictures
made under the occupation, but he had little luck in luring French
actors to Germany, with the exception of Harry Baur. This great

Harry Baur celebrates a musical triumph in his last film, Hans Bertram's *Symphonie eines Lebens* (1943).

performer was cast in the lead of Hans Bertram's *Symphonie eines Lebens* (*Symphony of a Life*), one of the genuine curiosities of the era. Produced at Tobis on a gigantic budget, the film boasted not only Baur, but a nonstop musical score lasting about 88 minutes composed by Norbert Schultze. The story concerned the life of a composer, which is shown in flashback as his symphony is performed for the first time. The film is pedantic and boring, and the music is an insufferable mixture of neo-Bruckner and Richard Strauss at their worst, compounded by choral passages of the greatest banality. The picture was passed by the censor in mid-November of 1942. Shortly thereafter, it was discovered that Baur's racial papers were not in order; indeed, a Jew had been allowed the leading role in a Nazi-financed extravaganza! The unfortunate actor was put in a concentration camp and eventually executed. If dates are to be trusted, it would seem that Goebbels, in one of his most cynical gestures, had the film released the day after Baur's death, on April 21, 1943. Business was business, and the film cost too much to keep it on the shelf.

Goebbels' wrath was not limited to French films; a good American picture could also send him into a true rage, even if his fellow-

countrymen were denied seeing it. The following entry from his diary
is especially revealing.

All motion picture producers visited me. In the evening we see the
American Technicolor picture *Swanee River*, which affords me an
opportunity for making a number of observations on the creation of a
new German film based on folk-songs. The fact of the matter is that
the Americans have the ability of taking their relatively small stock of
culture and by a modernized version to make it something that is very
*à propos* for the present time. We are loaded down with altogether
too much tradition and piety. We hesitate to clothe our cultural heritage in a modern dress. It therefore remains purely historical or
museum-like and is at best understood by groups within the Party,
the Hitler Youth, or the Labor Service. The cultural heritage of our
past can be rendered fruitful to the present on a large scale only if
we present it with modern means. The Americans are masters of this
sort of thing, I suppose, because they are not weighted down as much
as we are with historical ballast. Nevertheless we shall have to do
something about it. The Americans have only a few Negro songs, but
they present them in such a modern way that they conquer large parts
of the modern world which is, of course, very fond of such melodies.
We have a much greater fund of cultural goods, but we have neither
the artistry nor the will to modernize them. That will have to be
changed (May 3, 1942).[5]

The month of May, 1942, in which all entries cited above were
penned, marked the start of the British bombing raids on German
cities. These would, in time, cripple the Nazi film industry to such an
extent that production in many cases had to be moved to Prague,
Amsterdam, Budapest, and Rome.

One of Goebbels' pet projects of the period was the formation
of something called the International Moving Picture Association, a
protective group designed to insure that German films would dominate
European screens. To his chagrin, both Sweden and Switzerland refused to cooperate. Goebbels' diaries record his irritation on this
matter:

I saw the new American propaganda movie, *Foreign Correspondent*.
It is a first-class production, a criminological bang-up hit, which no
doubt will make a certain impression upon the broad masses of the

people in enemy countries. Significantly enough this film, with its absolutely anti-German tendency, was allowed to run for months in Sweden. The Swedes and the Swiss are playing with fire. Let us hope they will burn their fingers before the war is over (January 22, 1942).[6]

Sweden and Switzerland still haven't formally joined the International Moving Picture Association. I am now having these two states boycotted by not supplying them with raw materials. They will soon begin to feel the effects of acting in such an aloof way (April 23, 1942).[7]

Switzerland has recalled her representative in the International Motion Picture Association. It looks as though this stinking little country is trying to provoke the International Motion Picture Association. I am going to insist that the Association respond with a general boycott (May 7, 1942).[8]

In the evening I saw a Bolshevik propaganda picture, *One Day in the Soviet Union*. This movie is a first-class piece of agitation, although anyone who really knows conditions can easily contradict it. Undoubtedly it will be effective in neutral and enemy countries, as it was cleverly adapted to their mentality. It seems rather significant to me that this picture is running in Sweden with Swedish subtitles. That's how low the so-called Nordic States have sunk (March 4, 1943).[9]

Goebbels' organization and boycott of nonmembers both failed, but by 1943 he had more important things on his mind. On February 13, 1943, he gave his famous speech in the Sportpalast calling for total war on all fronts, the film world included. Stalingrad had proved a catastrophe for the German armies the month before. Goebbels was no fool and saw the seriousness of the situation far more clearly than most of those around him. It was his job to inform the German public of the Russian disaster without alarming them more than necessary, yet enough to increase popular zeal for the war. Newsreels of the period are of extraordinary interest in demonstrating his attempts in this direction, and it is hoped that they will be properly analyzed sometime in the future.

## II

The last six films Veit Harlan made under the Third Reich are of interest: *Pedro soll hängen* (*Pedro Must Hang*), (July 11, 1941); *Der grosse König* (*The Great King*), (March 3, 1942);

*Die goldene Stadt* (*The Golden City*), (November 24, 1942); *Immensee*, (December 17, 1943); *Opfergang* (*Sacrifice*), (December 8, 1944); and *Kolberg*, (January 30, 1945). Together, they form a curious sextet reflecting all aspects of this director's relationship to the Nazi regime.

Harlan referred to *Pedro soll hängen* as his "great, sad film," and regarded it as his masterpiece, telling me that it was the one film for which he would like to be remembered. Finished in the fall of 1939—before *Jud Süss*—its release was held up by the censors, who cut it down to a running time of barely sixty-eight minutes. Some of the missing footage was restored when the picture was rereleased in the early 1950's. It is unlike anything else in Harlan's work, and stands apart from other Nazi-era pictures as well because of the religious theme as originally filmed, plus the emphasis on human values.

The story takes place in a small Central American banana republic, where things are in a bad way. The United States has criticized the country's laws for their moral laxity, and the councilmen of the capital city decide that "the next man in town will be hanged for America." That man is a simple drunken waiter named Pedro (Heinrich George) who, despite his weakness for the bottle, is a profoundly Christian man.

In an impressive ceremony in which candles are extinguished one by one, he is condemned to death. But he states to the jury that his hope of immortality is sustained in the forthcoming birth of his mistress' child—"this is my eternity" he affirms in a moving speech.

Suddenly, an American woman arrives in an airplane and offers $90,000 for Pedro's life, after hearing the story of his arrest and trial. This sets up a beautifully written scene in which the town's sudden new crisis is discussed almost word for word from the dialogues of Socrates as reported by Plato. The town's dilemma is finally straightened out of some unusual arguments based on classical logic, and poor Pedro is freed.

At least this is the story the film was supposed to tell. Due to the numerous cuts made by the censor in the original negative on Goebbels' orders, Harlan had to shoot an entirely new ending to have the film make any sense at all, but he could not fill in the puzzling gaps in the narrative. Goebbels resented in particular the religious scenes and cut them along with a childbirth sequence crucial to the story.

If *Pedro soll hängen* presented religious censorship problems, Harlan's next film, *Der grosse König*, a biography of Frederick the Great, ran into historical censorship of an unusual variety. The director was not particularly interested in making yet another Fredericus movie and was even more annoyed when he was ordered on the project after making considerable preparations for a biography of Beethoven with Werner Krauss. As an alternative, he suggested the *Agnes Bernauer* film mentioned previously, but Goebbels could not be dissuaded, claiming that Hebbel's romance *cum* witchcraft drama should stay on the stage. As a reward for another Frederick picture, he held out the coveted project of remaking the *Nibelungen*, which apparently did not interest Harlan.

*Der grosse König*, with a script by Harlan and a cast including the usual Frederick, Otto Gebühr (replacing, on Hitler's direct order, the stubborn Werner Krauss), Kristina Söderbaum, Gustav Fröhlich, and Paul Wegener went ahead at enormous cost. It was one of the most lavish films of the Third Reich, with multitudes of extras and a battle sequence involving 5,000 horses. To Harlan's surprise, Goebbels viewed the completed picture and immediately banned it, turning it over to an equally mystified Emil Jannings, who was ordered, according to Harlan, to cut the print in line with the propaganda minister's directions. Jannings pleaded overwork, and the movie was consigned to the vaults.

Three days after the start of the war with Russia, Harlan was called to Goebbels' office and told that the film was to be released with some additional footage and editing. The character of the Russian general Chernichev, shown as a friend of Frederick, had to be removed, or at least altered. Goebbels apologized to Harlan that he had been forced to ban the film without explanation, but could not earlier reveal to him changes in the Russian policy. When Harlan remonstrated on grounds of authenticity, Goebbels remarked, according to Harlan, "Never mind, we'll change history."

The role of Chernichev was played by Paul Wegener, and when

told of Goebbels' decision, Harlan recalled that he "laughed so hard
the lights went out." Wegener demanded and received overtime wages
and told Harlan to tell "Mickey Mouse" (Goebbels) that he could
have anything he wanted as long as he paid for it. The extra scenes
were shot and the film was released with enormous popular approval.
With *Die goldene Stadt*, it was one of the most widely seen of all
Nazi pictures.

As history, the film is pure trash, and it is saved from dullness only
by the remarkably elaborate battle sequences. The problem of what
to do with the Chernichev character was finally solved by a narrator
who conveniently explained some scenes to the properly confused
viewer. In the palace of the Queen of Poland, Frederick finds docu-

Frederick the Great (Otto Gebühr, on white horse) rides again
in Veit Harlan's ambitious spectacle *Der grosse König* (1942).

ments which prove Poland's cooperation with Paris and London against him. The Russians have become Frederick's allies only in order to stab him in the back. After a great defeat, Frederick asks his commanders what he should do. They advise him to make peace. The following lines then occur:

*Frederick*: Capitulate? I take over the supreme command. We shall fight again! Whoever is afraid to accompany me may go home.
*Commentator in the Film* (following on these words): Frederick wages his wars not for the sake of war but from a historical necessity. Everyone knows that this great statesman would prefer to serve his people in peaceful work, that this great artist on the throne would prefer to stay with his beloved art than to carry out the cruel handicraft of murderous war.[10]

If Hitler saw himself as a reincarnation of Frederick, he had better luck than Mussolini, who had entered into a deal with the German film industry to write his own screenplay on the subject of Julius Caesar, to be made in late 1942. History prevented this project from being completed.

The second Agfacolor feature was *Die goldene Stadt*, based on a play by the Austrian dramatist Richard Billinger, *Der Gigant* (1937). Billinger was one of the few quality writers of the era, concerned with the plight of modern peasants and the breakthrough of paganism. The idea of the City (the "Giant" of the play's title) is usually portrayed in his works as a hostile force destroying those drawn to it from the country.

*Der Gigant* had to undergo some alterations to fit it in with propaganda lines. The family, German in the original, had its villainous members converted to Czechs. And the heroine had to commit suicide because she had committed the sin of race defilement. With Kristina Söderbaum in the lead, the method was obvious: drowning, as usual.

*Die goldene Stadt* became the story of a young German girl who resists the control of her father (Eugen Klöpfer). He wishes to keep her on their farm in a German-speaking area of Czechoslovakia from which her mother had fled many years before. But she falls in love with a visiting surveyor and flees to Prague, the all-devouring Golden City.

She cannot find him and goes to live at the house of her mother's sister, where her unruly cousin (Kurt Meisel) also dwells. She is seduced and forsaken by the young man, who marries a rich older woman. Ruined and alone, she returns to the farm where her father, who has just taken a second wife, refuses to speak to her. Broken-hearted, she goes to her mother's grave—in a swamp—and kills herself with the words, "Forgive me, father, for not having loved my native country as much as you did!"

The film has dated greatly, and seems today to be rather on the corny side. But at the time of its release it was an enormous success, both in and out of Germany. In Helsinki it ran for three years in the same cinema.

The most notable feature of *Die goldene Stadt* is the color, even judging it from the faded prints which survive. True to his word, Harlan worked for six months with the Agfacolor researchers to try to improve the process. It was decided to shoot as much as possible of the film outdoors, and to use Prague, an exceptionally beautiful city, for many backgrounds. As Harlan stated his views on the color-film: "The color film represents a complete artistic revolution. Although we have been able to photograph in color for some time, only the painter, so far, has been able to *think* and to express himself in color. . . . Our own awareness of color is stifled; we look at the world in daylight without considering its color."[11]

As a reward for the film, Goebbels allowed Harlan to make his next picture, *Immensee*, without interference. It is based on the classic novel by Theodor Storm and was selected by Harlan because, as he said to me, he wished to reflect in his picture his love for his wife. As Marcorelles described it, "*Immensee* is a film of peace and love. Its love story, filmed in the countryside where Storm himself lived, reflects the director's pagan and brutal lyrical streak. With Kristina Söderbaum in the leading role, *Immensee* conveys a strong feeling for nature and a fervent idyllic mood."[12]

This fifth color picture follows Storm's book only slightly, and is without propaganda content. It concerns a young girl torn between the love of two men, a music student and the master of a great estate. She prefers the former, but when they are separated by his travels, she marries his rival. The student returns a great conductor and begs his former sweetheart to leave her husband; the landowner, seeing the strength of their love, is prepared to renounce his own happiness. But she remains faithful to her husband, even after his death. If Goebbels had ordered a film extolling the purity of love and marriage, he could not have found anything better, and the film is still successful. It has been frequently revived and its original power remains undiminished.

*Opfergang*, based on R. G. Binding's popular novel, was also in color, and continues the romantic tradition. A young married man feels tied down by his wife and job, and returns to Hamburg, where he finds his old sweetheart still living next door to his old house. His wife realizes his feelings and resolves to help him as best she can. When she discovers that her rival's child, boarded elsewhere in the city, is in danger of an epidemic raging in the quarter, she prevails on her husband to rescue the child. He does so, but is himself infected. The child's mother is dying and when her former lover can no longer visit her, the faithful wife disguises herself as her husband and brings her comfort in her last moments. Before she dies, the sick woman writes a letter telling the sick man of his wife's sacrifices. At last he realizes her true worth and they are reunited.

The film was beautifully acted by Kristina Söderbaum, Irene von Meyendorff, and Carl Raddatz, photographed in remarkable color by Bruno Mondi, using the book's original locations. Harlan later said that he was astounded when the film was held up almost thirteen months after completion before it could be released; Goebbels was evasive about the reasons, and admitted to Harlan that he screened the film for his own enjoyment numerous times, and even repeated to the director an entire dialogue passage culminating in the words, "How long can this all last?"

Before the picture could be made, some plot changes had to be concocted, for the book was considered propaganda for possible desertion by soldiers. And Hitler himself said that a woman who destroyed a marriage must die—at least in books, plays and films produced in the Third Reich. Harlan said he was never satisfied with the required ending, which he regarded as "semisurrealist" and absurd, but thought he had solved the problems to the satisfaction of the censor.

According to Harlan, Goebbels began to show signs of a mental breakdown as the war turned against the Germans. A scene with a rainbow in *Opfergang* had a deep effect on him, and his talk turned more and more toward death. On one occasion he told Harlan that he was sure of going to heaven, for his favorite adjutant had just died and was preparing a place for him. These increasing confidences terrified the director, who was trying to get his wife and children out of Germany to Sweden, but Goebbels was not through with him as yet. As *Opfergang* waited for release, Goebbels put him on the biggest production ever made in Germany, *Kolberg*, designed as the Nazi answer to *Gone With the Wind* and *War and Peace*. It was the most insane project of a man on the verge of madness, a final monument to the folly and false grandeur of the Third Reich. *Kolberg* was to be Goebbels' cinematic testament, his celluloid warning to Germans of the future. It made no difference if the cost would virtually bankrupt the entire film industry, if thousands of soldiers were transferred from the front as extras. The film would be made before Goebbels' death, and nothing was allowed to stand in the way.

The film had been in preliminary planning stages as early as 1941, at the same time as *Der grosse König*, but had been shelved when Hitler personally ordered a film on the recent battle of Narvik in Norway. A script was prepared, but *Narvik* never got started, outside of some location work. The British announced, when they received word of the film, that they would never allow it to be made. Their threat to blow up the port if necessary alarmed Göring, who argued successfully that it was hardly worthwhile to divert sections of his forces in order to protect a movie company.

The production of *Kolberg*, the final Nazi film, is recounted at the close of this chapter.

### III

The two other major Nazi directors, Karl Ritter and Hans Steinhoff, continued their careers as the favored spokesmen of the regime. But apparently both men began to feel that it was time to start a gradual change in the subject matter of their films, just in case things did not turn out as expected.

Ritter, who in a good year could complete three propaganda vehicles, began to slow down, finishing only two more such epics: *G.P.U.* (August 14, 1942) and *Besatzung Dora* (*The Crew of the Dora*), (completed late 1943).

The former film was in the familiar mold, with a young girl joining the G.P.U. (Russian secret police) in order to betray them because of the murder of her family. The action jumps in the Ritter tradition of short incidents, from Riga to Sweden, Holland, France, and Russia. Instead of the usual decadent Englishmen, the audience is presented with the evil Russians, under the leadership of a Jewish agent named Spiegelglass. The height of decadence is suggested by a party in a Russian embassy, complete with Negro jazz band. The action is fast and furious: in the first reel someone is blown up by a bomb placed in an innocent-looking package, and the violence never ceases. The only interesting sequence, from a documentary point of view, is the performance of a cabaret number by Lale Andersen, the popularizer of the song "Lili Marlene." The technical work is less slap-dash than usual and the acting considerably above Ritter's usual low level.

*Besatzung Dora* was completed but never released, and I was unable to locate a print for appraisal. According to Blobner and Holba, "Here, too, human conflict and rivalry over a girl are set aside and forgotten through a united and successful trial of comradeship—an emergency landing in the desert."[13] It would appear that this is the only feature film which had as its setting the African front in 1942. In any case, it was banned by the Nazi censor for undisclosed reasons.

Ritter's last Nazi-era picture was *Sommernächte* (*Summer Nights*), (June 26, 1944), an idiotic comedy of mistaken identity in a resort community, using, with the exception of René Deltgen, a virtually unknown cast. The director was already reading the writing on the wall and making plans for his escape from Germany.

The final works of Hans Steinhoff include two major biographical films, *Robert Koch* (1939), completed before the ambitious *Ohm Krüger*, and *Rembrandt* (June 17, 1942). The Koch epic, based on the life of the proponent of the theory of germs as a cause of illness, and pioneer fighter against tuberculosis, was not as innocent as it seems on paper. A major part of the picture is devoted to the conflict between Koch (Emil Jannings) and Geheimrat Virchow (Werner Krauss). The script was based on an "idea" by Dr. Paul Cremers and Gerhard Menzel, both loyal propagandists for the regime, and stressed the perfidy of Virchow, whose name indicated his less-than-pure German blood. Outside of this political claptrap, which in this case is rather subtly introduced, the film moves with a stately grandeur not out of keeping with its subject matter. The tuberculosis germs are even shown in a two-color insert.

*Rembrandt* (June 17, 1942) was based on a biography of the artist by one V. Tornius, who stressed the conflict of a single-minded genius against the hostile forces of the painter's daily environment. It shows Rembrandt (Ewald Balser) as a spendthrift much in love with his wife. When she dies, she leaves him their house on the condition that he not marry again. His housekeeper (brilliantly played by Elisabeth Flickenschildt) hopes he will marry her, but when the painter falls in love with another servant, she brings action against him. The other woman has a child and dies; the creditors foreclose on the luckless man, and he is left broken and alone.

The film has little in common with the better-known Alexander Korda production made in England in 1936 with Charles Laughton. In that film, one is conscious of Laughton the actor *playing* Rembrandt, but Balser was a far more subtle artist and managed to delve deeply into the psychology of the painter. The theme of frustrated genius (German or not) was popular with writers who did not forget the early problems of Hitler as an artist and Goebbels as a novelist, but *Rembrandt* managed to sidestep some obvious propaganda pitfalls. The only objectionable scene shows two Jewish moneylenders.

The beauty of the film is due to Richard Angst's stunning camerawork, which makes the best of Walter Roehrig's handsome sets. No expense was spared on the production, which moved from the Ufa to Amsterdam and the Hague. The leading art forger of the period was released from prison to paint the "Rembrandts" used in the picture, and Angst vividly recalls watching him paint in the evening after the blackout, surrounded by candles. With the aid of several assistants, "The Night Watch" was recreated overnight in order to meet a deadline. Rather than attempting to show the subjects of Rembrandt's

Director Hans Steinhoff during production of *Rembrandt* (1942). (Photograph by Richard Angst).

work with live actors in the Hollywood manner, Angst and Roehrig more often concentrated on the recreation of period detail. There is an outstanding sequence of burghers bowling, using lighted candles as pins, to cite but one example.

Throughout the production, the cast and crew fought a running battle with Steinhoff, who was notoriously lacking a sense of humor. Roehrig, a famous practical joker, was at the bottom of most of the schemes against the director. When the company was in Amsterdam, Roehrig had an enormous nude statue in the hotel lobby removed, and when told that Steinhoff was returning, took off all his clothes and stood on the pedestal. Steinhoff was not amused.

Steinhoff's next project was *Gabriele Dambrone* (November 11, 1943), adapted from a play by Richard Billinger. But Steinhoff did not have the success that Harlan had in adapting one of the same author's works for *Die goldene Stadt*. The theme is once again the evil effects of city life on a girl from the country, this time a seamstress who wants a career in the theatre. Yet the film is convincing because of an excellent cast including Gusti Huber, Siegfried Breuer, Ewald Balser, and Eugen Klöpfer.

Another Billinger drama was the source of *Melusine*, Steinhoff's last completed film, banned by the Nazi censor in December of 1944 and released only after the war. The reason for the ban would appear to be on grounds of morality, as the drama concerns a man who falls in love with two women, unaware they are mother and daughter. The rather peculiar "happy ending" finds the hero married to the daughter, with the mother standing by; as the synopsis puts it, "Relieved, the young engineer recognizes the wisdom with which fate granted his love double happiness."[14] I have been unable to locate a copy of the film for analysis of exactly how Steinhoff treated this touchy subject.

As the war was coming to a close, Steinhoff at last realized his dream to make an elaborate color picture, *Shiva und die Galgenblume* (*Shiva and the Gallows Flower*), apparently a mystery film with Hans Albers. Because of the bombing of the German studios, the picture was made in Prague, where most of the color apparatus had been moved. When the film was about three-quarters completed, the Russians were virtually on the outskirts of the city. Steinhoff was highly regarded by the Nazi hierarchy, having served the regime faithfully since the days of *Hitlerjunge Quex* in 1933. Two SS men suddenly appeared on the set and escorted the director to a waiting airplane which was to take him to safety in Germany. He was never heard of again. The most commonly held belief was that he and his companions were shot down near Luckenwalde although apparently his body was never found. Other unfounded rumors reported he escaped with false papers. He was sixty-three when he vanished.

### IV

A more horrible fate was meted out to Herbert Selpin, whose earlier films have been discussed in some detail elsewhere in these pages. Although he directed one great film, *Heiratsschwindler* (1938), the majority of his work was capable without being particularly inspired or unusual.

Great success came to him because of his collaboration with Hans Albers in a series of five consecutive pictures, three comedies and two adventure pieces: *Sergeant Berry* (1938); *Wasser für Canitoga* (*Water for Canitoga*) (March 10, 1939); *Ein Mann auf Abwegen* (*A Man*

*Astray*) (February 16, 1940); *Trenck, der Pandur* (August 23, 1940); and *Carl Peters* (March 21, 1941).

During the period, Albers was with little question the most popular actor in Germany. Although Goebbels detested him because of his refusal to abandon his Jewish love (who was safe in London) and even more so because of his sharp business practices and even sharper sarcastic comments about the personalities of the regime, he was too big a personality to punish. As long as the actor took part in a propaganda vehicle now and then, the authorities were willing to look the other way as far as his political indiscretions were concerned.

Selpin was probably Albers' favorite director. Selpin's widow claims that both men despised the regime and enjoyed each other's company, especially at gargantuan drinking bouts. On the screen, Selpin would give Albers virtually complete freedom to depart from the script, and the two would improvise bawdy and often off-color moments placed in the innocent plot framework. Most of the time the censor let them pass.

Their first collaboration, *Sergeant Berry*, has been discussed elsewhere in these pages. *Wasser für Canitoga* was an adventure drama set in Canada at the turn of the century. The plot is complicated, defying rational synopsis, but culminates in Albers salvaging a caisson from the work of a saboteur, killing himself in the monumental effort. In between various deeds of derring-do Albers sings the famous song "Good-bye, Jonny" and drops the usual number of lewd asides.

*Ein Mann auf Abwegen* had Albers playing a Swedish millionaire named Percy who decides to visit the countryside incognito. He has numerous adventures, and the film is best remembered for a funny nude swimming sequence. There is also a great moment in which Albers plays a swing number on a huge pipe organ. The picture is better organized than most Albers-Selpin collaborations, with a coherent plot line and excellent secondary performers.

*Trenck, der Pandur*, although superficially a political biography, emerged as a clumsy and tasteless comedy with Albers out of control. Even Sybille Schmitz is terrible, mugging as runaway royalty and speaking her lines in an unbelievable Viennese accent. Despite the big budget and name players, it can be regarded as Selpin's worst film.

*Carl Peters* was hardly much better, being a wildly inaccurate biography of the nineteenth-century German colonialist who obtained large parts of Africa for his country in spite of lack of cooperation for his schemes at home. The film shows Peters as a benign bearer of Western virtues to the ignorant natives, although the historical Peters was relieved of his position of *Reichskommissar* because of his harsh treatment of the Africans. In the picture, this charge is brought against him by the false evidence of a Negro bishop in the pay of the British secret service.

*Carl Peters* was a box-office failure, despite Albers and a lavish production. Selpin was not particularly at home in this material and his disinterest in the story is painfully evident. The only scenes with any sparkle occur at the London "Piccadilly Club" where the infamous British agents are shown on their home ground, talking in English with German subtitles. With this film, Albers and Selpin came to the parting of ways.

In 1936, Selpin had met the screenwriter Walter Zerlett-Olfenius, a capable craftsman but also a fanatic Nazi. He scripted many of Selpin's films, and gradually managed to steer both their careers into the dangerous waters of the political propaganda genre, where Zerlett-Olfenius found himself at home.

With political control almost eliminating any personal expression at the studios, and Selpin now firmly entrenched in a genre of picture-making he despised, the director became increasingly morose, drinking heavily. However, he was greatly liked by his colleagues, who called him "hedgehog" due to his short stature and bristly working manner.

In 1941, Selpin was ordered to direct *Geheimakte W.B.1.* (*Secret Paper W.B.1.*), (January 26, 1942), a biography of the German inventor Wilhelm Bauer who perfected the first submarine. It was an enormously expensive film, but Selpin's talents seemed to work in inverse proportion to the amount of money given to his movies. The script of this epic, again by Zerlett-Olfenius, was awful, filled with long verbal explanations of submarine-building, and loaded with political references to the espionage activities of the British and the double-dealings of the Russians.

Trimmed down to its essentials, the plot shows Bauer at the court of the king of Bavaria, where he is able to finish his invention and

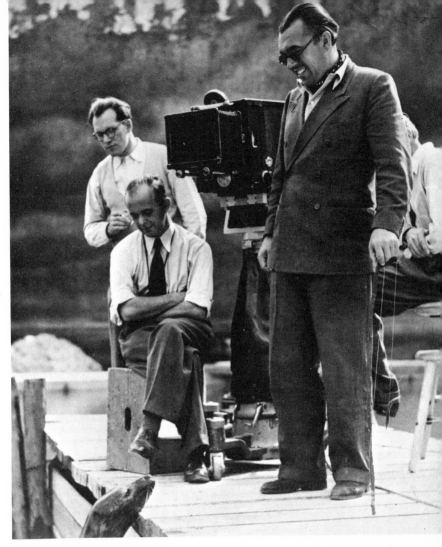

Herbert Selpin (right) and cameraman Franz Koch (seated) admire a seal during location work on *Geheimakte W.B.1.*, summer 1941.

test it in the Chiemsee, where he also demonstrates the techniques of underwater firing. Later experiments are sabotaged by a British agent, and Bauer accepts the invitation of the Grand Duke Constantine to continue his research at the Russian port of Kronstadt. All goes well until war breaks out in Germany, and Bauer and his workmen are refused permission to return to the fatherland. In an exciting finale, they board their improved submarine and break through the harbor gates. Their return, according to the script, marked the beginning of the new German navy, and the film closes with an epilogue superimposed over shots of Nazi U-boats: "It was still a long way from the first submarine to the present-day U-boat, and from the first underwater firing to the present-day torpedo, but a hundred years ago the deciding step was taken by Sergeant Wilhelm Bauer."

During his short career, Selpin directed three films set on ships, and Goebbels apparently took this in mind when he assigned him to the *Titanic* project. The epic theme of a great ship going down because of British pig-headedness appealed to him, and as a propaganda spectacle the subject could hardly be bettered. As his widow told me, Selpin found society and musical interludes to his liking; by this time he was getting adept at staging catastrophes of all kinds. Initially, she said, he greeted the project with enthusiasm; the lighter elements of the first part of the voyage would gradually give way to the suspense and danger and final tragedy, a most appealing progression.

But when the indefatigable Zerlett-Olfenius was through with the script, it was loaded with propaganda. The outlines of the story were generally historically correct, but the scenarist added a German first officer who warns the captain of the dangers of such a fast run. And when the sinking takes place, the German steerage passengers show much more bravery than the British in first class. For good measure there was a jewel robbery, and at the end of the film, a highly doctored version of the inquiry which exonerates the captain over the protests of the German witnesses.

The sheer size of the production was staggering. The interiors of the ship were built in Berlin, but it was decided to film a number of exteriors on a real vessel in the harbor of Gdynia (then "Gotenhafen"). According to Selpin's widow, early in May of 1942, Selpin had commenced shooting in Berlin. Zerlett-Olfenius, who had become a nuisance to the director, was sent to Gdynia with a shooting script, a second-unit crew and most of the extras, with instructions to do the preproduction work.

Several weeks later, with his Berlin shooting on schedule, Selpin took the train to Gdynia with his own entourage, and discovered to his surprise that Zerlett-Olfenius had done nothing, and furthermore seemed unconcerned with the costly delays that his inactivity would cause. The two men went to the nearby Kurhaus at Zoppot, where Selpin demanded to know why his instructions had been ignored. Zerlett-Olfenius told him that the local naval officers, who were under orders from the Propaganda Ministry to cooperate on the production, were interested only in romancing the girls from Berlin.

Selpin then asked why Zerlett-Olfenius did not put his foot down, since he had the necessary authority to do so. He answered that those who wore the *Ritterkreuz* (a German military decoration) were supermen, crusaders who could allow themselves what they wanted, and could spend the night with the whole crew of extras if they felt like. Selpin, who had managed to keep his temper under control during the interview, if not his drinking, snapped back that, as far as he could see, the decoration must certainly be awarded for the number of actresses seduced. When Zerlett-Olfenius continued to defend his "supermen," Selpin shouted at the top of his voice (according to witnesses at the postwar trial): "Ach du! Mit deinen Scheissoldaten, du Scheissleutnant überhaupt mit deiner Scheisswehrmacht!"

The next morning, Zerlett-Olfenius gave his notice, wrote to the head of the film company about what had happened, and took the train back to Berlin. On arrival, he went directly to SS Obergruppenführer Hinkel, a close friend, who in turn decided to report the incident to the *Reichssicherheitshauptamt* (Reich Security Office), which relayed it to Goebbels.

Wolfgang Liebeneiner, the actor-director who was head of the Ufa at the time and also director of the combined film companies, was summoned to the Wilhelmstrasse where Goebbels had his offices. Arriving there at 1 P.M. on July 30, he had no idea what was going on, and was astonished to find assembled in the anteroom Hinkel, von Demandowsky (vice-president of the Reich Kulturkammer), and Fritz Hippler (the Reich Filmintendant). Hinkel asked Liebeneiner if Selpin had contacted him, and upon receiving a negative answer, remarked, "Well, he will have to go directly to the minister and answer for himself."

At this moment, the group was ushered into Goebbels' office. Almost immediately thereafter, Selpin was led in, flanked by two SS guards.

Goebbels was in a difficult position. He was unwilling to stage a repetition of the Gottschalk affair, which had harmed his carefully prepared image as far as the Filmwelt was concerned. However, in this case he was cornered because of the interest of the Gestapo in the matter, and it was necessary to take some action. His intention was apparently to simply frighten Selpin slightly, give him a convenient excuse, and let him go with a warning.

Goebbels came from behind his desk—an unusual procedure as he preferred to hide his deformed foot—and told Selpin that he had a report that the director had made some remarks about the German navy at Gdynia, but that he was certain the whole incident had been misunderstood. Selpin told him that everything Goebbels had heard was true. Goebbels, making an attempt to control his temper, tried to give Selpin another chance to avoid a charge of treason. Selpin refused to take the bait.

Finally the propaganda minister shouted: "Do you really stand by those statements?" Selpin turned white and said, "Yes, I do." Goebbels turned to the SS guards and screamed, "Then arrest this man and take him where he belongs!" Selpin was dragged from the room while Goebbels, now in a frenzy, bellowed at the amazed Liebeneiner, "So these are the people you take under your wing!" The audience was dismissed.

What happened after this Thursday afternoon has been a matter of some conjecture. Normally, Goebbels would have turned the case over to Hippler, who did a large amount of his dirty work. But in this case Hippler had put in a request to begin his weekend that evening, apparently anxious not to be involved. Selpin's final hours were a tightly kept secret, but Veit Harlan and Selpin's widow told me in 1961 what apparently happened; Harlan said that the death scene was told to him by someone at the Propaganda ministry who read the report on the way to Goebbels' desk. Evidently, everybody told everybody else "in confidence" and soon it was all over Berlin.

Selpin was taken to a special prison and kept there while Goebbels —in a scene worthy of Schiller—made up his mind what to do with him. On the one hand, Selpin was unquestionably guilty of verbal treason, for the law was clear on this point. On the other hand, another death in the ranks of the Filmwelt would destroy the months of work Goebbels had put in to smooth over the Gottschalk matter, and ruin the paternal image he so greatly desired with his artists. In the end, he had to take the decision of Philip II in *Don Carlos*: the son must be sacrificed for the good of the state.

Sometime near midnight of Friday, July 31, 1942 (Hippler seemed to think it was the next day), two guards went to Selpin's cell and proceeded to tie his suspenders to the bars of a window high in the ceiling. They brought in a bench, told Selpin to stand on it and grasp the bars, then tied the suspenders around his neck and took the bench away. When the unfortunate man could no longer hold on, he was strangled to death.

Selpin's widow Anni was given a curt letter telling her of her husband's "suicide." With typical thoroughness, Goebbels had the death scene photographed, an incident which was to have a contrary effect to his original intentions—after the war.

Immediately the whole story was out and the entire Filmwelt carried out a coventry on Zerlett-Olfenius to such effect that a special order was issued by the Propaganda Ministry stating that anyone proved guilty of refraining to talk to Zerlett-Olfenius would have to explain himself to Goebbels in person; on the *Titanic* set a proclamation was posted forbidding mention of Selpin's name.

Director Werner Klingler (married to an American woman from Ohio who was playing a small role in the picture) was ordered to complete the film, which he did to the best of his ability under great pressure.

When the movie was at last finished, Goebbels screened it and decided it could not be released. Not only had the story of Selpin's end become public knowledge, but the terrified actions of the ship's passengers reminded him too clearly of how German people were reacting during the increased bombing raids. Selpin had the last grim laugh: his disaster sequences were too realistic to be shown in public.

The film had cost an enormous sum, and, to recoup some of the investment, *Titanic* was at last premiered in Paris on November 10, 1943, where it was a great success. German audiences saw it only after the war, and even then the release was abruptly terminated in the

Panic in the lifeboats as the great ship goes down, from Herbert
Selpin's spectacle *Titanic* (1943).

Western zones when the British complained of the propaganda content. Only recently has it been exhibited virtually intact before the
West German public. It is worth noting that *Titanic* had no such
trouble in the Eastern zone where the anti-British segments fitted
neatly into the current Communist line.

An investigation of the affair after the war (April 1947) did not
receive the publicity of the Harlan trials in Hamburg. The court
brought in a verdict against Zerlett-Olfenius, who was sentenced to
five years at hard labor plus partial confiscation of property; the repulsive "suicide" photograph was an important exhibit for the prosecution. It was reported that Zerlett-Olfenius escaped to Switzerland.

The story of Selpin's death is more dramatic than the plot of his last
film, but *Titanic* is worth a short synopsis. To quote the official program, which was apparently never issued:

The film uses as its material the historical tragedy of the Titanic
catastrophe of 1912. The maiden journey of the giant liner serves only

the speculative interests of the President of the White Star Line, which owns the ship. In order to save the company, which is on the verge of financial collapse as the result of the cost of building the liner, and in order to insure for themselves gigantic profits, President Ismay (Ernst Fürbringer) bribes the Captain (Otto Wernicke), to sail to New York at full speed along the northern route which was endangered by ice floes. The "Blue Ribbon" must be won, which will supposedly raise the stock of the company to its former level. At first, however, the shares fall and Ismay plans to buy them at a low price just before the ship arrives in New York.

On board during the journey a series of interesting individual stories take place, as interesting as the high society which is represented: Lord (Karl Schönböck) and Lady Astor (Charlotte Thiele), opponents of the President's business schemes; Gloria (Kirsten Heiberg), Ismay's mistress; Sigrid Oole (Sybille Schmitz), a young Danish woman unjustly reputed to be fabulously wealthy; a bankrupt Lord (Fritz Böttger) who tries to approach Lady Astor in order to get money from her husband; a German scholar, Counselor Bergman (Theodor Loos) with his assistant; a couple who are emigrating, the Captain of the ship, his first officer, the German Petersen (Hans Nielsen), and the little manicurist (Monika Burg).

All of their individual stories combine when the ship hits an iceberg, which sends it to the bottom of the ocean with the loss of 1600 lives. The panic that breaks out on board shows each person in his true colors. The great President of the company turns into a poor egoist clamoring for his own safety. The shallow Danish woman—who has spent most of her time flirting with the first officer—now devotes her full time to helping those in need.

Petersen, who throughout the journey has tried to keep the criminal speed of the ship's sailing to reasonable limits, makes sure that President Ismay is saved, and by doing so receives his punishment from the naval court of inquiry. Ismay is let off and only the Captain, who went down with his ship, is deemed responsible. The film closes with a heated attack by the German Petersen against the true guilty parties of this major catastrophe.[15]

Due to the hacking and chopping of the film by everyone from Goebbels to the postwar censorship boards, *Titanic* is a less than coherent picture. (I have seen both the original release print with French subtitles and the most recent reissue—the differences are slight.) Despite the often confusing intrigues of the plot line, it is hard to fault the acting, particularly that of Sybille Schmitz as the enigmatic Sigrid, per-

The beautiful Sybille Schmitz as the enigmatic Sigrid, the selfless heroine of *Titanic* (1943).

haps her best performance. Attired in a rather odd vampish black wig, she slithers through the picture with remarkable style and dominates every scene in which she appears.

The sinking of the ship, a combination of model shots and truly spectacular footage photographed by Friedel Behn-Grund in Gdynia and Berlin, can hardly be bettered. It is the highest praise to remark that some of it has the look of a nightmarish newsreel. These sequences were incorporated into the British picture *A Night to Remember* (1958) without credit.

### V

Short of suicide, there were other ways of bucking the system and getting away with it—at least most of the time. The finest director working in the Third Reich was Helmut Käutner, whose films could hardly be more different from those of Ritter, Steinhoff, Harlan, and Selpin discussed above.

Käutner is one of the few directors mentioned in this study still at work in the German film industry, but it would be hard to find a personality currently less fashionable. In this day of film research which brings forth illustrated monographs on everyone from Antonioni to Zurlini, the only serious study of Käutner would seem to exist in a Portuguese-language pamphlet so obscure that even someone interested in his films would find it virtually impossible to locate.

Käutner, to be sure, presents some severe problems to the researcher. His Nazi-period films, nine in number, have never been shown in the United States and several are almost unobtainable in Germany today. Further, he refuses to discuss them. His immediate postwar work was released in the United States and perhaps too highly praised; one has the impression that from 1950 on, with the exception of *Die letzte Brücke* (*The Last Bridge*), (1953), his films were mere anticlimax. To make matters worse, Käutner committed the critical sin of appearing commercial enough to be imported to the United States. Here he directed two films for Universal, which are better than the original reviews would indicate. His subsequent return to Germany has produced nothing of interest in the motion-picture medium, although his acting and stage direction have been superb. For some reason, he was selected as the particular *bête noire* of the young Marxist intellectuals who control contemporary German film criticism, and his name is usually mentioned with scorn as the foremost proponent of "Papas Kino."

To classify Käutner as the heir of Max Ophüls is not an exaggeration. Ophüls, like von Sternberg, had the ability to take a small situation and blow it up to enormous proportions, and Käutner carried on this tradition in his early films. It was once said of Ophüls that "he had nothing to say, but said it beautifully," a snide remark which can also be applied to Käutner.

Both men were supreme in depicting the problems of women; more specifically, women in love. For this reason it is too easy to dismiss their work as soap opera, placing undue emphasis on the subject matter of their films when in fact both men were far more concerned with form and style than content. While Ophüls has been adopted by the French critics and their disciples as a true *auteur*, they have yet to discover Käutner.

However, Käutner differs from Ophüls in several important ways. Most notable is an element of neuroticism which appears frequently in his work. His women are not only unhappy, but also slightly unhinged by the problems of the world around them. As a result they are, with a few exceptions, lonely introverts fighting a losing battle against extroverted husbands and lovers. In retrospect they reflect

Käutner, the introverted artist, beset by the almost impossible task of turning out "personal" films in the movie factory of the Third Reich.

While Goebbels personally detested most of Käutner's work— *Romanze in Moll* would seem to be the candidate for the top position on his private hate list—he was too shrewd to put the director out of business. There is also evidence that Goebbels had considerable personal respect for the director, although Käutner was known to be opposed to the Nazis and turned down many opportunities to advance his career by making political claptrap on the assembly line.

In the world of the Nazi film, Käutner's work stands out like some slightly unwholesome flower blooming in a field of hot-house weeds. Even his most ordinary works contain moments of personal involvement, which is more than can be said for the output of his contemporaries. The fact that most of his nine films of the 1939–1945 period are of some interest today while others of much more ambitious scope made during the same time are doomed to oblivion should give some hint that he is an artist to be reckoned with.

Käutner had entered the Filmwelt from the theatre and cabaret, following the usual pattern. In addition to writing various skits and reviews, he had shown considerable skill as an actor. The heritage of the cabaret is particularly important in his films, with a streak of cynicism often lurking in his scenarios. His career began with three film scripts written for other directors during 1938–1939, which are pleasant but hardly indicative of anything exceptional. However, Käutner was responsible for at least part of the scripts of all films he directed during the Third Reich.

His first film as a director was a harmless comedy, *Kitty und die Weltkonferenz* (*Kitty and the World Conference*), (August 25, 1939) about a young manicurist with romantic aspirations, set against the background of an international meeting in Lugano. It was based on a comedy by Stefan Donat, and the film rolls along in a pleasantly predictable manner—though with unusual style for the period—until a little scene which for a moment throws the mechanism out of order.

The heroine, through a series of absurd coincidences, is taken out to dinner by a British diplomat, who is unaware that she is an employee of the hotel in which he is staying. After the usual problems of finding a suitable dress for such an elegant evening out, she goes to the restaurant, hungry. Confronted with the menu, written in French, she is unable to order and has to settle for a bottle of wine and some small appetizers. The diplomat at last realizes her predicament and orders a full dinner. While this is an ordinary scene on paper, it is anything but ordinary on the screen, and is played in a manner completely different from the rest of the film. The heroine's false pride and very real hunger struggle with one another—a struggle reflected in her face, which at the end of the scene takes on an aspect of near-terror; the neurotic element has already crept in the side door. We are confronted for the first time with the hint that the woman is very different on the inside than her outward sophistication would indicate. In this sequence, an ordinary and not well-known actress, Hannelore Schroth, gave a tantalizing hint of her capabilities, which were to be realized at last in her superb performance as the heroine of *Unter den Brücken*.

The film had a curious fate. The day after its premiere in Stuttgart, it was banned because of the war situation; the British and French diplomats were shown as much too sympathetic characters. To all intents and purposes, the film was unknown until after World War II; the original story was used in a remake by another director in 1956.

The film that followed was *Frau nach Mass* (*Woman Made to Measure*), (March 23, 1940), an exceptionally silly comedy which might have been made by any talented director of the period. I have not been able to see *Kleider machen Leute* (*Clothes Make the Man*), (September 16, 1940), but it is based on a relatively familiar story by the Swiss writer Gottfried Keller concerning the adventures of a young tailor in a small town during the Victorian period. A review indicates that it might be of some interest in that it hints at the themes of *Auf Wiedersehen, Franziska*, but otherwise it would seem to be a typical vehicle for the comedian Heinz Rühmann.

After warming up on these three exercises, Käutner directed a film which is in every way mature and about as strong a statement on his view of the world as he was to give in any of his films. *Auf Wiedersehen, Franziska* (April 24, 1941) is his most Ophülsian work, and it is amazing that the film is almost completely unknown in and out of Germany. It escapes being a masterpiece only by its ending, but it is nevertheless a great film.

A newspaper and newsreel cameraman named Michael Reisiger

The best of Helmut Käutner's neurotic heroines, Marianne Hoppe, shown here with Hans Söhnker in a scene from the powerful *Auf Wiedersehen, Franziska* (1941).

lives in a small town between assignments which take him all over the world. One day he meets a young girl, Franziska Tieman, and follows her to her home, where she makes toys for a living. He flirts with her, and soon they fall in love. They go to his strange apartment, filled with Oriental bric-a-brac, and the girl admits her love for the first time. But no sooner have they become lovers than he must depart on another assignment, leaving her a note which bluntly states, "Don't write me; forget me soon." The girl is heartbroken and moves to Berlin.

In time, Michael finds her again, and persuades her to renew their affair. But he is off again on his job, this time to India, Africa, and America. Franziska waits and broods, creating her toys and building up a first-rate hysterical neurosis. On his return, he decides to marry her, but this hardly changes the situation. The lonely, introverted girl cannot understand her extroverted husband, who is always leaving her without warning. The years pass, two children are born, but Franziska cannot cope with her life. When Michael comes home from another trip, they quarrel, he boards a train, she runs after him but it is too late.

So far, so good, but in order to get the story on the screen, some propaganda was necessary. Michael arrives in China, to cover a Shanghai rebellion. His best friend is killed, but before dying tells him to return to the fatherland, "where great things are happening." (This whole section is directed without any conviction, and poorly acted.)

Michael comes home, this time for good, to judge from the dialogue, but the visuals simply do not match: Franziska is hollow-eyed, out of touch with the world, apparently on the border of insanity. The family is reunited but one wonders what is going to happen after the film is over. Obviously, nothing very good.

The strength of the film, outside of Käutner's script and direction, lies in the performance of Marianne Hoppe as Franziska. This actress was the best Germany had to offer, and her performance here is magnificent. The camerawork of the Czech photographer Jan Roth is also worthy of comment. *Auf Wiedersehen, Franziska* has nothing in common with other films of the period; it stands in lonely isolation as the work of an unhappy but superbly talented artist.

Käutner's next film, *Anuschka* (March 27, 1942), was made for the Bavaria Company, but shot in Prague at the Barrandow Studios, which were rapidly becoming the best equipped and staffed in Europe.

After a slow start, the film develops into a splendid romantic drama much in the Ophüls' manner. Anuschka, living in a small Slovak village, is unable to marry after her father's death because of his bad debt to her fiancé's mother. So the girl packs her bags and goes to Vienna, where she finds employment at the house of a well-to-do young doctor.

At the annual carnival, Anuschka meets a handsome young man who happens to be the lover of the doctor's wife. He slips a cigarette lighter which his mistress had given him into Anuschka's pocket. Drunk for the first time in her life, the girl sleeps it off in the park where she is arrested by a cynical policeman (apparently played by Käutner) and taken to headquarters. The lighter is found, the doctor is called and believes she has stolen it. To his surprise, his wife tries to defend the girl, but he fires her.

In the interim, Anuschka has put two and two together but refuses a bribe offered to her by the doctor's wife. Enter lover from the country who is furious that his fiancée is accused of theft. In the end, they locate the wife's paramour, she confesses her guilt to her husband, who forgives her as the affair is now over. Anuschka gets her man.

The film is more interesting than a synopsis indicates, largely because of the director's skill in switching rapidly back and forth between comedy and drama. Anuschka is another of Käutner's heroines unable to come to terms with a new environment, but in this case she has enough peasant good sense to avoid getting neurotic about the situation. Nonetheless, the film is probably the darkest photographed comedy (by Erich Claunigk) since *Bringing Up Baby*, with almost everything heavily shadowed or crammed with Victorian bric-a-brac. The period sense is marvellous, and the ball scenes at the Vienna Opera are worthy of Ophüls.

Käutner had an unfailing instinct for selecting the right actors, and in the case of *Anuschka*, the lovely Hilde Krahl was perfect in the title role, ably assisted by Siegfried Breuer and some relatively obscure performers better known for their stage work.

When it came time for Käutner's next film, Goebbels decided he should try a musical comedy in the American mold, as this was the period in which he was determined to do something about the dreadful state to which the genre had sunk in Germany. Zarah Leander was otherwise occupied on other projects, and her rival, Ilse Werner, who could look attractive in a tuxedo, belt out songs with enormous gusto, and deliver comic lines with style, was recruited for *Wir machen Musik* (*We Make Music*), (October 8, 1942).

The rather strange story concerns a girl who is a successful cabaret singer, taking harmony lessons from a frustrated opera composer who writes popular music on the side. They fall in love but the romance is nearly nixed when the young man's opera is a failure. (Again, the theme of bitterness and betrayal is evident for a few minutes in the middle of a comedy.) The happy ending is an excuse for a big *ersatz*-Warner Brothers musical number, showing that Käutner had studied his American models with considerable attention. Goebbels was highly pleased with the results.

It is curious to think that while this piece of silly froth was in progress, Käutner was planning his grim masterpiece, *Romanze in Moll* (*Romance in a Minor Key*; the term "romance" here refers to the musical composition), (June 25, 1943). The screen credits read that the script is by Willy Clever and Käutner, from an idea by Clever. The actual source was the short story "Les Bijoux" by Maupassant, an

The most elegant and artistic of all films made during the Third Reich, Helmut Käutner's *Romanze in Moll* (1943) with Marianne Hoppe.

author on the Nazi blacklist. The original tale, only a few pages in length (and not to be confused with "The Necklace") tells of a poor man who finds a strand of pearls among his wife's possessions after her death. Believing them to be paste, he takes them to a jeweler, who tells the astonished man that they are real. The reader is left to infer their source.

From this suggestion, Käutner went on to create a powerful film set in late nineteenth-century Paris. The opening sequence begins with the husband undressing after attending a concert which he had not wanted to hear. He carries on a monologue with his wife, who is lying in bed, having left the performance early. Suddenly we perceive that she is dead, a suicide. Then follows the incident with the jeweler, at which point the picture goes into flashback.

The woman, Madeleine, married to an elderly civil servant, lives a life of frugal unhappiness. One day, on the street, she meets a famous composer-pianist. Upon their initial encounter, he presents her with a valuable pearl necklace, and she, assuming him to be a thief, refuses to accept it. He agrees to take it back only if she will promise to pay him a visit at his home. It is at this appointed meeting that the composer plays his newest "romance" for Madeleine, who suggests improving on the theme by transposing it into a minor key. The two fall in love, and the composer ends his affair with his previous mistress, who was to have sung the new composition at its premiere. Then, returning from a party in the countryside with her lover, Madeleine is discovered by a young associate of her husband, who threatens to expose her unless she obliges him. This she does, but she feels that she has dishonored her lover and decides to commit suicide. Before she dies, however, she has the bittersweet pleasure of hearing the finished "romance" played for the first time in a minor key. When her lover learns of her death he challenges Madeleine's blackmailer to a duel. He manages to wound his rival but is himself seriously wounded in the hand, and, unable to accept Madeleine's death, can find solace only in drinking.

This most delicate and most French of all German films was an enormous public success at the time of its release. However, the subject matter of an unfaithful wife infuriated Goebbels, who was ready to hack the picture to pieces when Wolfgang Liebeneiner, now head of the Ufa, begged him to leave it alone as a superb work of art. After a heated argument, Goebbels agreed, but referred to the picture as "defeatist."

*Romanze in Moll* is the most complete statement of Käutner's desperately neurotic woman-in-love. Madeleine is a character of flesh and blood, played with almost unbearable intensity by Marianne Hoppe in the greatest single performance of the 1940's. Ferdinand Marian was properly shallow as the composer, and Paul Dahlke was an ideal choice for the lumpish husband. Käutner wrote a small scene for himself as a cynical poet, which reflected his personal philosophy.

As usual, Käutner's technical credits are beyond reproach, particularly the important musical score. The "Romanze," written by Lothar Brühe, has been published and is occasionally heard in concerts; the other music was by Werner Eisbrenner. For this film Käutner used

Georg Bruckbauer as his cameraman for the first time, one of his most fortunate discoveries.

Perhaps because the film is a costume piece, it has dated little, and it is surprising that it was never bought for American postwar release, particularly in view of the director's subsequent fame.

Goebbels ordered Käutner to make a film about the German Navy at war. Käutner said that he had no background to qualify him for such a project, so Goebbels agreed to let him do a film about sailors in Hamburg.

The picture was to be called *Die Grosse Freiheit* (*The Great Freedom*) after the name of the street in the middle of Hamburg's St. Pauli district, but the word *Freiheit* was taboo at the time and a compromise was worked out in which *Nr. 7* was added to the end of the title to avoid any conflict. The film was made in color, with a big cast including Hans Albers and Ilse Werner, Käutner again playing a bit part.

The story, by Käutner and Richard Nicolas, tells of a young girl who is sent to the city to live with her uncle, an accordion player at a nightclub located at the film title's address. She falls in love with a young sailor. The uncle, seeing that the boy will probably turn out to be little better than himself, tries to break up the romance, but at last gives his melancholy consent. Although the story was not particularly promising, the treatment of the characters is unusually tender, and the relationship between the proud yet sensitive uncle and niece—each in their own way true to their own ideals—is beautifully drawn.

There are delightful moments in the film, particularly a scene in an outdoor restaurant interrupted by a sudden summer shower, and the nightclub passages are engagingly vulgar. Hilde Hildebrand gives a fine cameo performance as a good-hearted tart, and the other supporting players are uniformly well cast. Ilse Werner proved too extroverted an actress to fit the usual Käutner neurotic mold, and it is the man in this case who seems to have enlisted the director's sympathies. For a change, Albers had a semiserious role, and made the most of this rare opportunity.

Käutner and Albers kept up a running battle with Goebbels, who was still trying to inject propaganda into the film after the script had been approved. When he decided that German battleships in the Ham-

Hans Albers
and Hilde
Hildebrand
have more on
their minds
than apples
in Helmut Käutner's
*Die grosse Freiheit*
(1944).

burg harbor should be used as a background, the director ordered fog machines and successfully obscured the waterfront. As Semmler reported in his diary, Albers was running a flourishing trade in selling French cognac at RM 300 a bottle until Goebbels caught him and made the actor pay a fine. This made Albers especially angry and he had a clever revenge. As Semmler described it:

He was earning a pretty good salary in his film work as well [as the brandy business]. In his contract for the color film *Die grosse Freiheit*, there was a clause saying that Albers would be paid RM 1500 a day until the film was finally ready for showing, regardless of whether or not he had to work daily in the studios. When the film was practically ready, Albers maintained that the film would not be "finally ready for showing" until Goebbels had seen it and approved release. Every day that passed with Goebbels prevented by one thing or another from seeing the film brought Albers RM 1500. Goebbels was furious about this sharp practice but did nothing about it. For his motto is like that of Frederick the Great: "Artists must not be bothered."[16]

At last Goebbels did see the film, and its excellence prompted him to an unusually petty act. To punish Käutner and Albers, he decided to ban the picture he knew they both liked very much. Since there was no excuse for this action on the basis of the picture's content, Goebbels forced Admiral Doenitz to write a letter to the effect that the film was harmful to the image of the German sailor, who was shown drinking and cavorting with prostitutes. Doenitz must have thought Goebbels was going mad when he received the order, but undoubtedly had more important matters on his mind and signed it.[17] The film was premiered in Prague on December 15, 1944, but was not seen in Germany until August 9, 1945.

Käutner's last Nazi-period film, *Unter den Brücken* (*Under the Bridges*) met a similar fate. Although passed by the censor in March of 1945, the fall of the Third Reich prevented its release until 1950. When finally screened, it was regarded by many as the director's finest work.

A tiny vein of neo-realism had always existed in the Nazi film but it was rarely exposed until the last few years of the Reich, as will be discussed shortly. Goebbels looked with disfavor upon films with serious contemporary subjects involving everyday life (as opposed to military action). *Die grosse Freiheit Nr. 7* had a modern and real setting of wartime Hamburg, but it was certainly an exception to the rule. Because of the chaotic state of the studios following the war's end, the German film was forced to adopt neo-realist techniques, and by the time *Unter den Brücken* saw the light of day, the genre was already somewhat old hat. However, this picture was a milestone of the German film in its use of familiar locations and situations with which the audience could strongly identify.

The film was scripted by Walter Ulbrich and Käutner from a *Manuskript* by Leo de Laforgue entitled "Unter den Brücken von Paris." The setting was moved to the Berlin area, where two barge workers, carrying coal on the series of canals about the city, save a young girl from suicide after she has jumped over a bridge. Both fall in love with her, although she is hardly shown as a paragon of virtue (nor are the two men, a refreshing change from the usual formula characters). She manages to break up the pair's friendship before making her choice for matrimony.

The girl is again one of Käutner's neurotic and tortured women, hiding her sensitivity beneath a mask of superficial toughness, which is gradually peeled away during the course of the film. Since there is almost no story, Käutner invented a wealth of details to keep the narrative going, such as the funny visit to a museum by the two sailors, which manages to make some tart comments on the official buxom-nude school of art favored by the Nazis. One feels that if Goebbels had seen the film, this one sequence would have been enough to have banned it in entirety; fortunately in March of 1945 his film viewing was severely curtailed. The three performers, Hannelore Schroth (Käutner's first heroine), Carl Raddatz, and Gustav Knuth, play with an excellent sense of ensemble. The film is also of interest for the debut of Hildegard Knef in a minor role.

From this point on, Käutner's career followed a downward path. It is perhaps an oversimplification to infer that he was able to make good films only under conditions which challenged his integrity, but this is probably not far from the truth. Given ample funds and freedom of expression his talent flickered and went out, film by film.

## VI

The Austrian-born director Gustav Ucicky, whose filmography during the Third Reich included such propaganda spectaculars as the previously mentioned *Flüchtlinge* (1933), *Morgenrot* (1933), and *Heimkehr* (1941), switched to noncontroversial features and completion of the last-named picture.

Ucicky is often underestimated as a creative artist of the period. In addition to his Nazi propaganda, he directed some of the best entertainment features of the era, *Der zerbrochene Krug* (1937), *Der Postmeister*, (1940) and *Ein Leben lang* (1940), which are still screened in Germany.

Unfortunately, his last four films, made in 1943–1944 were undistinguished with the possible exception of *Am Ende der Welt* (*At the End of the World*), which appears interesting on paper. It was banned by the censor in December of 1943 and not seen until after the war, in Austria, and I was unable to locate it for evaluation. Ucicky's postwar work fared poorly, although *Zwei blaue Augen* (*Two Blue Eyes*, released in England as *Christine*), (1957), showed that he had not lost his skill as an actors' director, rather in the Wyler tradition. Ucicky died in Hamburg in 1961, almost forgotten.

The case of G. W. Pabst is puzzling. He left Germany before the Nazi takeover, and, after an unsuccessful American film (*A Modern Hero*, 1934), went to France for a series of pictures which showed that either his talent was in decline or that he was simply not able to put together a satisfactory film for purely business reasons. By an unfortunate stroke of bad luck, he returned to Austria in 1938 to settle some matters of property, and was trapped by the *Anschluss,* unable to obtain an exit visa.

What happened between this date and the release of his first film under the Third Reich, *Komödianten* (*Comedians*), (September 5, 1941), is not clear. There is a dispute whether he aided in the production of "documentary" war films. I have been able to trace two short scenes in Leni Riefenstahl's *Tiefland* to his direction without credit.

*Komödianten* is a biography of Karoline Neuber, who founded the first German national theatre in the 1750's. She attempted to establish a serious repertory company by "banning the buffoon" as one biography puts it, but met with scant success. The Duchess Amalie von Weissenfels befriended her until her nephew fell in love with one of Karoline's actresses. This resulted in her expulsion and eventual exile to Russia, which proved an even greater disaster. She at last turned back to Germany to die alone and in poverty before seeing her advanced ideas come to fruition.

Pabst's film was based on a novel about Karoline entitled *Philine,* by one Olly Boeheim, and except for some possibly questionable romantic incidents, stuck to the depressing facts of the unfortunate woman's life. The film is not the failure which has been so often claimed, although it is hardly vintage Pabst. The cast alone lends interest to the project: Henny Porten, Käthe Dorsch, and Gustav Diessl— all in top form. Only Hilde Krahl disappoints the viewer.

There are at least two superb sequences. One is a fantastic orgy in the cellars of the Russian royal palace, obviously influenced by Sternberg's *The Scarlet Empress,* a picture which impressed Pabst. The other is a court performance of an exceptionally beautiful little opera which the bored audience finds inferior to the antics of a clown on the same bill whose major routine involves displaying a heart painted on his backside.

The film was not political except in the sense that it glorified a minor national cultural heroine, and contained some long-winded polemics on the future greatness of the German stage. Viewed today, *Komödianten* gives the impression that Pabst was not interested in the subject aside from its more baroque moments.

His second film, *Paracelsus* (March 12, 1943), is another lavish biography. It is not quite so politically innocent as some would have it. As Louis Marcorelles described it, *Paracelsus* is "a large-scale tribute to the Swiss healer of the Middle Ages who upheld the cause of natural medicine and, in reaction against contemporary authority, published his works not in Latin (which he didn't know), but in German. If Pabst finds obvious difficulty in transcending nationalistic claptrap, if he lacks the candor and conviction of a Harlan or a Steinhoff, he at least extracts some magical effects from medieval costumes and settings, and the completely mimed sequence of the appearance of Death would in itself justify the mediocrity of the rest."[18]

The passage Marcorelles cites is truly one of the greatest things Pabst put on the screen. In it, Paracelsus (Werner Krauss) has succeeded in keeping the plague out of Basel by the destruction of some goods which a merchant attempted to smuggle in, and caused the arrest of the man and his servants. The juggler Fliegenbein, attached to the caravan, manages to escape to a tavern, where he starts the infection of the city in a brilliantly choreographed *Totentanz* before the horrified Paracelsus, who realizes that the city is doomed. At the completion of the dance, the figure of Death is seen enjoying the entertainment. (This shot, introduced by the striking of an anvil, is one of the great shock moments in all film.) As danced by the late Harald Kreutzberg, the sequence ranks with the best ballet ever put on celluloid.

To the ordinary observer today, *Paracelsus* would probably appear innocent outside of some pompous dialogue about the superiority of the German language and the German citizen. But there is more to the situation. Five books about Paracelsus were published in 1941, all of them wildly nationalistic in nature, crediting him with Nazi ideals. (The fact that he had long been a Masonic hero was conveniently overlooked.) As one postwar critic wrote about the curious Paracelsus revival:

The great dancer Harald Kreutzberg leads the Dance of Death in
G. W. Pabst's *Paracelsus* (1943).

Paracelsus as a force in modern German literature, quite apart from
his influence on medical writings, presents an interesting problem for
the literary historians and critics. It must be assumed that his influence
will wane from now on, or at least until such time as the political
motives of his admirers will have been erased from all connotations of
his name; the recent Paracelsus revival can therefore be reviewed now
with some detachment. German novelists did not take to Paracelsus
simply because his colourful life lent itself to epic dramatization . . .
with Paracelsus there is the possibility of a national theme or myth,
and that he allows the Germans to rewrite Goethe's *Faust*, at any rate
the titanic Faust of the German commentators on new terms. This
is a classical instance of masked literary imitation, of switching from
one national symbol to another without an essential change in meaning. For you can give Paracelsus all the impestuousness and defiance
of Faust and at the same time have the satisfaction of planting a new
furrow.[19]

A careful reading of Kurt Heuser's script reinforces the contention
that Paracelsus was a sort of substitute Faust with Nazi attributes. (It

might be noted that the film is excessively talky and after a while the viewer's attention wanders to Pabst's superb décor and costumes, ignoring the dialogue.) In all fairness to Heuser, some of the dialogue is on a remarkably high literary level considering the period, but the rancid odor of political dogma soon stifles one's interest. Oddly enough, the film seems to have escaped postwar censorship. In any case the appeal of *Paracelsus* was far too highbrow for the general audience, and it met with scant success.

Pabst's last Nazi-period film, *Der Fall Molander* (*The Molander Trial*), a melodrama about a false Stradivarius, was apparently destroyed when the studio where it was being cut was bombed. The synopsis is not very promising, and Pabst himself dismissed the work as inconsequential.

Reviewing the two surviving films, one gets the impression of a tired director occasionally rising to brilliance, a pale shadow of a once great talent reduced to the position of a studio hack. If Pabst willingly returned to work in Germany, he deserved the historical consequences of this deed. If this was not the case, he deserves our pity.

### VII

Only a few films were made during the period of World War II showed German life with any semblance of reality. Real people in real settings were hardly to Goebbels' taste, and even tentative steps in this direction ran into opposition, sometimes from peculiar quarters.

The Zarah Leander musical *Die grosse Liebe* (*The Great Love*), (June 12, 1942), is an interesting case in point. The pilot line involved a romance between a young German air officer (Viktor Staal) who falls in love with a beautiful revue actress (Zarah Leander) while on furlough, and their continuing problems as the war interrupts their liaison. Director Rolf Hansen managed to infuse the rather banal story with a convincing aura of the hysteria of war and its effects on the civilian population. Despite falling in the "musical" genre, *Die grosse Liebe* is a rather grim and pessimistic picture, and the propaganda content was so negligible that it was possible to rerelease the film after the war with an introductory title explaining that the time in which it was made necessitated some slight military sentiments which could be ignored.

Goebbels recorded in his diary:

I had a telephone conversation with the Reich Marshall [Göring] who complained about the OKW because it protested against the new Leander film. This picture shows an aviator spending a night with a famous singer. The OKW considers itself insulted morally and insists that an aviation lieutenant wouldn't act that way. Opposed to this is the correct view of Göring that if an aviation lieutenant didn't make use of such an opportunity, he simply wouldn't be an aviation lieutenant. Göring pokes fun at the sensitiveness of the OKW. That's fine grist for my mill, since the OKW creates a lot of difficulties for me in my movie work. In this case we can depend upon Göring as the better expert on the Luftwaffe and won't have to fear any jurisdictional difficulties.[20]

Perhaps because of the adult theme, *Die grosse Liebe* was the most successful of all Leander pictures and holds up better today than most of the "costume" musicals in which she appeared.

Some interesting glimpses of Berlin at war are provided in *Grossstadtmelodie* (*Big City Melody*), (October 4, 1943), directed with unusual skill by Wolfgang Liebeneiner. This picture shows the adventures of a young girl (Hilde Krahl) who wins a photo contest in a small town and moves to Berlin hoping to get a job on a big magazine. Her first assignment, to cover a bicycle race, ends in disaster when she brings in the film twelve hours too late. She tries to earn a living photographing children in a park, but has to stop because she has no license—a nice comment on Nazi bureaucracy. She ruins her best assignment when the mysterious millionaire she is to trap into a photo turns out to be the wrong man. She finally succeeds in her career and wins the man she loves.

The film rambles on in a pleasantly episodic style until about the ninth reel, which is blatant propaganda—a newsreel montage of Goebbels, Furtwängler conducting in a factory, and so forth. There is considerable historical interest in this material, but the scenes of everyday life are more valuable for their candid glimpses of wartime Berlin.

The earlier *Zwei in einer grossen Stadt* (*Two in a Big City*), (January 23, 1942), is a more modest effort, but equally fascinating. This time, the plot concerns a young soldier on leave in Berlin searching for his pen pal Gisela, whom he has never met. There are numerous complications, but he at last ends up with another girl named Gisela from the German equivalent of the USO. Director Volker von Collande recorded the mood of Berlin in the summer of 1941 with great skill and managed to draw charming performances from two usually uninspired performers, Monika Burg and Karl John.

Unfortunately, there were few other films of this type. Boleslav Barlog's *Junge Herzen* (*Young Hearts*), (November 30, 1944), is reportedly a remarkable little picture about a bittersweet love affair set in Berlin and its environs, and has one scene in which the lovers on a visit to Potsdam "skate irreverently down the galleries at Sans Souci behind the guardian's back."[21] The plot synopsis gives a tantalizing hint that the picture might also be a rather devastating commentary on student morals of the period; regrettably, the film proved impossible to locate.

The realistic technique could also be misapplied, as in Wolfgang Staudte's debut picture as a director, *Akrobat schö-ö-ön* (*Bravo Acrobat!*), (December 1, 1943). This was a misguided comedy featuring the real circus clown Charlie Rivel in what was apparently a semi-biographical drama of his rise to stardom. Despite his deadpan antics, Rivel was no Keaton, and Staudte's leaden film gave no hint that he was to become the most important postwar German director. Part of the fault lies in Georg Bruckbauer's gloomy camerawork; his particular style was far more suited to Helmut Käutner's romantic melodramas.

### VIII

The 1942–1945 period brought forth some surprisingly good pictures which properly fall into the category of "sleepers"— films hardly noticed at the time of their release and virtually forgotten today. Several of these deserve mention here.

Geza von Bolvary was one of Germany's most prolific directors, turning out three or four pictures a year, usually musicals or light romantic dramas. Most of these are of little interest, but occasionally

Bolvary directed an important work. His pre-Nazi *Der Raub der Mona Lisa* (*The Theft of the Mona Lisa*), (1931), was a musical with moments worthy of René Clair, and his *Dreimal Hochzeit* (1941) was mentioned earlier in these pages.

*Schicksal* (*Destiny*), (March 18, 1942), comes as a surprise, a powerful drama from a Gerhard Menzel script with a superb cast and brilliant use of exotic locations, photographed by Hans Schneeberger.

The father of two small children, a boy and a girl, is hanged during an attack on a Bulgarian castle which he is defending. His steward (Heinrich George) adopts them, taking a job as a waiter and working for the local political underground on the side. Many years later the girl (Gisela Uhlen) falls in love with a lieutenant of the occupying powers and agrees to marry him. When the steward sees her fiancé, he recognizes him as the man responsible for her father's death. On the day of the wedding he goes to the bridegroom's hotel, kills him and is jailed. The years pass, and at last the old steward is released from prison. He climbs the long hill to the castle where the story started, now inhabited by the girl and her brother. The three are reunited, but it would seem the girl is tubercular. The futility and stupidity of the Teutonic "code of honor" mentality is bitterly exposed, much in the same style as in *Liebelei*. While *Schicksal* contains some propaganda —enough to have the picture banned after the war—it seldom intrudes upon the relentless course of the story. The performance by Heinrich George was one of the best of his career, understating the melodrama in favor of creating a truly human character.

Walter Felsenstein, considered by many to be the finest opera director of our time on the basis of his work with the East Berlin Komische Oper, made a memorable film debut with *Ein Windstoss* (*A Gust of Wind*), (August 9, 1942), adapted from Giovacchino Forzano's popular comedy *Un colpo di vento*. There is plenty of evidence that Felsenstein, had he decided to make his career in the film medium, might have become another Lubitsch.

Forzano's play is based on the old gag of a man locked out of his apartment while wearing only his nightshirt, and the outraged reaction of his neighbors who refuse to believe his excuse that the door blew shut while he was emptying the morning trash in the hall. The comedy served as a vehicle for numerous actors on the German and Italian stage, and Paul Kemp was perfectly cast in the film version. Some lovely Florentine locations helped the picture. It is unfortunate that because of copyright problems the film can not be rereleased today.

Ibsen's *A Doll's House* was another extremely successful adaptation from the stage, under the title usually used for the play in Germany, *Nora* (February 14, 1944). The film is slightly disconcerting to the American viewer as Nora and her husband are reconciled at the end, and the famous door is never slammed. However, Ibsen wrote this alternate finale at one point in his career, and this was the version performed on the stage during the Nazi era when the doctrine of the sanctity of marriage was enforced. Luise Ullrich was a fine heroine, with Viktor Staal and Gustav Diessl supporting her in great style. Harald Braun directed as well as wrote the screen adaptation, using some inventive devices to "open" the play for film use.

One of the last films made under the Third Reich, and certainly one of the strangest, was Josef von Baky's *Via Mala*. The script by Thea von Harbou was based on John Knittel's famous novel of violence and retribution, a worldwide bestseller of the mid-1930's. Almost entirely shot in the studio, the picture looks like a vintage Ufa horror drama of the silent period, complete with bizarre neoexpressionist decors, heavy shadows, dripping water, and a villain straight from the *Nibelungen*.

Even with some plot changes from the original novel the film proved unacceptable to the censor because of religious material in the script. Completed late in 1944, *Via Mala* was forbidden in February of 1945, and, while in storage, the second and third reels were destroyed in a bombing raid. After the war, Baky took his actors to the East German Defa studios, reshot the missing footage, and the film was released at last in early 1948. Despite these difficulties *Via Mala* is a highly successful picture, with some of the most frightening sequences I have ever seen on the screen. Knittel's novel has been filmed again and Baky's version can not be revived.

### IX

In March 1943, Ufa was scheduled to celebrate its twenty-fifth anniversary, and Goebbels decided that the company should produce a super spectacle in honor of the occasion. The project was initiated as early as 1941, when Josef von Baky was selected for the task on the basis of the great success of *Annelie*. The subject of the picture proved somewhat of a problem until Goebbels saw the English film *The Thief of Baghdad* and decided that something along this line might be appropriate.

One of Baky's close friends was Erich Kästner, writer of numerous popular books and plays, including *Emil and the Detectives*. Because of a political indiscretion Kästner was unable to write under his own name, being on the official blacklist, but the censors looked the other way if the writer decided to use a pseudonym. (Nazi censorship appears today incomprehensible as far as general standards were concerned.) The director suggested that Kästner might be the ideal scriptwriter, and Goebbels agreed—so long as Kästner's name didn't appear on the credits.

When the director approached the writer for suggestions, Kästner said, "Well, your commission has come from the world's greatest liar—why not do a film about his closest competitor, the Baron Münchhausen?" Without being told the exact genesis of the subject, Goebbels agreed and allocated a budget of RM 5 million, with permission for Baky to use any stars he wanted for the color production.

Kästner, under the pseudonym of Berthold Bürger (a typical joke, as the first name was apparently borrowed from Goebbels' arch enemy Brecht, and the last name of course meant "citizen"), penned an enormously complex story which would depend a great deal on trick photography and special effects. In addition, there were numerous cameo roles so that as many Ufa stars as possible could take part in the picture.

It took five months to prepare the sets and costumes, and the Agfacolor laboratories went on an overtime schedule to manufacture the necessary raw stock. Another ten months were required to stage and edit the trick shots alone; it should be mentioned that this kind of thing had not been attempted since the silent-film period, and there were few technicians with any knowledge of the complex processes required. The Korda *Thief of Baghdad* was carefully studied, in addition to numerous Disney pictures procured by Goebbels' agents in neutral countries.

*Münchhausen* begins with a gala eighteenth-century ball at the Bodenwerder castle, presided over by the jovial but somewhat sinister Baron Münchhausen and his wife. There is a sudden lovers' quarrel between two of the young guests; the girl flees the party and jumps into her Mercedes. We have been viewing a costume party, and the period is very definitely the present.

The baron and his much older wife attempt to reconcile the pair. He tells them of the adventures of his "ancestor," the fabulous Baron Münchhausen, and the film goes into flashback, this time to the real eighteenth century.

Münchhausen (Hans Albers) and his servant Christian (Hermann Speelmans) are visiting the baron's father, who is puzzled over his son's invention of a rifle which can see and shoot a distance of 200 kilometers. After a series of surrealist sight gags (including the blasting of some clothing which has suddenly come to life in a closet), the pair decide to go to Braunschweig on the invitation of the local prince (Michael Bohnen), whom the Empress Catherine the Great has offered the command of a Russian regiment. The prince asks for Münchhausen's help in convincing his lovely mistress Louise la Tour (Hilde

In the more intimate surroundings of her boudoir, Catherine (Briggitte Horney) does a strip-tease for the Baron (Hans Albers) in *Münchhausen*.

von Stolz) to make the trip, and when this is accomplished the group sets off for Russia.

The dealings at the Russian court are devious. The magician Cagliostro (Ferdinand Marian) tries to enlist Münchhausen in a plot against the empress, but without success. At a carnival (the sets modeled after those of Benois for *Petrouchka*), the baron meets a young girl named Kätchen, who is later revealed to be Catherine (Brigitte Horney) in disguise. Münchhausen becomes Catherine's new lover, kindling the jealousy of the former favorite, Prince Orlov (Andrews Engelmann), who challenges the baron to a duel, wounding him slightly. Münchhausen goes to the strange house of "Doctor" Cagliostro to get patched up, and while there warns Cagliostro that he is about to be arrested. Although the magician knows this, he rewards the baron with the secret of eternal youth, and also gives him a ring that will make him invisible for one hour. As the secret police break into the house, the pair make a fast getaway, using magic.

Catherine soon tires of Münchhausen and sends him to Turkey in command of a regiment. As a joke, he is shot on a cannonball to Constantinople where he becomes a prisoner of the sultan (Leo Slezak). After a period of imprisonment he is reunited with his servant and a friend who proves to be the fastest runner in the world. The baron is offered his freedom if he will convert to the Moslem religion. He explains to the sultan that this would be impossible because he would have to drink water instead of wine, but the sultan tells him he does not really have to abstain—and gives him a sample of his private stock of Tokay. Münchhausen insists that the Tokay he drank at the palace of the Empress Maria Theresa in Vienna was twice as good. This leads to a bet in which the baron promises to provide the sultan with a bottle of the wine from Vienna in an hour. If he wins the bet he will have his freedom. Thanks to the wonderful runner, the bottle is produced, leading to a second wager. If the wine is indeed better than the sultan's, Münchhausen will be rewarded with the beautiful Princess Isabella d'Este (Ilse Werner), a prisoner in the harem. Münchhausen wins this bet too, but the sultan reneges on his promise, attempting to pass off another girl as Isabella. Using the magic ring, the baron invades the harem, abducts the real princess, and sets sail for Venice.

The court theatrical scene from Josef von Baky's *Münchhausen* (1943), cut from the film before release. Note the prompter.

Director Josef von Baky puts the finishing touches on the Man in the Moon's Daughter (Marianne Simson) —who boasts a removable head— from *Münchhausen*.

He learns that the girl's family had planned to marry her to an old man. She fled the city but was abducted by pirates who sold her to the sultan. Her sudden return is no joy to her family, and her wicked brother Francesco (Werner Scharf) has her kidnapped a second time and locked up in a convent. Isabella's last meeting with Münchhausen is one of the darker moments of the film, a mood which is quickly dispelled when the baron fights a duel with Francesco that results in the latter's clothes being cut to ribbons.

Münchhausen and Christian, with the d'Este family in hot pursuit, escape Venice in a giant balloon conveniently anchored in the Grand Canal. Their vehicle takes them to the moon. There, in a surrealist landscape, Christian ages and dies, because one day is equal to a year on earth—but Münchhausen is of course immortal. His gloom is dispelled by the presence of the daughter of the Man in the Moon (Marianne Simson). She can be in two places at the same time by separating her head from her body. But even her charms soon pale, and the baron returns to Germany.

The scene now shifts back to the present, where Münchhausen tells the startled young couple that he and his distinguished "ancestor" are one and the same. Thoroughly frightened, they flee the castle. The baroness, having observed that her husband is attracted to the girl, tells him to follow his new love. But instead, he renounces the gift of eternal youth to grow old with her.

After almost two years' work, the film was completed early in 1943. The finished print ran two and one-half hours, which everyone felt was too long. The first scene to go was a court theatrical at the start of the story, of which only stills remain (see illustration). Other small cuts were made here and there, and the original German release copy ran about 130 minutes. However, three different versions were prepared, two for export, which differ slightly from each other. The version in current release also seems to be missing a delightful sequence with a living musical clock, and a Venetian commedia dell'arte passage is sheared. Some enterprising foreign distributors further complicated the situation by printing parts of the nude harem-bath episode *twice*, while in more prudish lands the naked girls are missing. I have seen five different prints, no two alike.

The Baron and his fast-aging servant Christian (Hermann Speelmans) visit the moon, from *Münchhausen*.

As Pauline Kael remarked, the film looks as though it was edited with a meat cleaver. This was a result of using the Agfacolor stock; the director ruefully recalled in 1964 that no two takes of the same scene seemed to match in color tone because of the inexperience in using the new film, which was extremely sensitive to differences in color temperature. On the whole, the color was not bad, and safety-film prints were made after the war which give some indication of how it originally looked. *Münchhausen* was carefully color-coordinated in design, reflecting the change in locations and seasons: autumn tints for the Braunschweig court, wintry whites and blues for the Russian episodes, brilliant golds and red for the Turkish campaign, darker tones of the Renaissance painters for the Venetian interlude, and a bizarre mixture of almost everything for the lunar landscape. As usual, the exteriors using natural sunlight appear more realistic than the interiors.

The trick work, even by modern standards, is outstanding. In the wild race to Vienna, ten runners were placed a short distance apart and photographed at one frame per second as they popped in and out of concealed holes. Crude though this method seems, it worked very well. Only the cannonball ride to Turkey reveals obvious back projection. The director himself could not remember exactly how the business of the girl with the removable head was managed, but it is a great technical feat.

Wartime conditions added further complications. For the banquet in the Russian palace, virtually every candle in Berlin was requisitioned. The sumptuous place settings were borrowed from museums and palaces and were real Meissen, with silver and gold tableware. The flunkies standing behind the guests were recruited from the SS, the producer believing that they would be less likely to take home souvenirs after the day's shooting.

Albers, difficult as usual, insisted on doing his own stunts and at one point seriously injured his leg in a jump, holding up production while he insisted on being paid his daily salary though unable to work.

Considerable location work was shot in Venice, including a regatta of great splendor. Although it is seen on the screen for only a few minutes, more than four hours of color film was made of the event. For the duel at the Venetian island, a number of technical innovations were introduced, including hand-held cameras to give a dizzying feeling of first-person participation.

The musical score by Georg Haentzschel is outstanding, with a particularly lovely waltz theme to link the various scenes together. An orchestral suite was later arranged for concert performance, and it is still occasionally performed, although it has never been heard in the United States.

The March 5 premiere of the film was an enormous success. An elaborate ceremony was held in the afternoon before the screening. As Goebbels recorded in his diary:

Klitzsch [executive director of the Ufa] delivered a long but interesting speech about the history of the Ufa. He showed how exceedingly hard a few patriots had to fight against Jewish-American efforts at control of the German motion picture during *Systemzeit* [the Weimar Republic]. I was able to announce a number of honors conferred by the Führer. Hugenberg received the Eagle Shield, Klitzsch and Winkler the Goethe Medal, and Liebeneiner and Harlan appointments as professors. As these honors had been kept secret they made the men thus distinguished very happy. Hugenberg was simply flabbergasted at the public tribute paid to him. I treated him with special friendliness and courtesy and made a deep impression on him.[22]

After the film was screened he goes on to record:

Late at night I went for a short visit to Professor Froelich. All the bigshots of the Ufa were assembled there. They were very happy that I sat down with them for an hour. . . . People, on the whole, are of good will. That applies even to the intelligentsia.[23]

In the welter of awards and honors only one person seems to have been overlooked: Josef von Baky, the director of *Münchhausen.*

A confused legal situation over the postwar rights to the film caused *Münchhausen* to be publicly shown only once in the United States, and then in a dubbed print released in Milwaukee. It was immediately withdrawn because of a law suit by two other companies which claimed exclusive American rights. The case has never been settled, and it is unlikely that the picture will ever be seen again on American screens.

### X

It has often been asked if the Nazi film industry turned out any anti-American pictures. With certain qualifications, the answer would have to be no. This was a reflection of Hitler's strange attitude toward the United States. As one harassed book reviewer pointed out, having read three studies of Hitler's views on the matter, the Nazis simply didn't have any American policy.

Two short subjects, reportedly exist entitled *Amerikanische Unkulturen, Rund um die Freiheitstatue* and *Herr Roosevelt Plaudert.* I have been unable to locate copies for evaluation, but official postwar critiques indicate they are directed more against specific personalities than Americans at large. No information is available on date of issue or director.

There is one real curiosity piece, Hans Schweikart's *Der unendliche Weg* (*The Endless Road*), (August 24, 1943), which is a pro-American biography of Friedrich List. List emigrated to the United States from Germany in the first half of the nineteenth century and set up the first railway system in Pennsylvania. For sheer historical lunacy, the film stands in a class by itself. The viewer is treated to scenes of Andrew Jackson, complete with plaid vest, straw hat, and enormous cigar. Frontiersmen keep appearing during the story, sing-

The Wild West—of Pennsylvania—as Friedrich List (Eugen Klöpfer, right) meets Andrew Jackson! From Hans Schweikart's *Der unendliche Weg* (1943).

ing a weird mixture of out-of-period songs and generally extolling the virtues of German-American cooperation. If there is an explanation for the film at all, it might possibly lie in the fact that many high-ranking Nazis believed that the day would come when the Americans would join with the Germans to fight the Soviet Union, and anything to encourage this possibility was promoted in certain quarters.

A film about Thomas Paine was scripted but never made, and this project was even more pro-American (or, more properly, anti-British) than the List movie. A stageplay on the subject was popular in Nazi Germany and appeared in the repertoire of almost every major company.

### XI

The apotheosis of the Nazi film is unquestionably *Kolberg*. As mentioned earlier, it was Goebbels' favorite project, an attempt to equal in scope and grandeur the American film *Gone With the Wind*. And much to the amazement of those few who saw it, he nearly succeeded in his aim.

The story is based on a relatively obscure historical incident. In 1806, after the battles of Jena and Austerlitz, Napoleon's armies almost wiped Prussia off the map. The small fortress town of Kolberg stood in the way of complete victory for the French. The local government, realizing the inevitability of the French advance, decided to surrender the town, but the citizens revolted and set up their own army. With great courage they managed to hold out until they were overwhelmed.

When the *Kolberg* project was initiated in 1941, the fortunes of the German army were at their high point. The possibility of a foreign invasion of modern Germany seemed remote, and the original script was apparently little more than that of a monster spectacle extolling the courage of the historical Kolbergers. However, by the time the film started production in 1943, the situation was different. Goebbels, who never trusted the army, decided to place the emphasis on propaganda aimed at promoting popular resistance should the army be on the defensive.

With the enormous technical drain of making *Münchhausen* out of the way, it was at last possible to use the full facilities of the Ufa for *Kolberg*, which was to be even bigger in scope. There were numerous delays caused by the size of the production, the constant changes made in the script, and the unavailability of various actors who were committed to other pictures. These problems were finally solved and Veit Harlan was ordered to direct the epic. By this time, everyone involved was nervous about the military situation, making private plans of what to do in the event of a German defeat; the last thing most actors desired was to be tied up in a film which was going to take almost a year to complete.

But there was no stopping Goebbels on the *Kolberg* project. An enormous set was built in Neu-Stettin near the actual site of the battle, the modern Kolberg being unsuitable for the picture. A budget of RM 8½ million was allocated. More than ten thousand costumes were made, 6,000 horses were found somewhere for the battle sequences, and (in Harlan's final count) more than 187,000 persons were involved at one time or another, including whole army units assigned to the film as extras. At a time when every soldier possible was needed on the Eastern front, Goebbels thought nothing of diverting crucial manpower to his insane project. Although the railroad system was in chaos and people were going hungry because it was impossible to ship foodstuffs into the cities, one hundred railcars of salt somehow found their way to the set to provide the necessary "snow."

Harlan told me these numerous details of the nightmarish situation, made all the worse by Goebbels' daily calls to rush the completion of the film in the face of the Russian advance. The battle scenes had to be photographed before all the costumes had arrived, and the troops in the rear were forced to dye their military uniforms overnight and wear sashes improvised from toilet paper. There was a shortage of ammunition in the East, but factories were put on overtime to make the necessary blank bullets for this movie. Millions of feet of color negative film had to be especially prepared and developed at a staggering cost.

The final script of the film had little resemblance to the 1941 version or, for that matter, to actual history. The biggest problem was the simple fact that the French won the battle of Kolberg and even Goebbels could not find a way to rewrite this historical fact. To get around this, a compromise was reached in which, although the city is destroyed, it would seem that the population escaped with minimum casualties. To cap the picture, the battle of Leipzig was added so that the defeat of Napoleon could be made clear. Although this sequence was photographed, it was not included in the final cut.

Harlan's script (co-written with Alfred Braun) shows the events through the eyes of a young girl (Kristina Söderbaum), the daughter of the mayor of Kolberg (Heinrich George), Joachim Nettelbeck. Nettelbeck is alarmed at the poor preparations for the town's defense in the face of the French invasion. But the fortress is commanded by an old Colonel Lucadou (Paul Wegener), who is apparently determined to let the enemy pass through without resistance. Nettelbeck sends his daughter with a message to the Queen of Prussia (Irene von Meyendorff) telling her of the situation, and she delegates the young officer von Gneisenau (Horst Caspar) to organize the resistance. When the army refuses to cooperate, Nettelbeck organizes the citizens into a local militia, some armed only with pitchforks. They open the dikes around the city and build a moat. At last the French arrive, and there is a terrible battle. The city is virtually destroyed, but the French

Napoleon's cavalry makes its charge in *Kolberg* (1945).

*Blitzkrieg* is at least temporarily halted. One of the casualties is a pacifistic young violinist (Kurt Meisel) who is killed while trying to save his instrument.

There are numerous impressive passages scattered through the nearly two-hour-long film. An ominously silent Napoleon is seen at the tomb of Frederick the Great. The battle sequences, with hundreds of magnificently costumed officers on white horses charging up the sand dunes, are unforgettable. *Kolberg* also contains one of the most perfect bits of sentimentality attempted on the German screen. In this scene Nettelbeck comforts his heartbroken daughter in the smoking ruins of the city, while the remaining inhabitants sing the familiar Thanksgiving Hymn "We gather together" under the blasted roof of the cathedral.

The film has numerous weaknesses. The script is far too talky, and it takes an interminable amount of time to get the action going. Kristina Söderbaum has an embarrassing musical number, and the scene between her and the Queen of Prussia, complete with a celestial choir, is ludicrous.

*Kolberg* is full of propaganda songs and slogans, designed to cheer up the *Volkssturm*. In addition to the constantly sung *"Ein Volk steht auf!"* ("A people rise up!") refrain, there are lines such as ". . . *lieber in den Trümmern unserer Stadt begraben als sie dem Feind übergeben!"* ("We would rather be buried in the ruins of our city than to give it up to the enemy.") Norbert Schultze, of *Lili Marlene* fame, was responsible for the score, which is heavy with choral music.

It would seem that cameraman Bruno Mondi at last solved most of the problems of the tricky Agfacolor film. Flesh tones are remarkably real, and the exteriors have a vivid quality quite unlike previous attempts with the new stock. Only the interiors tend to be unpleasant, with a predominance of pink hues.

When the film was completed, Goebbels cut out RM 2 million worth of film which he considered too demoralizing, most of it devoted to the horrors of the battle within the town. Aside from this, he was pleased with the picture. The premiere was scheduled for the *Atlantikfestung* at the city of La Rochelle, on January 30, 1945, the anniversary of the Nazi takeover of power. Unfortunately, La Rochelle was by this time completely encircled by the enemy, and the film had to be parachuted onto the battlefield. Almost all Berlin cinemas were closed by this date, but one was found for a dual premiere. *Kolberg* ran but a few days and appears to have been viewed only by government officials and a handful of viewers brave enough to venture out of the air-raid shelters.

Goebbels unquestionably saw himself in the character of Nettelbeck. On April 17, 1945, he lectured his staff after screening *Kolberg* for them:

Gentlemen, in a hundred years' time they will be showing another fine color film describing the terrible days we are living through. Don't you want to play a part in this film, to be brought back to life in a hundred years' time? Everybody now has the chance to choose the part which he will play in the film a hundred years hence. I can assure you that it will be a fine and elevating picture. And for the sake of this prospect it is worth standing fast. Hold out now, so that a hundred years hence the audience does not hoot and whistle when you appear on the screen.[24]

According to Semmler, Goebbels' listeners hardly knew whether to laugh or swear at the end of this extraordinary speech. Most were far too concerned about saving their necks to worry about the movies of the future.

In the spring of 1966 the film was rereleased in Germany in a specially edited version which was interspersed with newsreel footage of Nazi Party leaders speaking the same slogans used in the picture. The public reception was mixed: Older viewers apparently attended out of a sense of nostalgia for "the good old days" to see their favorite actors of the period; younger members of the audience found the melodramatics ridiculous. Communist and left-wing political groups picketed cinemas which showed the picture. After a short revival, *Kolberg* was withdrawn from circulation.

## XII

The final scene in the film history of the Third Reich occurred in the flaming ruins of Berlin, with the Russians already in the suburbs. Goebbels, in the company of General von Oven, was busy destroying his personal papers and momentoes of office.

He suddenly stopped, a large autographed photo in his hand. "*Sehen sie, das ist eine vollendet schöne Frau,*" ("Now, there's a beautiful woman") he remarked. Von Oven saw it was a picture of Lida Baarova. Goebbels looked at it a moment longer, then tore it into pieces and threw it into the fire.[25] It was April 18, 1945.

On May 1, Goebbels and his family were dead, their charred remains found by the Russians in the smouldering gardens above the *Führerbunker*.

# EPILOGUE

It would take another book to record the story of the postwar German film industry.* And the story would not be a happy one.

The late spring of 1945 found many studios in ruins although the Ufa plant had suffered little damage. The German journalist Erich Kuby, in his study *The Russians and Berlin* (1968), published the following extract from the diary of one Frau K., a resident of Babelsberg, who reported on the situation of April 24 when the Russians occupied the town:

> It was like living on an island. When we went out of the front door before retiring at night we could see signs of spring . . . [The next day the Ufa film studios were handed over to a Russian commissar.] On Monday morning SS-Obergruppenführer Dr. G., president of the company, injected poison into his children, wife, mother, and governess, and blew himself up in his own home.[1]

Apparently the message of *Kolberg* had found one listener.

The enormous studios in Prague likewise escaped damage; they had been in operation to the last minute, and it was there that the expensive Agfacolor equipment and laboratories were situated. The invading

* For the 1946–1948 period, see Peter Pleyer's *Deutscher Nachkriegsfilm* (1965).

Russians took this plant over, sending most of the technical machinery to the USSR where something called Sovcolor soon appeared.

Commissions were hastily set up to clear or condemn the film personalities of the Third Reich. A few artists were placed on the blacklists, but most were allowed to return to work. The British, French, Americans, and Russians each established their own film-review committee, lacking common standards of evaluation. It was thus possible for some persons to be forbidden employment in one zone, while being cleared in another.

On the whole, the Russians were the most liberal in their policy of artistic clearance. The Ufa was renamed Defa, and it was there that the first postwar film, *Die Mörder sind unter uns* (*The Murderers Are Among Us*) was completed. The picture was billed as an East German-West German coproduction, directed by Wolfgang Staudte, and was premiered in East Berlin on October 15, 1946.

Paul Wegener was put in charge of establishing a center for stage and screen artists in East Berlin, where, to quote Ruth Andreas-Friedrich, he presided over all "like God the Father."[2] The choice of Wegener for this post would seem odd, since he had both acted in and directed propaganda features for the Nazis. However, his selection might confirm rumors that the former star of *Hans Westmar* had been a Russian informant of sorts during the Nazi period.

But the Western powers were less casual in their investigation procedures. Thousands of films were shipped to the United States for analysis, where many remain today; the British located their censorship office in Hamburg.

With American money, the Bavaria Studios were restored to service. Further plants were constructed in Hamburg and West Berlin on a smaller scale, splitting the industry into numerous separate units. The old, compact Filmwelt was shattered. Animosity promptly flared between artists working in the East and those in the West. Chaos became the normal state of affairs almost at once.

Directors Staudte, Lamprecht, Käutner, Klingler, von Baky, Rabenalt, Hoffmann, Marischka, Pabst, (Rolf) Meyer, Martin, Stemmle, and others were back to work by 1948. Among those blacklisted were Leni Riefenstahl, Veit Harlan, Wolfgang Liebeneiner, Gustav Ucicky, and a few others who had produced Nazi propaganda. Karl Ritter fled to Argentina by way of Portugal to avoid prosecution, but returned to West Germany and somehow managed to direct two pictures during 1953–1954.

After some discussion between the French, British, and American authorities, Veit Harlan was selected as the film director to go on trial for crimes against humanity, mainly for having made *Jud Süss*. After two sensational hearings, he was acquitted of the charges in 1950 due to lack of sufficient evidence, went promptly back to his old occupation, and directed nine other pictures between 1950 and 1958.

Most actors were able to resume their careers on screen and stage after perfunctory examination of their work during the Third Reich. Only a few were banned, notably Emil Jannings and Werner Krauss. Heinrich George died in a Russian-occupied concentration camp. Gustaf Gründgens became the target of his former brother-in-law, Klaus Mann, and had a difficult time explaining his peculiar career under the Nazis. Ferdinand Marian, who had taken the title role in *Jud Süss*, committed suicide in a car crash due to feelings of guilt as mentioned earlier. Other Nazi propagandists melted away into obscurity, emerging only when the heat was off. Even Lida Baarova had a comeback of sorts when Fellini cast her in a small part in *I Vitelloni*.

A few films made immediately after the end of the war raised the hope that a rebirth of the German film was impending, but this hope was quickly dashed. To quote Erich Kuby again:

> Nowadays, it is customary to talk with bright-eyed enthusiasm about Berlin in the summer of 1945, to say that, after the end of Nazi rule, the intellectual and artistic life of Berlin, which had been dammed up for so long, burst forth with irresistible force, that there was a brief renaissance reminiscent of the twenties, the only time a German city had been an international centre of culture. But people who talk like that are travellers in the desert, enthusing about a glass of brackish water after two parched days, water that would normally be thrown away. If the truth be told, there was no cultural renaissance worth mentioning in Berlin. Or, for that matter, anywhere else in Germany.[3]

After 1950, the most talented personnel employed in the Eastern Zone of Germany returned to the West, their places taken by Communist party hacks willing to turn out propaganda vehicles for the new regime, which was fast proving itself as reactionary as the Nazis in choice of subject matter and political controls.

The *coup de grâce* was delivered by the introduction of television. Film attendance fell drastically, and the few movies that drew good audiences were foreign products. One of the formerly best organized film industries in the world found itself on the edge of extinction. Following the failure of an enormously expensive film, *Das Wunder des Malachias* (*The Miracle of Father Malachias*), made in 1961, the great Ufa company (or what remained of it in the West), went into bankruptcy with the exception of its newsreel division and theatre circuit. The Bavaria studios, where it was hoped the new German films would be made under first-rate technical conditions, gradually became a foreign arm of American companies attracted by the appeal of saving money by "runaway" production.

By 1960, the German film industry was virtually a thing of the past. A new generation of filmmakers had begun to emerge, but it is difficult to guess if they will produce anything of lasting value. In any case, the highly organized German film industry, as it existed from before World War I to 1950, would seem to be dead.

# NOTES

NOTES FOR PROLOGUE (pp. 1–9)

1. Siegfried Kracauer, *From Caligari to Hitler,* p. 5.
2. Rudolf Semmler, *Goebbels, the Man Next to Hitler,* pp. 149–150.
3. Information Services Division, Control Commission for Germany, *Catalogue of Forbidden German Features and Short Film Productions Held in Zonal Film Archives of the Film Section.*

NOTES FOR 1933: THE SUBVERSION OF THE FILM INDUSTRY (pp. 10–41)
1. Semmler, *Goebbels, the Man Next to Hitler,* p. 161.
2. The two best biographies of Goebbels are by film historians: Rober Manvell and Heinrich Fraenkel, *Dr. Goebbels;* and Kurt Riess, *Joseph Goebbels.*
3. Joseph Goebbels, *Vom Kaiserhof zur Reichskanzlei,* translated as *My Part in Germany's Fight.*
4. Louis P. Lochner, ed., *The Goebbels Diaries.*
5. Siegfried Kracauer, *From Caligari to Hitler.*
6. *Ibid.,* p. 262.
7. Goebbels, pp. 228–229.
8. Josef Wulf, *Theater und Film im Dritten Reich,* p. 335.
9. Kracauer, p. 270.
10. New York *Times,* March 19, 1933, IX, p. 4.
11. New York *Times,* February 11, 1933, p. 10; February 14, 1933, p. 19; February 19, 1933, II, p. 2.
12. Wulf, p. 265.
13. *Ibid.,* pp. 327–328.
14. Goebbels, p. 271.
15. New York *Times,* April 2, 1933, p. 1.
16. Wulf, p. 267.
17. New York *Times,* April 16, 1933, IV, p. 2.

18. Wulf, p. 268.

19. *Ibid.*, p. 266.

20. New York *Times*, May 14, 1933, IX, p. 4.

21. Wulf, p. 328.

22. *Ibid.*, p. 376.

23. *Ibid.*, p. 277.

24. *Ibid.*, p. 385.

25. Roger Manvell and Heinrich Fraenkel, *Dr. Goebbels*, p. 132.

26. Wulf, p. 305.

27. New York *Times*, October 10, 1933, p. 12.

28. New York *Times*, February 4, 1934, X, p. 4.

29. Wulf, p. 350.

30. Gregory Bateson, "Cultural and Thematic Analysis of Fictional Films," *Transactions of the New York Academy of Sciences*, February 1943, pp. 72–78.

31. New York *Times*, December 3, 1933, IX, p. 8.

32. Traub, quoted in Wulf, p. 330.

33. Richard Roud, *An Index to the Work of Max Ophüls*, pp. 8–9.

34. Lang has told various versions of this story to different writers, and even once in person on a television program. The most complete version is included in Kracauer, pp. 248–250.

35. Wulf, p. 329.

## NOTES FOR 1934: GOEBBELS SHOWS HIS TEETH (pp. 42–67)

1. William Shirer, *The Rise and Fall of the Third Reich*, p. 296.

2. Wulf, *Theater und Film*, p. 284.

3. *Ibid.*, p. 271.

4. See *Jahrbuch der Reichsfilmkammer, 1934*, for full legislation.

5. New York *Times*, February 17, 1934, p. 3.

6. *Ibid.*, February 19, 1934, p. 6.

7. *Ibid.*

8. *Ibid.*, March 11, 1934, p. 26.

9. *Ibid.*, March 30, 1934, p. 26.

10. Wulf, p. 280.

11. *Ibid.*, p. 280.

12. New York *Times*, March 24, 1934, p. 7.

13. Wulf, p. 273.

14. New York *Times*, May 2, 1934, p. 13.

15. *Monthly Film Bulletin*, December 31, 1934, pp. 104–105.

16. John Altmann, "Movies' Role in Hitler's Conquest of German Youth," *Hollywood Quarterly*, III, no. 4, p. 381.

17. New York *Times*, May 21, 1934, p. 7.

18. Wulf, p. 284.

19. New York *Times*, November 30, 1934, p. 22.

20. *Ibid.*, December 30, 1934, IX, p. 4.

21. *Ibid.*, December 3, 1934, p. 33.

22. Wulf, p. 385.

23. *Ibid.*, p. 385.

24. *National Film Theatre Program*, November–January 1963–1964, p. 20.

NOTES FOR 1935: INTERLUDE (pp. 68–88)

1. New York *Times*, January 9, 1935, p. 26.
2. *Ibid.*, February 2, 1935, p. 2.
3. *Ibid.*, April 25, 1935, p. 19.
4. *Film-Welt*, May 5, 1935.
5. New York *Times*, April 28, 1935, p. 34.
6. *Film Comment*, Winter 1965, p. 29.
7. Wulf, *Theater und Film*, p. 294.
8. *Ibid.*, p. 281.
9. *Ibid.*, p. 274.
10. New York *Times*, August 7, 1935, p. 2.
11. *Ibid.*, August 25, 1935, p. 7.
12. Wulf, p. 414.
13. *Ibid.*, pp. 295–296.
14. *Ibid.*, p. 285.
15. *Film-Welt* clipping, n.d., n.p.
16. National Film Theatre Program, April 1964, p. 3.
17. Donald Costello, *The Serpent's Eye*, p. 42.


NOTES FOR 1936: GOEBBELS ABOLISHES THE CRITICS (pp. 89–106)

1. New York *Times*, February 2, 1936, p. 4.
2. *Ibid.*, May 14, 1936, p. 1.
3. *Der Deutsche Schrifsteller*, I: 12, reprinted in George L. Mosse, *Nazi Culture*, pp. 162–163.
4. New York *Times*, November 28, 1936, p. 1.
5. *Ibid.*, p. 4.
6. *Ibid.*, November 29, 1936, p. 31.
7. *Ibid.*, March 16, 1937, p. 15.
8. For the official Nazi description of the party, see article from *Der Angriff*, August 18, 1936, reprinted in Mosse, pp. 53–54.
9. See especially Manvell, *Dr. Goebbels*, pp. 151–157.


NOTES FOR 1937: GOEBBELS ABSORBS THE INDUSTRY (pp. 107–125)

1. New York *Times*, March 26, 1937, p. 9.
2. *Ibid.*, May 11, 1937, p. 31.
3. *Ibid.*, May 19, 1937, p. 25.
4. *Ibid.*, May 6, 1937, p. 22.
5. *Ibid.*, April 28, 1937, p. 6.
6. *Ibid.*, May 23, 1937, p. 29.
7. *Ibid.*, April 11, 1937, p. 12.
8. *Monthly Film Bulletin*, July 31, 1937, p. 151.
9. Altmann, "Movies' Role . . . ," *Hollywood Quarterly*, p. 382.
10. *Ibid.*, p. 383.
11. *Illustrierter Film-Kurier*, no. 2643.
12. Altmann, p. 383.
13. *Ibid.*, p. 383.

NOTES FOR 1938–1939: WAR AND ESCAPISM (pp. 126–156)

1. New York *Times*, September 25, 1938, IX, p. 2.
2. Manvell, *Dr. Goebbels*, p. 157.
3. New York *Times*, January 24, 1939, p. 17.
4. *Ibid.*, January 31, 1939, p. 5.
5. *Ibid.*, March 28, 1939, p. 8.
6. *Ibid.*
7. *Ibid.*, August 9, 1939, p. 15.
8. Gordon Hitchens, "An Interview with a Legend," *Film Comment*, Winter 1965, p. 9.
9. Ulrich Gregor, "A Comeback for Leni Riefenstahl?" *ibid.*, p. 25.
10. Robert Gardner, "Can the Will Triumph?" *ibid.*, p. 30.
11. *Ibid.*, p. 23.
12. Lochner, *Diaries*, pp. 246–247.
13. Altmann, "Movies' Role . . .", p. 384.
14. *Ibid.*, p. 385.
15. Clipping in the British Film Institute files.
16. Interview between Veit Harlan and myself, July 20, 1963.


NOTES FOR 1939–1940: THE ANTISEMITIC FILM (pp. 157–177)

1. Helmut Blobner and Herbert Holba, "Jackboot Cinema," *Films and Filming*, December 1962, p. 16.
2. *Filmpress*, No. 27a, July 22, 1950, p. 7. (Mimeographed.)
3. *Ibid.*, p. 8.
4. Blobner and Holba, p. 16.
5. Wulf, pp. 9–10; see also the legend to an illustration showing Werner Krauss as Rabbi Loew in *Jud Süss*, which reads: "Antisemitic movies prepared the ground for the annihilation camps; sometimes they pointed directly to the gas chambers. Thus, *Jud Süss* was shown in the eastern territories always when a new deportation was imminent. Under these circumstances it is not surprising, to hear, again and again the question, whether the actors in these movies are not also responsible for the murder of millions of people."
6. Maurice Bardèche and Robert Brasillach, *Histoire du cinéma* (1948 edition), p. 508.
7. *Variety*, April 7, 1958, December 12, 1959, and May 8, 1968.
8. For full description of this film, see Kracauer, *From Caligari . . .*, pp. 275–331.
9. Blobner and Holba, pp. 16–17.
10. Howard K. Smith, *Last Train from Berlin*, pp. 155–156.
11. Ernest K. Bramsted, *Goebbels and National Socialist Propaganda, 1925–1945*, p. 402.


NOTES FOR 1940–1941: FILMS OF THE EARLY WAR PERIOD (pp. 178–205)

1. Semmler, *Goebbels, the Man Next to Hitler*, p. 15.
2. *Ibid.*, p. 162.
3. Louis Marcorelles, "The Nazi Cinema," *Sight and Sound*, Autumn 1955, p. 68.

4. Control Commission, *Catalogue of Forbidden German Features*, p. 68.
5. Paul Joseph Cremers, "Zum Schiller Film," clipping in British Film Institute files.
6. *Illustrierter Film-Kurier*, no. 3186.
7. Smith, *Last Train*, pp. 121–122.
8. Blobner and Holba, "Jackboot Cinema," p. 18.
9. A. U. Sander, *Jugend und Film*, pp. 47–49.
10. *Ibid.*, pp. 118–128.
11. *Illustrierter Film-Kurier*, no. 3134.
12. Smith, p. 121.
13. Blobner and Holba, p. 20.
14. Gerald Reitlinger, *The Final Solution*, p. 132.
15. François Bayle, *Croix gamée ou caducée*, p. 781.
16. *Ibid.*, pp. 843–844.
17. Marcorelles, "The Nazi Cinema," p. 67.

NOTES FOR 1942–1945: FILM IN TWILIGHT (pp. 206–266)

1. *Vertriebsprogram der Deutschen Filmvertriebs-Gesellschaft, m.b.H., 1942/1943.*
2. Lochner, *Diaries*, p. 213.
3. *Ibid.*, p. 215.
4. *Ibid.*, p. 221.
5. *Ibid.*, pp. 203–204.
6. *Ibid.*, p. 138.
7. *Ibid.*, p. 181.
8. *Ibid.*, p. 208.
9. *Ibid.*, p. 272.
10. Heinrich Fischer, "The Theatre and Film in Nazi Germany," *Tricolor*, July–August 1945, p. 117.
11. Marcorelles, "The Nazi Cinema," p. 68.
12. *Ibid.*, p. 68.
13. Blobner and Holba, "Jackboot Cinema," p. 19.
14. *Deutscher Film Katalog*, p. 292.
15. *Illustrierter Film Kurier*, no. 3336.
16. Semmler, *Goebbels, the Man Next to Hitler*, pp. 149–150.
17. Fraenkel, *Unsterbliche Filme*, II, 131.
18. Marcorelles, p. 68.
19. Boechenstein, *The German Novel, 1939–1944*, pp. 36–37.
20. Lochner, p. 230.
21. Marcorelles, p. 69.
22. Lochner, p. 273.
23. *Ibid.*, p. 274.
24. Manvell and Fraenkel, p. 243.
25. Wilfred von Oven, *Mit Goebbels bis zum Ende*, II, 304.

NOTES FOR EPILOGUE (pp. 267–270)

1. Erich Kuby, *The Russians and Berlin, 1945*, p. 236.
2. *Ibid.*, p. 327.
3. *Ibid.*, p. 324.

# BIBLIOGRAPHY

Allgeier, Sepp. *Die Jagd nach dem Bild.* Stuttgart: J. Engelhorn, 1931.

*Almanach der Deutschen Filmschaffenden 1943.* Berlin: Max Hesses Verlag, 1943.

Altmann, John. "Movies' Role in Hitler's Conquest of German Youth," *Hollywood Quarterly,* Vol. III, No. 4. Berkeley, Calif.

Bardèche, Maurice and Robert Brasillach. *Histoire du cinéma,* Vol. 2. Paris: Les Sept Couleurs, 1964.

Bateson, Gregory. "Cultural and Thematic Analysis of Fictional Films," *Transactions of the New York Academy of Sciences,* Series II, Vol. V, No. 4. New York: February 1943.

Bauer, Alfred. *Deutscher Spielfilm-Almanach 1929–1950.* Berlin: Filmblätter Verlag, 1950.

Bayle, François. *Croix gamée ou caducée.* Freiburg: 1950.

Belling, Curt. *Der Film in Staat und Partei.* Berlin: Verlag "Der Film," 1936.

Bennett, E.K. and H.M. Waidson. *A History of the German Novella.* Cambridge: Cambridge University Press, 1961.

Blobner, Helmut and Herbert Holba. "Jackboot Cinema" in *Films and Filming,* Vol. VIII, No. 3. London: December 1962.

Boeschenstein, H. *The German Novel, 1939–1944.* Toronto: University of Toronto Press, 1949.

Bramsted, Ernest K. *Goebbels and National Socialist Propaganda 1925–1945.* Ann Arbor: Michigan State University Press, 1965.

Brenner, Hildegard. *Die Kunstpolitik des Nationalsozialismus.* Hamburg: Rowohlt, 1963.

British Film Institute. "The 30's Part One: Germany." Program notes for screenings April–May 1964. (Mimeographed.)

276

British Film Institute Clipping Files. These include numerous articles on German film, many unidentified as to original published source or date.

Carlson, John Ray (pseud. of Derounian, Arthur). *Under Cover.* New York: Dutton, 1943.

Clark, Barrett H. and George Freedley. *A History of Modern Drama.* New York: Appleton Century, 1947. See especially the sections on Germany by Franz Rasp, and on Austria by Henry Schnitzler.

Control Commission for Germany, Information Services Commission, *Catalogue of Forbidden German Features and Short Film Productions Held in Zonal Film Archives of the Film Section, Information Services Division.* Hamburg: 1951.

Costello, Donald. *The Serpent's Eye.* Notre Dame: University of Notre Dame Press, 1966.

Cremers, Paul Joseph. "Zum Schiller Film." Unidentified clipping of unknown source in British Film Institute Files, c. 1940.

*Deutscher Film-Katalog 1930–1945 (Ufa, Tobis, Bavaria).* Frankfurt/Main: K. L. Kraatz. Short synopses of feature films in German and English.

*Deutschland und der deutsche Film.* Berlin: Neue Film-Kurier Verlagsgesellschaft, 1935.

Drews, Berta (ed.). *Heinrich George, Ein Schauspielerleben.* Hamburg: Rowohlt, 1959. Various essays on the actor, edited by his widow.

Ebermayer, Erich and Hans-Otto Meissner. *Evil Genius.* Freely adapted by Louis Hagan. London: Allan, Wingate, 1953.

Esslin, Martin. *Brecht, the Man and His Work.* Garden City: Doubleday Anchor Books, 1961.

*Film-Welt* 1934, 1935. Weekly magazine. Berlin.

*Film-Woche* 1934. Weekly magazine. Berlin.

*Filmpress.* No. 27a (July 22, 1950). Mimeographed copy of issue devoted to the trial of Veit Harlan in my possession. This weekly journal was published in Hamburg, Heimhunderstrasse 58; it is now extinct.

Fischer, Heinrich. "The Theatre and Film in Nazi Germany," *Tricolor,* Vol. III, No. 16. New York: July–August 1945.

Fraenkel, Heinrich. *Unsterbliche Filme,* Vol. II. München: Kindler Verlag, 1957.

Freeden, Herbert. *Jüdisches Theater in Nazideutschland.* New York: Leo Baeck Institute, n.d.

Gardner, Robert. "Can the Will Triumph?" *Film Comment,* Vol. III, No. 1. New York: Winter 1965.

Goebbels, Joseph. *My Part in Germany's Fight.* London: Hurst and Blackett, 1935.

Gotz, Karl August. *Der Film als journalistisches Phänomen.* Düsseldorf: Dissertations-Verlag G. H. Nolte, 1937.

Gregor, Ulrich. "A Comeback for Leni Riefenstahl?" *Film Comment,* Vol. III, No. 1. New York: Winter 1965.

Günter, Walther. *Der Film als politisches Führungsmittel.* Leipzig: Robert Noske, 1934.

Hale, Orton J. *The Captive Press in the Third Reich.* Princeton: Princeton University Press, 1964.

Harlan, Veit. *Im Schatten meiner Filme.* Gütersloh: Sigbert Mohn Verlag, 1966.

Herzfeld, Friedrich. *Lexikon der Musik.* Berlin: Ullstein Verlag, 1961.

Hippler, Fritz. *Betrachtungen zum Filmschaffen.* Berlin: Max Hesses Verlag, 1942.

Hitchens, Gordon. "An Interview with a Legend," *Film Comment,* Vol. III, No. 1. New York: Winter 1965.

*Illustrierter Film-Kurier.* Berlin. Issues devoted to synopsis and stills of specific productions. Usually undated, but numbered.

*Jahrbuch der Reichsfilmkammer 1937.* Berlin-Schöneberg: Max Hesses Verlag, 1937.

*Jahrbuch der Reichsfilmkammer 1938.* Berlin-Schöneberg: Max Hesses Verlag, 1938.

Kalbus, Oscar. *Vom Werden deutscher Filmkunst.* 2 vols. Altona: Behrenfeld, 1935.

Knittel, John. *Via Mala.* New York: Gosset and Dunlap, 1934.

Koch, Heinrich and Braune, Heinrich. *Von deutscher Filmkunst.* Berlin: Verlag Hermann Scherping, 1943.

Kolb, Richard and Heinrich Siekmeier. *Rundfunk und Film im Dienste nationaler Kultur.* Düsseldorf: Friedrich Floeder Verlag, 1933.

Kracauer, Siegfried. *From Caligari to Hitler.* Princeton: Princeton University Press, 1947.

Kuby, Erich. *The Russians and Berlin, 1945.* New York: Hill and Wang, 1968.

Leander, Zarah. *So bin ich und so bleibe ich.* Berchtesgaden: Vier Falken Verlag, 1958.

Lochner, Louis P. (ed.). *The Goebbels Diaries.* Garden City: Doubleday and Doran, 1948.

Manz, H.P. *Ufa und der frühe deutsche Film.* Zürich: Sanssouci Verlag, 1963.

Manvell, Roger and Heinrich Fraenkel. *Dr. Goebbels.* New York: Pyramid Books, 1961. (Originally published New York: Simon and Schuster, 1960).

Marcorelles, Louis. "The Nazi Cinema," *Sight and Sound,* Vol. 25, No. 4. London: Autumn 1955.

Möller, Kai. *Paul Wegener: Sein Leben und seine Rollen.* Hamburg: Rowohlt, 1954.

*Monthly Film Bulletin.* London: British Film Institute, 1933 to present. Some reviews of German films released in England.

Mosse, George L. *Nazi Culture.* New York: Grossett and Dunlap, 1966.

*National Film Theatre Programs.* London: British Film Institute. Various issues, unnumbered but dated, contain capsule descriptions of German films.

Neumann, Carl, Curt Belling, and Hans-Walther Betz. *Film "Kunst", Film-Kohn, Film-Korruption*. Berlin-Verlag Hermann Scherping, 1937.

Oven, Wilfred von. *Mit Goebbels bis zum Ende*. 2 vols. Buenos Aires: Dürer-Verlag, 1950.

Pardo, Herbert. *Jud Süss, historisches und juristisches Material zum Fall Veit Harlan*. Hamburg: Auerdruck, 1949.

Pfeiler, William K. *War and the German Mind*. New York: Columbia University Press, 1941.

Pilgert, Henry P. *Press, Radio and Film in West Germany*. Bonn: Historical Division, Office of the Executive Secretary, Office of the United States High Commissioner for Germany, 1953.

Pleyer, Peter. *Deutscher Nachkriegsfilm 1946–1948*. Münster: Verlag C. J. Fahle, 1965.

Rabenalt, Arthur Maria. *Film im Zwielicht*. München: Copress Verlag, 1958.

Rathgeb, Kaspar. *Die Filmindustrie als Problem der Handelspolitik*. Birkeneck: Druckerei St. Georgsheim, 1935.

*Reichswoche für den deutschen Kulturfilm, München, 12–18 November 1943. Presse Almanach*. München: Grassinger, 1943.

Reitlinger, Gerard. *The Final Solution*. New York: Barnes, 1961.

Riess, Kurt. *Das gab's nur einmal*. Hamburg: Verlag der Sternbücher, 1956.

————. *Gustaf Gründgens*. Hamburg: Hoffman und Campe Verlag, 1965.

————. *Joseph Goebbels*. London: Hollis and Carter, 1949.

Roud, Richard: *An Index to the Work of Max Ophüls*. London: British Film Institute, 1957.

Sadoul, Georges. *Le cinéma pendant la guerre: 1939–1945*. Paris: Denoel, 1954.

Sander, A.U. *Jugend und Film*. Berlin: Zenterverlag der NSDAP, Franz Eher Verlag, 1944.

Semmler, Rudolf. *Goebbels, the Man Next to Hitler*. London: Westhouse, 1947.

Shirer, William. *Berlin Diary*. New York: Knopf, 1941.

————. *The Rise and Fall of the Third Reich*. Greenwich: Crest Books, 1964. (Originally published New York: Simon and Schuster, 1960).

Siska, Heinz W. (ed.). *Wunderwelt Film*. Heidelberg: Verlagsastalt Hüthig, 1943.

Smith, Howard K. *Last Train from Berlin*. New York: Popular Library, 1962. (Originally published New York: Knopf, 1942).

Stephan, Werner. *Joseph Goebbels: Dämon einer Diktatur*. Stuttgart: Union Deutsche Verlagsgesellschaft, 1949.

Thomas, Hans Alex. *Die deutsche Tonfilmmusik*. Gütersloh: C. Bertelsmann Verlag, 1962.

Traub, Hans. *Der Film als politisches Machtmittel*. München: Münchner Druck- und Verlagshaus, 1933.

————. *Die Ufa*. Berlin: Ufa-Buchverlag, 1943.

*Vertriebsprogram der Deutschen Filmvertriebs-Gesellschaft m.b.H., 1942/ 43.* n.p., n.d. [1942].

Wesse, Kurt. *Grossmacht Film.* Berlin: Deutsche Buch-Gemeinschaft, 1928.

Wolf, Kurt. *Entwicklung und Neugestaltung der deutschen Filmwirtschaft seit 1933.* Heidelberg: Druckerei Hermann Meister, 1938.

Wollenberg, H.H. *Fifty Years of German Film.* London: Falcon Press, 1948.

Wulf, Joseph. *Die bildenden Künste im Dritten Reich.* Gütersloh: Sigbert Mohn Verlag, 1963.

————. *Theater und Film im Dritten Reich.* Gütersloh: Sigbert Mohn Verlag, 1964.

# INDEX

281

## ABOUT THE AUTHOR

David Stewart Hull was born in Wisconsin. He is a graduate of Dartmouth College and did post-graduate work at the University of London, where research on this book began. He has written widely on the film for *The Guardian, The New York Times, Film Quarterly,* and numerous magazines in the United States and Europe. Mr. Hull is vice-president of James Brown Associates, authors' representatives.